MW00452761

Begin to explore the DESQview multitasking environment immediately ...

Order the *DESQview* disk today!

This companion disk includes all of the DESQview API programs developed in the book. You'll find programs that control the size, position, and color of DESQview windows; start and stop separate tasks and processes under DESQview; read keyboard, mouse, and timers; and give you control of EMS memories, control of DESQview .PIF files from application programs, and control of displays using DESQview panels. All of these programs are presented in a demo version of DESQview. Also included are project files used by some of the programs. All programs require DESQview 2.0 or better. The C source code will compile under Turbo C 2.0 and Microsoft C 5.0.

To order, simply return this postage-paid self mailer with your payment of $20, plus sales tax if you are a California resident, to: M&T Books, 501 Galveston Drive, Redwood City, CA 94063. Or, call toll-free 800-533-4372 (In CA 800-356-2002) between 8 a.m. and 5 p.m., Monday through Friday, Pacific Standard Time. Ask for **Item #040-0**.

YES! Please send me the *DESQview* Disk for $20 _____

California residents add applicable sales tax _____ % _____

TOTAL _____

Check enclosed. Make payable to **M&T Books**.

Charge my _____ VISA _____ MasterCard _____ American Express

Card # _____ Exp. date _____

Name _____

Address _____

City _____ State _____ Zip _____

7019

BUSINESS REPLY MAIL

FIRST CLASS PERMIT 871 REDWOOD CITY, CA

POSTAGE WILL BE PAID BY ADDRESSEE

M&T BOOKS

501 Galveston Drive
Redwood City, CA 94063

PLEASE FOLD ALONG LINE AND STAPLE OR TAPE CLOSED

DESQview

A Guide to Programming the DESQview Multitasking Environment

Stephen R. Davis

M&T BOOKS

M&T Publishing, Inc.
Redwood City, California

M&T Books
A Division of M&T Publishing, Inc.
501 Galveston Drive
Redwood City, CA 94063

M&T Books
General Manager, Ellen Ablow
Editorial Project Manager, Michelle Hudun
Editor, Dave Rosenthal
Cover Designer, Cynthia Engler
Cover Art Director, Michael Hollister

Library of Congress Cataloging in Publication Data

Davis, Stephen R., 1956—
    DESQview : a guide to programming the DESQview multitasking environment.

    Bibliography : p. 337
    Includes index.
    1. Object-oriented programming (Computer science)
2. Desqview (Computer program) I. Title. II. Title:
DESQview
QA76.6.D375   1988   005.4'46   88-32586

ISBN 1-55851-028-1 (book) $24.95
ISBN 1-55851-006-0 (book/disk) $39.95
ISBN 1-55851-040-0 (disk) $20.00

93   92   91   90   89   5   4   3   2

Limits of Liability and Disclaimer of Warranty

How to Order the Accompanying Disk

The DESQview companion disk includes all of the DESQview API programs developed in the book. You'll find programs that control the size, position, and color of DESQview windows; start and stop separate tasks and processes under DESQview; read keyboards, mouse, and timers; and give you control of EMS memories, control of DESQview .PIF files from application programs, and control of displays using DESQview panels. All of these programs are presented in a demo version of DESQview. All programs require DESQview 2.0 or better. The C source code will compile under Turbo C 2.0 and Microsoft C 5.0.

The disk price is $20.00. California residents must add the appropriate sales tax. Order by sending a check, or credit card number and expiration date, to:

DESQview Disk
M&T Books
501 Galveston Drive
Redwood City, CA 94063

Or, you may order by calling our toll-free number between 8 A.M. and 5:00 P.M. Pacific Standard Time: 800/533-4372 (800/356-2002 in California). Ask for **Item #040-0**.

Contents

To

the memory of J.C. Blackwell,
loving husband, father, and grandfather

Introduction

Why this Book?

This book is intended for users of the API C Library distributed by Quarterdeck Office Systems. The API C Library is a software set that allows the C programmer convenient access to the programming capabilities of the DESQview operating environment. With this package, programmers can add the impressive capabilities of DESQview to their own programs.

Quarterdeck supplies excellent manuals with the API C Library (and with the Pascal and assembly language API libraries). However, these manuals are reference works, much like a dictionary. Functions are described in alphabetical order without much discussion of how they interrelate or how they may be used in a real program.

This can make learning the DESQview API more difficult. DOS for the IBM PC is a comparatively simple operating system lacking many of the concepts of more modern environments. Programmers whose experience is limited to writing programs for DOS have a certain amount of learning to do before they can begin writing effective programs for DESQview, one of the new generation of operating systems for the PC.

If you want to learn Spanish, you don't start with a Spanish dictionary, but rather with an introduction to the language. This book is designed to introduce the programmer to DESQview. Not every function call is covered in this book. Mastering the principles of a modern operating system such as DESQview is more important. Once the programmer has become familiar with these concepts, Quarterdeck's "dictionary-style" manuals will prove to be useful and trusted tools, providing any details that may not be discussed here.

(As a further aid, paragraphs in the earlier chapters that deal specifically with the details of implementation have been separated from paragraphs that deal more with concepts and have been shaded.)

Why DESQview?

With DOS in such a preeminent position in the PC world today, why should anyone worry about other operating systems, such as DESQview? Designed in a time when the demands of users on their PCs were considerably more modest, DOS has some serious limitations—limitations that place on the shoulders of the applications programmer the ever-increasing burden of more and more user demands. The pressure to replace DOS comes not only from its much maligned user interface, but also from the fact that it makes writing the powerful applications that today's users demand too difficult. It is clear that DOS is ailing—it is not clear which of the contenders to the throne will succeed it.

DESQview started life in July 1985. DESQview 1.0 was written as a clone of the then newly introduced IBM operating system, Topview. Although well-designed, Topview suffered from some serious implementation problems, including size and incomplete DOS compatibility. Thus, while Topview faded away, DESQview flourished, being named an InfoWorld Product of the Year for 1986 and 1987, Best Operating Environment in *PC Tech Journal*'s System Builder Contest, and Best Alternative to OS/2 by *PC Magazine* for 1987. This early success was due primarily to DESQview's user interface. In early 1988 Quarterdeck began to market the DESQview API Reference and the companion DESQview API C Library, making available to programs written in C the advanced user capabilities of DESQview. (This interface had always been available to the assembly language programmer, although DESQview had not completely documented it.)

DESQview has advantages over other operating systems. It offers pre-emptive multitasking, intertask communication, message passing, semaphores, and advanced memory management, which includes paging of applications on 80386-based computers or PCs outfitted with EEMS or EMS 4.0 memory. (If these features are unfamiliar to you, don't worry—each is covered within the chapters of this book.)

Of course, these features come standard issue on modern, second generation PC operating systems. What makes DESQview unique is its complete DOS compatibility. DOS is generally maligned for what it does not provide rather than for what it does. DESQview runs "on top of DOS," allowing applications to continue to access those features of DOS which it does handle (primarily a reasonably well-developed file system). DESQview's features are added to those already present in DOS. Applications that limit themselves to DOS continue to see DOS just as they would without DESQview present.

Beyond this, DESQview is considerably less expensive. By this I mean not only its sales price, which is competitive with other systems, but also that DESQview requires less host computer. Many in the trade press have recommended at least 3MB of internal RAM to support OS/2 with Presentation Manager. Although not quite that hungry, DOS under UNIX requires in excess of 1MB to execute properly. DESQview adds a scant 145K of overhead to that required by DOS itself (this 145K does not necessarily come from the lower 640K).

In addition, OS/2 requires an 80286 CPU or better, while DOS under UNIX requires no less than an 80386. DESQview supports the 8088 CPU found in the most inexpensive PCs and their clones. While DESQview does not make use of the 80286's extended features, DESQview does put many of the 80386's advanced features to good use when combined with the separately available QEMM386. DESQview allows the user and the programmer to put all of available memory to good use (not just the first 640K) while executing DOS programs.

This makes the DESQview API an ideal platform for learning how to program on second generation operating systems for the hobbyist and educational environment where the cost of the development hardware is a consideration. Knowing that the resulting product has the widest range of possible customers open to it makes it desirable for the commercial applications developer.

Why Multitasking?

Multitasking is the aspect of DESQview with which its users are most familiar. They know the concept of executing programs "in the background" while they whisk over to begin work on another program in the foreground. Skeptics have pointed out that this is not the way in which users of DOS typically work. While it should be pointed out that maybe people don't work that way today because the option has not been available to them with DOS, there is some justification to the complaint.

Conventional single-tasking applications do not execute very well in a multitasking environment. They make no attempt to take advantage of the multitasking and sometimes do things that are downright unfriendly to their neighbor applications executing simultaneously. How can executing two applications simultaneously be any faster if they only execute half as fast? "Compiling in the background" is not the shining promise of multitasking and may actually serve to give it a bad name by trivializing the concept. The real advantages of multitasking lie in two other areas.

The first promise of multitasking is the switch operation. It can be very frustrating to be deeply buried in some application only to find that a number is required that can only be retrieved from some other application. With DOS, users must exit the current application—being careful to save their work—to bring up the new application, retrieve the number, and reverse the process. With a switcher such as DESQview, users do not need to exit the current application before bringing up the new one. They need only to pop up the new application to retrieve the needed value and then instantly switch back to the suspended application to plug it in.

Some applications programmers have attempted to address this problem by writing large and involved Terminate and Stay Resident utilities that users can pop-up to handle the more obvious operations, such as listing a file to the screen. Others attempt to address the problem with large do-it-all Integrated Environments. These are just band-aid fixes to the real problem: this important feature is missing from DOS.

Even more important than this, however, is the power that multitasking offers the programmer. Multitasking allows the programmer to divide the program into several independently executing applications. This multitasking paradigm allows the programmer a degree of modularity and control that is not possible under single-tasked DOS. I will be discussing the multitasking paradigm throughout this book, as this is one of the most attractive features offered by the DESQview API.

Programs in this Book

The programs in this book are simple and demonstrative. Each program attempts to demonstrate a single principle or API call. Programs should be tackled in order. Later programs borrow freely from programs found earlier in the book. Explanation is limited to the sections of code that are new.

Authors of programming books are always torn between incredibly simple example programs and examples that actually perform some useful function. Of course, the best examples are those that qualify under both descriptions; unfortunately, this is not usually possible.

In this book, I have leaned toward the simple. The example programs only attempt to develop the principle far enough for the reader to see it and, just as important, to recognize its significance. There is not much chance that I can anticipate the reader's need and produce just the program desired. It's much better for readers to understand the examples sufficiently to be able to write the needed program themselves.

To keep things as simple as possible, all of the programs in this book follow the pattern shown in INTRO.C below.

```
 1[ 0]: /*******************************************************************
 2[ 0]:    Intro - a brief explanation of the function goes here
 3[ 0]: *******************************************************************/
 4[ 0]:
 5[ 0]: #include <stdio.h>
 6[ 0]: #include "dvapi.h"
 7[ 0]:
 8[ 0]: /* prototype declarations of user functions*/
 9[ 0]: void main (void);
10[ 0]: void program_body (void);
11[ 0]:
12[ 0]: /*minimum API version required is DESQview 2.00*/
13[ 0]: #define required 0x200
14[ 0]:
15[ 0]: /*main - standard pattern for DESQview programs*/
16[ 0]: void main (void)
17[ 0]: {
18[ 1]:   int  version;
19[ 1]:
20[ 1]:   version = api_init();
21[ 1]:   if (version < required)
22[ 1]:       printf ("This program requires DESQview %d.%02d or later.\n",
23[ 1]:               required >> 8, required & 0xff);
24[ 1]:   else {
25[ 2]:       /* tell DESQview what extensions to enable and start application
26[ 2]:       api_level (required);
27[ 2]:       program_body();
28[ 1]:   }
29[ 1]:   /*if DESQview present (even if wrong version), shut it down*/
30[ 1]:   if (version)
31[ 1]:       api_exit();
32[ 0]: }
33[ 0]:
34[ 0]: /*Program_body - a more detailed explanation of what the
35[ 0]:                 main program does*/
36[ 0]: void program_body (void)
37[ 0]: {
38[ 1]:   /*the actual program begins here*/
39[ 0]: }
40[ 0]:
```

All programs begin with the include file DVAPI.H, which is included with the DESQview C Library. This include file defines the constants to which Quarterdeck refers in its documentation. The API calls look like any other function calls except that they always start with three letters followed by an underscore and a name. The first three letters are an overall grouping and are the same among all functions of the same general type.

The first API call is always *api_init()*. This call turns on the DESQview system and returns the version number of the DESQview currently running. All programs in this book have been tested with version 2.2x of DESQview but do not require features beyond 2.00. The program then informs DESQview as to what level of features it intends to use via the *api_level()* API call. The program is then ready to execute the user code by calling *program_body()*. Once the code has finished, the DESQview system is turned off via the *api_exit()* call.

In general, a figure such as Figure I.1 is given when new API functions are being discussed. This figure lists the arguments to each function as well as a short description of what it does and what it returns. This information may also be found in the API C Library documentation, but it is listed here so that the reader may avoid constantly referring back to that manual.

Figure I.1—Prototype Declarations for *api_init()*, *api_level()*, *api_exit()*, and *api_shadow()* API calls

```
                             /*disable DESQview prior to
                               terminating application*/
void   api_exit              /*returns nothing*/
         (void);             /*takes no arguments*/

                             /*initialize DESQview API*/
int    api_init              /*returns level of DESQview running*/
         (void);             /*takes no arguments*/

                             /*enable DESQview features*/
void   api_level             /*returns nothing*/
         (int  level);       /*level of features to enable*/

                             /*allocate a virtual screen for
                               direct manipulation*/
char *api_shadow             /*returns address of virtual screen*/
         (void);             /*takes no arguments*/
```

To compile the example programs, a few tips are in order. Most important, DESQview uses 32-bit addresses exclusively. While it might be possible to carefully define long pointers in all the proper places (including to the functions themselves), this would be exceedingly difficult to get right. In practice, the programs in this book and any other DESQview specific programs should be compiled using the LARGE memory model. This insures that only 32-bit addresses are passed between functions. (Under Turbo C, select the LARGE model from the compile option of the Options menu. For Microsoft C, use the /AL switch during compilation.

In addition, DESQview packs tables on byte boundaries to save space. Most compilers attempt to pack fields on word boundaries since word accesses on even boundaries may be faster than those on odd boundaries. Such compilers must be instructed to override this feature and pack fields within structures on byte boundaries. (With Turbo C this is in the Options Menu; with Microsoft C use the */Zp* compile option.) This is only critical with those programs that define DESQview structures.

It will also be necessary to disable warnings concerning the number and type of arguments passed to functions. As noted, the DVAPI.H file does not include prototype declarations. Compilers that comply with the ANSI C Draft Standard generate warnings when such a function is called without a prototype declaration appearing previously. If these warnings are not disabled, it may become difficult to see real warnings or error messages. This is only a suggestion, as it does not affect the code generated.

The code for the API functions is included in the files *API1.OBJ* and *API2.OBJ* included with the API C Library. Versions of the object files for the C compilers from Borland, Microsoft, Metaware, and Lattice are included. The source files are also included so other compiler users may generate their own object files (here again, be sure to compile using the LARGE memory model).

For Turbo C, *API1* and *API2* may be included in a separate link step such as that in Figure I.2.

Figure I.2—Example Link Command for Turbo C

```
LINK EXAMPLE.OBJ+API1.OBJ+API2.OBJ,,,CL.LIB /ST:32768
```

The *CL.LIB* is Turbo C's large memory model library. A project file may be used instead. A sample project file appears in Figure I.3.

Figure I.3—Sample Project File for the Sample Programs

```
api1.obj api2.obj
example.c
c:\turboc\lib\cl.lib
```

The Microsoft C link command looks similar except that object *SLEEP.OBJ* must be included as well. *SLEEP.OBJ* adds the *sleep()* function, which some of the example programs use to slow down output. SLEEP.C appears in Figure I.5.

Notice in both cases that the default stack size has been increased using the */ST* link switch. The default allocation of 2K is not sufficient for the multitasking example programs.

Figure I.4—Example Compile and Link Command for Microsoft

```
CL /AL/Zp /c EXAMPLE.C
LINK EXAMPLE.OBJ+API1.OBJ+API2.OBJ+SLEEP.OBJ,,,/ST:32768
```

Figure I.5—Source for SLEEP.C Required for Compilers Lacking *Sleep()*

```
/*SLEEP—this function should be compiled into a .OBJ
        file and included in the link step for environments
        that have no sleep() function */
```

```
void sleep (int secs)
{
    long int j,k;
    for (j=10000L*secs;j;j--)
        k=5*j;
}
```

In addition, it may be necessary to increase the common memory and system memory sizes for some of the example programs. Common memory is adjusted using the SETUP program. The example APPTST1.C requires 25K. Other programs use less. Two of the example programs, PRCTST2.C and PRCTST3.C, require *.DVP* files to execute. These may be created using the Add a Program option from the Open command. Once created, their name and path must match the name within the example programs (either the filename or the example programs may be changed).

All of the programs in this book were checked out with Turbo C Version 2.0 and Microsoft C Version 5.0. No calls were made anywhere in the example programs that are specific to any particular compiler, therefore any ANSI C compiler should work fine.

Modifying Existing Applications to Use DESQview

This book is directed primarily to authors of new applications. However, existing applications may be modified to execute under DESQview as well. In fact, since DESQview supports all DOS programs, your existing DOS applications already support DESQview! There are only two places where changes may be required: memory and direct screen access. DESQview reduces slightly the amount of conventional memory available on systems not equipped with EMS memory or an 80386 processor. If your application is borderline, there may not be enough room for it and DESQview together. There is not much that can be done other than buying EMS 4.0 memory or an 80386-based PC, or else reducing the size of your application.

The second problem stems from the fact that DESQview cannot supervise programs that directly access screen memory. DESQview cannot compel their output into windows. Such programs must be given the entire screen when they execute, lest they "bleed" onto the displays of other applications. Fortunately, this problem can be handled quite easily.

This is not a problem on processors equipped with an 80386 processor as DESQview can use the paging capabilities of the CPU to force direct screen writes into virtual display memory. Other programs may solve the problem using the *api_shadow()* API call. This function call returns the address of a virtual display. Your program may then access this virtual display directly, just as if it were the real thing. Each application is afforded its own virtual display. DESQview periodically copies the contents of these virtual displays into the windows on the real display. This is described in the DESQview API Reference.

Conclusion—Elegance

Elegance, when applied to software, has been defined as the universal application of a small set of rules. While it may not seem that DESQview has a small set of rules, I hope the reader will be impressed with the fact that the principles embodied in DESQview are reasonably few in number. This gives the large number of DESQview API functions available a considerable amount of order. So much so that the reader will soon find them easy to remember.

Of the universal applicability of these principles, there is no doubt. As you proceed through this book, it will become clear how these principles interact to produce the user interface that has made DESQview famous and that are now available to enhance your application.

Application Program Interface and DESQview

What is an API?

There are many facets to an operating system. The most obvious one is that which the user sees from behind the keyboard, the so-called "user interface." People's opinions of an operating system are generally formed purely from interaction with the user interface.

The standard user interface for the PC has been IBM's PC-DOS and its twin MS-DOS from Microsoft. While acceptable for its time, time has not been kind to DOS. Other user interfaces adopting different user paradigms conspire to highlight the deficiencies of DOS's simple, single-task command-line interface.

DESQview's interface is user-friendly, yet is geared to the high speed power user. DESQview supports a windowed, multitasking environment. The user may load multiple DOS applications into memory at one time, switching back and forth between them with simple keyboard commands or by clicking on the applications with the mouse.

DESQview supports:

1) true, preemptive multitasking of multiple applications with user control of time slicing
2) swapping of applications to disk to make room for new applications, a process known as *overcommitting*
3) simple Cut and Paste between DOS applications
4) paging of data using Expanded Memory Specification (EMS) 3.2 memory and paging of data and code on EMS 4.0 and 386 memory

But this is not the interface to which this book is directed. While some familiarity with the DESQview user interface is assumed, this book is concerned primarily with the interface that programs see: the Application Program Interface (API). It is this software interface with which programmers must interest themselves.

While DOS might mean the *C>* prompt and all that goes with it to the user, it means something quite different to the programmer. Like all operating systems, DOS actually consists of several loosely interlinked parts. It is the program COMMAND.COM which displays the user prompt and which accepts and processes DOS commands such as *CD*, *DIR*, and the ubiquitous *ERASE *.**.

COMMAND.COM, however, is not much more than a simple program; a program that you might write. COMMAND.COM rests upon a lower DOS substrate. When the user requests DOS to list out a directory or delete a file, COMMAND.COM makes system calls into DOS to actually perform the function. COMMAND.COM is merely an interpretive shell between the user and this lower level.

When COMMAND.COM is instructed to load a program, it politely steps out of the way. The features found within COMMAND.COM are not normally available to the application program. When the user program wants to read the disk, output a string to the screen, or read the keyboard, it may execute the same system calls to DOS to perform the function as

COMMAND.COM. The DOS program rests upon the same DOS bedrock. This is the DOS API.

Other packages besides operating systems may have APIs. For example, programmers may decide that writing their own library of graphics routines to build three-dimensional images on the screen is too much effort. They may choose to purchase one instead. This library will undoubtedly come with a manual that lists a plethora of different functions that the software may access in the library. These interface functions are the API of the graphics library.

The DESQview API is more like that of an operating system. Like DOS, DESQview consists of two parts: a user interface, very similar in theory but different in practice from that of DOS, and a series of system calls. These are the same system services which the DESQview interface uses to perform its magic.

DESQview is unusual among operating systems in that it is not designed to operate by itself. DESQview binds with a DOS substrate to form a single operating system, one which is compatible with—but is an extension of—the basic DOS services. DOS is always present, so programs may access the DOS API in the same way that they do without DESQview. In addition to these basic services, however, DESQview-specific programs also have a suite of additional API services at their disposal. Programs executing under DESQview can do almost anything that the user can do by entering DESQview commands. The DESQview API also gives programs capabilities that the user does not have from the keyboard.

What function does the API of an operating system serve? It is certainly not necessary. There are programs that execute under DOS that make no calls at all to the underlying DOS operating system other than to exit when they complete. Most programs rely very heavily on operating system calls, however. The operating system API forms a shield between the application program and the underlying hardware. This interface is designed to both make the job of writing a program easier and to protect applications from minor differences between models or manufacturers of the base computer.

As hardware platforms evolve, the operating system provides a single point where changes can be made to mask any differences that the application software sees. Most operating systems, including DOS, allow device drivers to be installed to integrate previously unanticipated hardware into the existing operating system.

In addition, the interface that an operating system's API provides to the programmer is much simpler than the interface provided by the hardware itself. This allows more applications to be built with less development cost. (As you read through the DESQview API's capabilities in successive chapters, think about how much it might cost to write these capabilities into the user program.)

Interfacing to an Operating System

Making a system call to the operating system from an application program is not the same as calling a function within the program. Calls within a program are made using the symbolic names of the functions involved. During the link step, the addresses of all of the functions called within the program are calculated and written into the object code. Each functional reference becomes a reference to a fixed address within the program.

Providing fixed addresses of operating system functions in order to call them is not acceptable, however. First of all, this puts a very large burden on the programmer to be familiar with the address of each operating system function. Additionally, operating systems undergo updates, some of which are major. As long as these updates retain compatibility with earlier versions, applications written for the old operating system are expected to execute without incident on newer versions. Since updates are likely to change the offset of functions within the operating system, software developers must use a call mechanism that's independent of fixed addresses within the operating system itself.

DOS uses the interrupt structure of the 8086 microprocessor. Interrupts are external events that require immediate CPU attention. The 8086 family of processors can support up to 256 different interrupts. Each of these numbered interrupts has associated with it a fixed location in lower memory. Each of these locations contains the address in memory of the handler for that interrupt. When an interrupt occurs, signaling some external event such as a character received from the serial port or a timer tick, the current address being executed is saved onto the stack and control is immediately passed to the address associated with that interrupt.

Figure 1.1—Invoking an 'INT' Instruction on the 8086

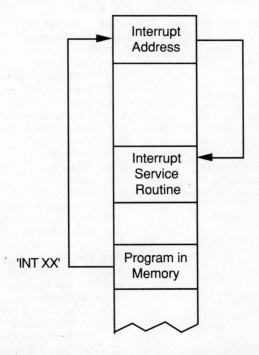

Interrupt routines can also be invoked from software. Executing the instruction *INT 21H*, for example, causes the CPU to save the location of the next instruction and jump to the interrupt 21 service routine exactly as if an external interrupt 21 had occurred.

DOS uses these so-called soft interrupts to provide address independence. When DOS is loaded into memory, it places the address of its main entry points into interrupts 20 hex through 27 hex. To make a DOS system call, an application program loads the number of the function to be performed into the AH register and then invokes interrupt 21. This invokes DOS like a function call since DOS has already placed its own address into this interrupt. The application neither knows or cares where interrupt 21 points as long as DOS receives and honors the request.

Figure 1.2—List of DOS Interrupt 21H Calls

System Call	Function	System Call	Function
0*	Terminate	21*	Read Random
1	Keyboard Input w/ Echo	22*	Write Random
2	Display Output	23*	Get File Size
3	Serial Input	24*	Set Relative Record
4	Serial Output	25	Set Interrupt Vector
5	Printer Output	26*	Create New PSP
6	Direct Console I/O	27*	Read Random Block
7	Direct Keyboard Input w/o Echo	28*	Write Random Block
8	Keyboard Input w/o Echo	29	Parse Filename
9	Display String	2A	Get Date
A	Buffered Keyboard Input	2B	Set Date
B	Check Keyboard Buffer Status	2C	Get Time
C	Clear Keyboard and DO Function	2D	Set Time
D	Reset Disk	2E	Set/Reset Verify Flag
E	Select Drive	2F	Get Disk Transfer Address
F*	Open File	30	Get DOS Version Number
10*	Close File	31	Terminate and Stay Resident
11*	Find First	33	Get/Set Control Break Check
12*	Find Next	35	Get Interrupt Vector
13*	Delete File	36	Get Disk Free Space
14*	Read Sequential	38	Get Country Data
15*	Write Sequential	39	Create Directory (MKDIR)
16*	Create File	3A	Remove Directory (RMDIR)
17*	Rename File	3B	Change Current Directory (CHDIR)
19	Report Current Drive	3C	Create Handle (Create File)
1A	Set Disk Transferr Address	3D	Open Handle (Open File or Device)
1B	Get Default Disk Data	3E	Close Handle (Close File or Device)
1C	Get Disk Data	3F	Read Handle (Read File or Device)

System Call	Function	System Call	Function
40	Write Handle (Write File or Device)	54	Get Verify State
41	Delete Directory Entry (Delete File)	56	Change Directory Entry (Rename File)
42	Move File Pointer	57	Get/Set Date/Time of File
43	Get/Set File Attributes	58	Get/Set Allocation Strategy
44	I/O Control	59	Get Extended Error
45	Duplicate File Handle	5A	Create Temporary File
46	Force Duplicate File Handle	5B	Create New File
47 *	Get Current Directory	5C	Lock/Unlock
48	Allocate Memory	5E	Get Machine Name
49	Free Memory	5F	Newtword Assign List Entry Access
4A	Set Block	62	Get PSP
4B	Load and Execute Program	65	Get Extended Country Information
4C	End Process	66	Set/Set Global Code Page
4D	Get Return Code of Child Process	67	Set Handle Count
4E	Find First File	68	Committ File
4F	Find Next File		

Note that system calls beginning with 59 were first introduced with DOS 3.0. System calls 65 through 68 are only defined under DOS 3.3. Those system calls marked with an asterisk have been replaced by a later (larger numbered) system call.

DOS has an assembly language-oriented API. Most of the system calls accept their arguments in the 8086 registers. The system call itself is indicated by the contents of the AH register. C, Pascal, and most other high-level languages are stack oriented, preferring to save values on the stack before performing function calls. To interface between C programs and DOS, an assembly language translation routine must load values from stack memory (where C stored them) into the registers (where DOS expects them) before performing the system call, and then reverse the process before returning. In Microsoft C and compatible compilers, this function may be performed using the *bdos()*, *intdos()*, or *int86()* library functions.

DESQview has three different calling mechanisms, each with a different specialty. The first, known as the assembly language interface, is similar to DOS in that it is controlled through soft interrupts with the AH and AL registers indicating the actual function to be performed. To simplify the interface, however, Quarterdeck provides in the DESQview API package a set of assembly language macros defined in the include file *DVAPI.INC* to access this interface. Commands such as *@CALL* and

@SEND partially conceal the underlying interrupt nature of the inter-face.

DESQview functions which must be accessed very rapidly, such as those required in interrupt service routines or those whose effect is globally rather than specifically directed, are accessed via the *@CALL* macro. Most of these Direct Call functions access DESQview by invoking interrupt 15, but some use interrupt 10 or 21. The details of which interrupts are used for which functions is hidden by the *@CALL* macro.

Direct Call functions are also similar to DOS calls in that communication is primarily through registers. The value of the call is loaded into the AX register by the *@CALL* macro. The other registers are loaded by the application program and their meaning is dependent upon which call is being performed.

Less time-critical DESQview functions are accessed with the *@SEND* macro. The send macro defines a set of twenty different operations, called messages, which can be performed on six different types of objects. The different messages are shown in Figure 1.3. Also listed are the different types of objects plus several object aliases that may be used with the *@SEND* interface.

Figure 1.3—The DESQview Messages and Objects Used in the Assembly Language (@SEND) Interface

Messages		Objects
HANDLE	CLOSE	OBJECT QUEUE
NEW	ERASE	WINDOW
FREE	STATUS	MAILBOX
ADDR	EOF	KEYBOARD
DIR	AT	TIMER
READ	SETSCALE	POINTER
APPLY	SETNAME	PANEL
WRITE	READN	
SIZEOF	GETSCALE	
LEN	REDRAW	
ADDTO	SETESC	
SUBFROM	LOCK	
OPEN		

The concept is object-oriented in that DESQview defines six different types of objects: windows, mailboxes, keyboard, timer, pointer (mouse), and panel. Each of these object types will be discussed in detail in ensuing chapters. Notice that the operations are fairly generic in nature. Their exact meaning depends somewhat on the type of object being operated on. For example, WRITEing an object of type WINDOW causes output to the screen, while WRITEing a MAILBOX object sends a message to be picked up by another task, and WRITEing a POINTER object moves the mouse pointer to a particular location on the screen.

Objects are 32-bit values and do not, therefore, fit easily into the 8086 registers (which are 16-bits in length). Therefore, *@SEND* passes objects, not in the registers, but pushed onto the stack. To aid in manipulating these 32-bit values, *DVAPI.INC* defines the 32-bit macros *@PUSH*, *@POP*, *@MOV*, and *@CMP* to perform operations analogous to their 8086 instructional counterparts. The programmer is not compelled to use these macros, however, as long as the 32-bit handles find their way onto the program stack properly.

The *@SEND* interface is designed to add a level of consistency to the DESQview API. For example, the operations NEW, OPEN, READ, WRITE, CLOSE, and FREE can be applied to all six different types of objects. In addition, the result of these operations can be accurately guessed in every case by merely knowing what the object type is. This is designed to make the DESQview API easier to use.

It is worth noting that the *@SEND* interface does not actually perform a "send" of a message in the sense which we will examine in Chapter 5. The terms "send" and "message" are used in this context only to be consistent with object-oriented languages, such as C++ and SmallTalk, which this interface attempts to emulate in some ways. Sending a message in the SmallTalk sense is too time consuming to sit well with DESQview's high-performance concepts.

To this Quarterdeck adds a second interface designed primarily for the C language known as the C interface. These functions are defined to the compiler in the include file DVAPI.H.

Of course, a C program can also access the assembly language interface routines. Since registers cannot normally be loaded nor values PUSHed and POPed from C, an assembly language interface module would have to be written to make the conversion from C calling conventions to those used by the *@CALL* and *@SEND* routines. In fact, the functions defined in *DVAPI.H* make just such conversions.

The C interface provided by Quarterdeck is nothing more than a set of conversion functions that provide easy access to the assembly language and stream interface functions. Rather than copy the assembly language routine names and functions identically, however, the C interface routines are organized slightly differently. The C functions fall into thirteen broad categories that are differentiated by the first three letters of their names. The "direct call" routines all begin with *api_*. The send routines begin with letters indicative of the type of object or handle upon which they work. For example, the window-related functions begin with *win_*, the timer functions with *tim_*, etc.

Since the C conversion routines are not built into DESQview, programs which wish to use the C interface must also include the file *API2.OBJ* during the link step.

A third interface, the streams interface, is designed to allow the user to embed DESQview instructions into a data stream. It is often desirable to be able to make system calls from within a data stream. As a programmer, for example, I often wished for the ability to change output colors in the middle of an output string by embedding some special flag. I could then print out a line or two, change colors, print out a critical value, and then change the colors back before continuing without resorting to multiple *printf()* calls.

The concept of embedding commands within data strings is also not foreign to mini- and mainframe computer users. Having only one interface, remote terminals can only be commanded via Escape sequences embedded within output strings. An Escape sequence to switch to inverse video, for example, may appear in the middle of a stream of ASCII output.

DESQview allows operating system commands to be made in the middle of output strings as well. Commands may be inserted to open windows, close windows, place them on the screen, etc. As we will see, placing commands within the data using the Panel Design Tool allows a level of generality in the software and an ease of modification that is not attainable in any other system.

This book concerns itself primarily with the C interface. Only in our discussion of Panels will we examine the streams interface. Although we will not study the assembly language interface directly, the similarity of principles with the C interface should make the transition from the C to the assembly language interface a simple one, if the need to access DESQview from assembly language should arise.

chapter 2

Windowing

The only view users have into the goings on within their computers is through the video screen. All information that the operator receives, short of the occasional beep or click, must be communicated through the 80-column-by-25-line-display. Little wonder then that major sections of a program fight for this precious resource like siblings for parental attention.

To understand that this competition exists, we must remember that the application which we are executing is not a monolithic whole. Let us consider, for example, a word processor. While a word processor may be a single program, there is more information displayed than just the file being edited. There is a small command display area which displays a help screen of possible commands. There may be a status display that keeps the user up to date on which line is currently being edited, how large the file is, whether Caps Lock is engaged, etc. In addition, entering commands may cause other displays to appear as well. Each of these display areas is a separate entity maintained by a different software functional group within the executing program. These functional groups are, in effect, competing for the screen resource.

One way to handle these requests is to give the entire display over to each different function upon request. Using our word processor example, the display might be consumed with nothing but the text of the current file.

Entering a command key would then bring up a help screen of all possible commands which entirely blot out the text display. Another key might bring up a status display, showing the size of the file, the current line, etc. Each of these displays entirely consumes the screen so that only one is visible at any given time. Developing software using this display model is fairly easy. Functions do not need to worry about what might already be on the screen when they execute. They simply overwrite anything there.

A more pleasing approach is to rigidly divide the display into functional areas. Commands always appear on this line, status on that line in columns A through B, etc. Staying within these boundaries is the responsibility of the software routines that create the different displays in the first place. Developing applications like this can be quite difficult. Either the display divisions must be quite rigid, or the application routines must constantly be concerned with meshing its data properly with what is already being displayed.

It is possible, however, to divide the real display up into smaller "subscreens" that are managed by a windowing package. Each of these smaller screens, also known as virtual displays or windows, appear to the software to be an entire display. This approach has several advantages over its predecessors.

Windowing allows each functional area of a program to ask for just the amount of screen it needs to display its information. Since each of these windows appears to be an entirely independent—albeit somewhat smaller—display, software is easier to develop as it need not concern itself with fitting into displays that precede it. In fact, it need not have any idea of what the screen looks like outside the confines of its own, single purpose window.

Software also need not worry as much about restricting itself to its display area. Since all screen access is through these windows, the windowing package makes sure that the functional group does not write outside of its windowed borders and spill over into applications behind it. Text that threatens to extend beyond the borders is either wrapped around onto successive lines or is clipped to fit. In addition, scrolling is only within the confines of the window. Once the functional group has out-lived its usefulness, its window can be removed by restoring to the screen any data that it may have temporarily covered.

Windows have a psychological advantage as well. Somehow replacing the entire display with a completely new one is disrupting and momen-tarily confusing to the user, even if the user entered the key to bring up the new display and completely anticipates its appearance. By leaving the larger window visible behind the smaller one just opened, users have a reference point to use in understanding where they are within the pro-gram. This aids users in understanding the program displays more rapidly.

General purpose, commercial windowing packages are available for al-most every environment, including the PC and its clones. Modular, ob-ject-oriented methodologies are greatly enhanced through the use of these packages. Since functional groups within the program can address their own window, which is completely independent of other windows on the screen, they may be written as general-purpose as desired. In this way, each functional group may be written as an independent module, capable of inclusion into other, perhaps dissimilar, programs. This modularity is enhanced by the fact that the windowing functions themselves are written as general purpose as possible. (In addition, companies that offer such packages for more than one environment often attempt to make the interface as common as possible between all machines supported.)

A common example of such modularity is the drop-down menu. A function to place such a menu on the screen could be written to open a window with almost any menu desired. This function might be used in several different programs requiring drop-down menus.

The use of windowing packages at the application software level carries some limitations with it, however. Since the windowing is being han-dled at the application level, the advantages of windowing cannot extend from one application to another. That is, a user may open up a window within one application on top of another within the same application, but a user may not open up a window from one application on top of a window from another. When the operating system provides the windowing, windows from different applications may be opened on top of each other in any order desired.

DESQview provides a complete windowing environment. At the user level, multiple applications may be executed under DESQview's multitasker, with each confined to its own window. This is true both for DESQview-oblivious applications that were never designed to use windowing and those which utilize their own, internal windowing package.

The DESQview API also provides support for windowing. Applications may use these API routines to open windows, access them, and eventually close them. Since DESQview's windowing support is provided at the operating system level, functional groups from different applications can interact on the same screen.

Simple Windows

Creating a window on the screen generally consists of executing some type of *open()* function call, passing it the height and width of the window to be opened. This function must allocate sufficient space to save details about the window as well as its contents. The amount of space required is a function of how large the window is and the resolution of the display. High resolution graphics windows require much more memory than text-only type windows. The *open()* call returns some type of handle to the caller. Other windowing routines use this handle to determine on which window to operate. Generally, this handle is nothing more than the location of the window's stored information. No matter what it actually is, the user software must save this handle as long as the window is open.

Under DESQview, windows are created using the *win_new()* call. In addition to the size and location, the user may also specify the title of the window. This title appears in the upper left corner of the window and may be used to explain the function of the window. *win_new()* returns the handle of the window created. Like all handles under DESQview, a window handle is a 32-bit entity of type unsigned long. The *DVAPI.H* file defines a type *ulong*, which may be used in declaring handles. Unlike other handle types, the lower 16-bits of a window handle are always zero.

Figure 2.1—Prototype Declaration of *win_new()*

```
                               /*open a new window*/
ulong win_new                  /*return window handle*/
            (char *title,      /*title of new window*/
             int  ltitle,      /*length of title*/
             int  rows,        /*height of window*/
             int  cols);       /*width*/
```

Windows are created in the upper left corner of the screen. Windows may be positioned as desired by passing the row and column location of the upper left corner of the window to the *win_move()* API call.

Figure 2.2—Prototype Declaration of *win_move()*

```
                               /*position a window on the screen*/
void win_move                  /*returns nothing*/
            (ulong winhan,     /*window to place*/
             int   row,        /*row (zero relative)*/
             int   col);       /*column ( " )*/
```

All output under DESQview is through the DESQview windowing system. This implies that a window must be opened automatically and given to the application program when it is invoked from the DESQview menu. In fact, this is the case. The handle of this initial window, also known as the default window, is returned by the API call *win_me()*. The label of this window is the name of the application and the size of this window is defaulted to some value if not specified by the user in the *.DVP* descriptive file created by the Add a Program selection of the DESQview menu. Output using conventional "nonwindowing" function calls, such as printf(), is to this default window.

Figure 2.3—Prototype Declaration of *win_me()*

```
                              /*return default window handle*/
  ulong win_me                /*return window handle*/
          (void);             /*takes no arguments*/
```

Creating a window does not necessarily cause it to be displayed on the screen. There are often many details to be attended before a window is ready for display. Text must be written out, colors must be selected, and the window must be properly placed. If the window is visible as soon as it is opened, these operations become visible to the user. The programmer may prefer to create a window, but leave it invisible until it has been placed and text has been written to it. Only after the window is ready does the application software execute a final window call to make the now complete window visible. The effect appears more refined to the user.

Newly created windows are not visible under DESQview. First, a window must be marked unhidden with the *win_unhide()* call and then drawn to the screen using the *win_redraw()* API call. As we will see, most window changes (such as unhiding it) do not have an effect on the display screen until they are redrawn. Here again, the primary reason for this is to allow the user to make several changes to the display and make them all visible at once with a single redraw. Not only is this faster, but the effect is more striking. Writing text is one exception to the redraw rule. Text written to a window appears on the screen immediately and does not require a redraw.

A window is normally created as the bottommost window of the application. A window may be brought to the top of the application via the *win_top()* API call. A window may also be forced below all windows opened by the current application via the *win_bottom()* call. A window that is completely covered by another window will have no effect on the display when it is redrawn unless the user moves the obscuring window out of the way, so it is generally a good idea to *win_top()* a new window.

Both the *win_top()* and *win_bottom()* API calls automatically redraw the window.

Figure 2.4—Prototype Declarations for *win_unhide()*, *win_redraw()*, *win_top()*, and *win_bottom*

```
                              /*mark a window unhidden*/
void win_unhide               /*returns nothing*/
         (ulong winhan);      /*window to unhide*/

                              /*draw a window to the screen*/
void win_redraw               /*returns nothing*/
         (ulong winhan);      /*window to draw*/

                              /*draw window above other windows*/
void win_top                  /*returns nothing*/
         (ulong winhan);      /*window to draw*/

                              /*draw window below other windows*/
void win_bottom               /*returns nothing*/
         (ulong winhan);      /*window to draw*/
```

A simple sequence for opening and displaying a 15 row high by 50 column wide window at row 5, column 10 on the screen is shown in the following code segment:

```
ulong win1;                    /*declare a window handle*/
win1 = win_new ("Window #1", 9, 15, 50); /*open a 15 x 50 window*/
win_move (win1, 5, 10);        /*position it on row 5, col 10*/
win_unhide (win1);             /*mark it unhidden*/
win_top (win1);                /*and draw it on top*/
```

Windowing packages may provide new functions for writing to windows or they may replace the existing standard C output functions, such as *printf()*. Replacing *printf()* provides the distinct advantage in that the programmer has nothing to relearn. Programs written for nonwindowing environments may not even need changes and may be portable to other environments. However, *printf()* and other standard output routines do not provide the special arguments that windowing routines do. In particular, *printf()* does not accept a window handle, so the package must guess as to which window is to receive the output. Programmers must learn new functions with packages that provide new output routines, but these functions can be customized to the particular environment.

DESQview provides both mechanisms. Since DESQview is designed to work with standard DOS programs, output routines must be replaced at the lowest level possible. DESQview replaces the BIOS output routine with a windowed version. Programs that call *printf()*, which eventually invoke the screen output BIOS call or the BIOS call themselves, are automatically compatible with DESQview's windows. (Output is made to the default window in the current application.)

Accommodation is even made for programs that manipulate the screen directly. On computers that use the 80386 processor, output may be virtualized (this is an option in the *.DVP* file created by the Add a Program utility under the DESQview window). Virtualizing a program allows its output to be windowed, even if it writes directly to screen memory. This is handled by using the paging registers of the 80386 to map the video RAM space into some other physical memory. An operating system demon then copies the video spaces of the different application into the proper windows in the real video memory.

In addition, the API call *api_shadow()* returns the address of a logical screen buffer. A program may call *api_shadow()* and then use the received address exactly as if it were the actual display. DESQview periodically copies the contents of the logical buffer into the application's window on the actual display. This allows programs which directly manipulate screen memory to be converted to execute in a window under DESQview on any microprocessor (such programs are called DESQview *aware programs*).

The DESQview API provides a windowing print function, *win_printf()*. This function accepts all the same arguments as *printf()* with the addition of a window handle as the first argument. (*win_printf()* does have the two curious limitations: the string to be printed is limited to 256 characters in length, and *win_printf()* does not return the number of characters printed.) Programs may also use the simpler *win_swrite()*.

This function may be faster for simple output requirements as it does not perform the character conversions that *printf()* does.

The situation is the same with character output. Programs may use the standard *putc()* and *putchar()* functions to output to the topmost window, or they may use the API version *win_putc()* to output individual characters to any window desired; however, *win_putc()* also outputs the attribute of the character.

Figure 2.5—Prototype Definitions for *api_shadow()*, *win_printf()*, *win_swrite()*, and *win_putc()*

```
                                /*return the address of a logical
                                  video buffer*/
char *api_shadow                /*returns the address of a video
                                  buffer which looks exactly like
                                  video RAM*/
            (void);             /*takes no arguments*/

                                /*printf to a window*/
void win_printf                 /*returns nothing*/
            (ulong winhan,      /*window to be printed to*/
             char *control,     /*control string*/
             ...);              /*variable arguments*/

                                /*write a string to a window*/
void win_swrite                 /*returns nothing*/
            (ulong winhan,      /*window to write to*/
             char *string);     /*string to write*/

                                /*write char/attribute*/
void win_putc                   /*returns nothing*/
            (int  character,    /*character to write*/
             int  attribute);   /*attribute to write*/
```

Positioning of the cursor in a non-windowed system is relative to the upper left or lower left corners of the screen. It is, therefore, natural for cursor positioning in windowed systems to be relative to the corners of the window. Memory-mapped systems such as that found on the PC also differentiate between the logical and physical cursor. The physical cursor is the small, blinking underline. The logical cursor is the location on the screen where the next output call will place a character. After each output, the logical cursor is left just beyond the last character printed. In a serial terminal the logical and physical cursor are always in the same location, but in a monitor which is driven from a memory-mapped video card, the two may be disconnected. In addition, the video hardware on the PC only supports one physical cursor, whereas each window has its own logical cursor.

Under DESQview, the API function *win_cursor()* places the logical cursor at the specified row and column (zero relative) from the upper left corner of the window. The next call to *win_printf()* begins at that location. The physical hardware cursor is not updated by the *win_cursor()* call; however, it may be repositioned by following it with a call to *win_hcur()*.

Figure 2.6—Prototype Declaration for *win_cursor()*, *win_hcur()*, and *win_free()*

```
                              /*place the logical cursor*/
    void win_cursor           /*returns nothing*/
            (ulong winhan,    /*handle of cursor to place*/
             int row,         /*row and column*/
             int col);

                              /*place hardware cursor at current
                                location of logical cursor*/
    void win_hcur             /*returns nothing*/
            (ulong winhan);   /*handle of hardware cursor*/

                              /*close a window and free handle*/
    void win_free             /*returns nothing*/
            (ulong winhan);   /*handle to free*/
```

Once a functional group is finished with a window, it must close it to remove it from the screen. Any text which was obscured by the window is rewritten to the screen and any memory that was used to store the window is returned to the system for use by future window opens.

DESQview uses the API function *win_free()* to close a window and free its memory and handle. After the *win_free()* call, the window is immediately removed from the screen without the need for a *win_redraw()* call. A handle which has been freed must not be used again. Freeing the default window handle which was opened when the application was initially started (the one returned from *win_me()*) terminates the current application.

If you forget to remove a window, all of an application's windows are automatically removed when the application is exited. If you want to temporarily remove a window from the screen, the API call *win_hide()* followed by a call to *win_redraw()* is a better approach. This way, the window can be brought back by simply calling *win_unhide()* and *win_top()*.

Assume that an application program has four different menus that may be brought up by the user. At initialization, the program could create these windows by calling *win_new()* and fill them in with the proper menu choices via calls to *win_printf()*, but not unhide them. When the user entered the proper key to display a menu, all that the application must do is unhide the proper menu and *win_top()* it to the screen. Once the menu selection has been made, calls to *win_hide()* and *win_redraw()* remove it. Merely making the windows appear and disappear is faster than creating the windows from scratch, which gives the application program faster response time. The listing of WINTST.1 below shows a simple program which opens two windows, writes to them and then terminates.

```
 1[ 0]: /*****************************************************************
 2[ 0]:     Windowing Program #1 - put some windows up on display,
 3[ 0]:                 write text to them and then take them down.
 4[ 0]: *****************************************************************/
 5[ 0]:
 6[ 0]: #include <stdio.h>
 7[ 0]: #include "dvapi.h"
 8[ 0]:
 9[ 0]: /* prototype declarations of user functions*/
10[ 0]: void main (void);
11[ 0]: void program_body (void);
12[ 0]: void display (ulong, int);
13[ 0]:
14[ 0]: /*minimum API version required is DESQview 2.00*/
15[ 0]: #define required 0x200
16[ 0]:
17[ 0]: /*main - standard pattern for DESQview programs*/
18[ 0]: void main (void)
```

```
19[ 0]: {
20[ 1]:    int  version;
21[ 1]:
22[ 1]:    version = api_init();
23[ 1]:    if (version < required)
24[ 1]:        printf ("This program requires DESQview %d.%02d or later.\n",
25[ 1]:                    required >> 8, required & 0xff);
26[ 1]:    else {
27[ 2]:        /*tell DESQview what extensions to enable and start application
28[ 2]:        api_level (required);
29[ 2]:        program_body();
30[ 1]:    }
31[ 1]:    /*if DESQview present (even if wrong version), shut it down*/
32[ 1]:    if (version)
33[ 1]:        api_exit();
34[ 0]: }
35[ 0]:
36[ 0]: /*program_body - open two window handles, place them, turn on logical
37[ 0]:                     attributes and display them.  Then write to them both
38[ 0]:                    and close them*/
39[ 0]: void program_body (void)
40[ 0]: {
41[ 1]:    ulong win1, win2;
42[ 1]:
43[ 1]:    /*go through the opening sequence for a window*/
44[ 1]:    win1 = win_new ("Window #1", 9, 15, 50);
45[ 1]:    win_move (win1, 5, 10);
46[ 1]:    win_logattr (win1, 1);
47[ 1]:    win_attr (win1, 1);
48[ 1]:    win_unhide (win1);
49[ 1]:    win_top (win1);
50[ 1]:
51[ 1]:    display (win1, 30);           /*write to window*/
52[ 1]:    sleep (1);
53[ 1]:
54[ 1]:    /*now open a second window and reveal it*/
55[ 1]:    win2 = win_new ("Window #2", 9, 7, 20);
56[ 1]:    win_move (win2, 7, 20);
57[ 1]:    win_logattr (win2, 1);
58[ 1]:    win_attr (win2,2);
59[ 1]:    win_unhide (win2);
60[ 1]:    win_top (win2);
61[ 1]:
62[ 1]:    display (win2, 50);          /*write to this window*/
63[ 1]:    sleep (1);
64[ 1]:
65[ 1]:    display (win1, 50);          /*now write to the first window*/
66[ 1]:    sleep (1);
67[ 1]:
68[ 1]:    /*finally release them and git*/
69[ 1]:    win_free (win1);
70[ 1]:    win_free (win2);
71[ 0]: }
72[ 0]:
73[ 0]: /*display - write some output to the window long enough to allow the
74[ 0]:                user to examine it*/
```

```
75[ 0]: void display (winhan, length)
76[ 0]:   ulong winhan;
77[ 0]:   int length;
78[ 0]: {
79[ 1]:   int i,j,k;                    /*use for indexes*/
80[ 1]:
81[ 1]:   k = win_len (winhan);
82[ 1]:   for (i = 0; i <-length; i++)
83[ 1]:     for (j = 0; j < k; j++)
84[ 1]:       win_printf (winhan, "%d", (i+j) % 10);
85[ 0]: }
```

Intermediate Windows

DESQview supports several operations on windows that fall into the realm of more advanced operations. While not required to use the windowing interface, their use can improve the appearance of an application.

One of the more exciting aspects of monitors available for the PC is color, as it has a powerful sensory impact that should not be ignored. Video memory includes room for two bytes per character position on the screen in text mode. The first byte contains the ASCII character, while the second byte, known as the attribute, contains the color information. The attribute byte is further divided into two nibbles, one dedicated to the foreground (that is, the character) and the background (the field around the character). These nibbles specify the color on a color monitor and such characteristics as underline, full-bright, inverse video, and flashing on a monochrome monitor.

Figure 2.7—Attributes of the Color Graphics Array (CGA)

```
BIT  7   6   5   4   3   2   1   0
     BL  R   G   B   I   R   G   B
         ------------------   ------------------
            background           foreground
```

where
```
        BL - blinking
         I - 0 -> half bright, 1 -> full bright
         R - red
         G - green
         B - blue
```

Figure 2.8—Representative Monochrome Display (MDA) Attributes

Attribute	Meaning
0x00	black on black (no display)
0x01	underlined normal
0x07	normal
0x0f	high intensity
0x70	inverse video
0x78	high intensity inverse video
0x81	blinking underlined
0x87	blinking normal
0x8f	blinking high intensity
0xf0	blinking inverse video

The EGA and VGA monitors are somewhat more flexible. In their case, the color nibble is simply an index into a color palette containing up to 64 different colors (in CGA-compatible mode).

The user may specify the default attribute of a window via the *win_attr()* API call. Subsequent output to the window will use this attribute unless another is specifically provided by the API call. For example, as already noted, the *win_putc()* API call outputs both a character and an attribute. By comparison, *win_printf()* uses the default attribute for output. Strings of characters and attributes may be output using the *win_addto()* call. Notice that if the attribute string is shorter than the character string, it is reused until the character string is exhausted. Therefore, a single attribute may be passed to *win_addto()* and it will be applied to the entire character string.

The user may write just the attribute field by using either the *win_repattr()* or *win_subfrom()* function calls. The *win_repattr()* writes a single attribute as often as desired, while the *win_subfrom()* writes an attribute string to the window much like *win_write()* writes a character string. Erasing a window with the function *win_erase()* replaces all of the characters in the window with spaces and replaces all of the attributes with the current default attribute.

On the other hand, a function may specify that the attributes of its window are frozen when characters are drawn by using the *win_leave()* function call. The default condition is for the attributes to not be frozen.

Figure 2.9—Prototype Declarations for *win_addto()*, *win_repattr()*, *win_subfrom()*, and *win_leave()*

```
                             /*write char.s and attributes*/
void win_addto               /*returns nothing*/
        (ulong winhan,       /*window handle*/
         char *string,       /*characters to write*/
         int  stringlen,     /*length of string*/
         char *attrstring,   /*string of attributes*/
         int  attrlen);      /*length of attribute string*/

                             /*set the default output attribute*/
void win_attr                /*returns nothing*/
        (ulong winhan,       /*window handle*/
         int   attr);        /*attribute to use*/

                             /*erase a window and set background
                                to current attribute*/
void win_erase               /*returns nothing*/
        (ulong winhan);      /*window to erase*/

                             /*(un)freeze window attributes*/
void win_leave               /*returns nothing*/
        (ulong winhan,       /*window handle*/
         int   on);          /* 1->attributes frozen, 0 otherwise*/

                             /*fill window with attribute by
                                writing attribute 'count' times*/
void win_repattr             /*returns nothing*/
        (ulong winhan,       /*window handle*/
         int count,          /*number of times to write attr*/
         int attr);          /*attribute to write*/

                             /*write an attribute string*/
void win_subfrom             /*returns nothing*/
        (ulong winhan,       /*window handle*/
         char *attrstring,   /*attribute string*/
         int  attrlen);      /*length of string*/
```

In addition to specifying the attribute field directly, the user may choose to indicate the output attribute indirectly through the use of logical attributes. Logical attributes are enabled with the *win_logattr()* call. Once enabled, the attribute field specified during output becomes an index into an attribute lookup table. The values in this 16-position lookup table are the attributes which are actually output to the screen. A different lookup table is maintained for monochrome displays, CGA text and all EGA and VGA displays, CGA displays in high resolution mode, and CGA displays in low resolution mode.

When a program is started, DESQview assigns default physical attributes to each logical attribute in the lookup table. The user may modify these values, however, using the *win_color()* API call. The user specifies which table to modify by passing a bit field to *win_color()* call with a different bit being assigned to each table.

The physical attributes which correspond to each of the logical attributes are specified via the *win_color()* API call. Changing the color of a logical attribute does not change colors already written to the window until a redraw is performed, although all subsequent output uses the new color. By specifying different lookup tables, the user program may map the same logical attribute to different physical attributes on different monitors.

Logical attributes have several advantages. First, they may be changed to match the preferences of either the user or the software. For example, suppose the program maps two different logical attributes, Normal and Special, to the physical attribute normal white. Some fields may be written in Normal and some in Special, but as long as both are mapped to normal white, the user notices no distinction. To highlight special fields, however, the program needs only to remap the logical attribute Special to red and redraw the window. Instantly, those fields written in Special appear red. Remapping Special back to normal white masks any differences in fields just as rapidly.

This remapping of attribute Special may be the result of a safety limit being exceeded. In order to call attention to the problem, the program may alternately map Special from green (when it was safe) to yellow and then to red. Remapping may just as well be performed when the user selects a menu item such as Highlight limits.   Selecting the highlight or unhighlight options induces a call to *win_color()* to set Special to either red or normal white, respectively, but the remainder of the program needs only to output attribute Special without regard to its actual color.

Second, logical attributes can mask differences in hardware from the underlying software.   Continuing the example above, a monochrome monitor cannot display objects in red.   It can display things in full bright (as opposed to the normal half bright), however this does not always stand out sufficiently.   The user program might map Special to blinking or underline on the monochrome monitor, as these characteristics readily standout, while retaining the red mapping on color terminals.   Other functions need only to select attribute Special without worrying about the type of display that may be in use and what attributes will be used to make Special noticeable.

Figure 2.10—Prototype Declarations for *win_logattr()* and *win_color()*

```
                            /*select physical attribute for a
                             given logical attribute*/
void win_color              /*returns nothing*/
        (ulong winhan,      /*window handle*/
         int    display,    /*indicate display types affected
                             1xxxxxxx  - monochrome
                             x1xxxxxx  - text, EGA, VGA
                             xx1xxxxx  - medium CGA graphics
                             xxx1xxxx  - hi res CGA graphics*/
         int    logattr,    /*logical attribute*/
         int    physattr);  /*corresponding physical attribute*/

                            /*select logical or physical
                             attributes*/
void win_logattr            /*returns nothing*/
        (ulong winhan,      /*window handle*/
         int    logical);   /* 1->logical, 0->physical*/
```

```
 1[ 0]: /****************************************************************
 2[ 0]:     Window Program #2 - Example Use of Logical Attributes for
 3[ 0]:                         Highlighting.
 4[ 0]: ****************************************************************/
 5[ 0]:
 6[ 0]: #include <stdio.h>
 7[ 0]: #include <dos.h>
 8[ 0]: #include "dvapi.h"
 9[ 0]:
10[ 0]: /* prototype declarations of user functions*/
11[ 0]: void main (void);
12[ 0]: void program_body (void);
13[ 0]: void wfield (ulong, char *, int, int, int);
14[ 0]:
15[ 0]: /*minimum API version required is DESQview 2.00*/
16[ 0]: #define required 0x200
17[ 0]:
18[ 0]: /*main - standard pattern for DESQview programs*/
19[ 0]: void main (void)
20[ 0]: {
21[ 1]:   int version;
22[ 1]:
23[ 1]:   version = api_init();
24[ 1]:   if (version < required)
25[ 1]:       printf ("This program requires DESQview %d.%02d or later.\n",
26[ 1]:                 required >> 8, required & 0xff);
27[ 1]:   else {
28[ 2]:       /*tell DESQview what extensions to enable
29[ 2]:         and start application*/
30[ 2]:       api_level (required);
31[ 2]:       program_body();
32[ 1]:   }
33[ 1]:   /*if DESQview present (even if wrong version), shut it down*/
34[ 1]:   if (version)
35[ 1]:       api_exit();
36[ 0]: }
37[ 0]:
38[ 0]: /*program_body - open a window, write several fields using
39[ 0]:                  different logical attributes and then remap
40[ 0]:                  the logical attributes*/
41[ 0]:
42[ 0]: #define NORMAL  1
43[ 0]: #define SPECIAL 2
44[ 0]: int color [] = {0x17, 0x40};
45[ 0]:
46[ 0]: void program_body (void)
47[ 0]: {
48[ 1]:   ulong winhan;
49[ 1]:   int i;
50[ 1]:
51[ 1]:   /* create the menu window and set it to use logical attributes */
52[ 1]:   winhan = win_new ("Example Colors", 14, 15, 50);
53[ 1]:   win_move (winhan, 5, 10);
54[ 1]:   win_unhide (winhan);
55[ 1]:
56[ 1]:   /*first map both NORMAL and SPECIAL to the same color*/
```

```
 57[ 1]:   win_logattr (winhan, 1);
 58[ 1]:   win_color (winhan, 0x00f0, NORMAL, color [0]);
 59[ 1]:   win_color (winhan, 0x00f0, SPECIAL, color [0]);
 60[ 1]:   win_attr (winhan, NORMAL);
 61[ 1]:   win_erase (winhan);
 62[ 1]:
 63[ 1]:   /*now write several fields, one of which is special*/
 64[ 1]:   wfield (winhan, " here is field 1 ", NORMAL,  3,  2);
 65[ 1]:   wfield (winhan, " here is field 2 ", NORMAL,  8,  2);
 66[ 1]:   wfield (winhan, " here is field 3 ", NORMAL, 13,  2);
 67[ 1]:   wfield (winhan, " here is field 4 ", NORMAL,  3, 25);
 68[ 1]:   wfield (winhan, " here is field 5 ", SPECIAL, 8, 25);
 69[ 1]:   wfield (winhan, " here is field 6 ", NORMAL, 13, 25);
 70[ 1]:
 71[ 1]:   /*make visible and wait for users to see*/
 72[ 1]:   win_top (winhan);
 73[ 1]:   sleep (2);
 74[ 1]:
 75[ 1]:   /*now change the color of logical attribute SPECIAL*/
 76[ 1]:   win_color (winhan, 0x00f0, SPECIAL, color [1]);
 77[ 1]:   win_redraw (winhan);
 78[ 1]:   sleep (2);
 79[ 1]:
 80[ 1]:   /*switch it back and forth - adding a delay within this
 81[ 1]:      loop helps to see the two different colors*/
 82[ 1]:   for (i = 100; i--; ) {
 83[ 2]:      win_color (winhan, 0x00f0, SPECIAL, color [i & 1]);
 84[ 2]:      win_redraw (winhan);
 85[ 1]:   }
 86[ 1]:
 87[ 1]:   /*now put it back and then quit*/
 88[ 1]:   win_color (winhan, 0x00f0, SPECIAL, color [0]);
 89[ 1]:   win_redraw (winhan);
 90[ 1]:   sleep (2);
 91[ 1]:
 92[ 1]:   win_free (winhan);
 93[ 0]: }
 94[ 0]:
 95[ 0]: /*wfield - output a string at the specified location with
 96[ 0]:             the specified logical attribute*/
 97[ 0]: void wfield (winhan, string, attribute, yloc, xloc)
 98[ 0]:   ulong winhan;
 99[ 0]:   char *string;
100[ 0]:   int attribute, yloc, xloc;
101[ 0]: {
102[ 1]:   /*set the current output attribute for this window*/
103[ 1]:   win_attr (winhan, attribute);
104[ 1]:
105[ 1]:   /*now set the logical cursor location*/
106[ 1]:   win_cursor (winhan, yloc, xloc);
107[ 1]:
108[ 1]:   /*and then write string*/
109[ 1]:   win_swrite (winhan, string);
110[ 0]: }
```

Since windows may overlap in any random fashion, the user needs some help in determining the borders of windows. On color monitors, this can often be handled by differences in background colors, but this is not possible on a black-and-white screen. Most windowing packages offer at least the option for frames about windows. A window frame is nothing more than a line written around a window to delineate its boundaries.

On pure graphically oriented systems, the host may draw any pattern of pixels it desires. Drawing sweeping lines that vertically and horizontally crisscross the screen to create a frame is not a problem. Drawing these lines on text-oriented systems (as are most terminals) is sometimes a problem. Boxing in windows using nondescript characters such as Xs has an unpleasing appearance.

The normal ASCII character set is based on 7-bits and includes only 128 characters. This includes all of the letters of the alphabet (both upper- and lowercase), and the numbers and control characters. IBM designed the PC with an 8-bit ASCII character, which has a full 256 characters. Fortunately, some of the extra 128 characters that IBM introduced include special framing characters for enclosing screen windows. Windowing packages designed to work on the PC in text mode use these extended characters to build either single-lined or double-lined frames.

DESQview uses the API function *win_frame()* to specify whether a window is framed or not. The default for a new window is to be framed. In addition, the color of the window frame may be specified with the *win_frattr()* API call. Neither function has any effect until the window is redrawn.

DESQview uses both single- and double-lined frames. A window is framed using double lines when it belongs to the currently active application. All other windows are single-lined.

Windows may be placed on the screen either relative to the physical screen (absolutely) or relative to another window (relatively). Absolute placement is most useful when the windows are independent entities.

Relative placement is useful when the different windows are strongly
related. Either way, a windowing package must concern itself with
windows that exceed the boundaries of the video display. Windows
must either be truncated to fit or forced to a position where the entire
window fits.

Figure 2.11—Prototype Declarations for *win_frame()* and *win_frattr()*

```
                                /*specify framing or no*/
void win_frame                  /*nothing returned*/
        (ulong winhan,          /*window to frame*/
         int   on);             /* 1->frame, 0->no frame*/

                                /*specify window frame color*/
void win_frattr                 /*returns nothing*/
        (ulong winhan,          /*window frame to color*/
         int   vid,             /*specify which monitor types to
                                  effect (same as win_color)*/
         int   attr);           /*attribute to use for window frame*/
```

Under DESQview, all windows are opened in the upper left corner of the
screen. They can be positioned anywhere on the screen before being made
visible using the *win_move()* API call. Once placed by the program, the
user is free to move a window as desired using the Move command in
the Rearrange option of the DESQview menu. DESQview truncates
whatever does not fit on the screen after being placed by *win_move()*.
Truncated sections reappear if the user moves the window on the screen
to fit.

DESQview also allows windows to be placed relatively using the
win_poswin() API call. The position may be absolute or relative to the left
or right side, or the middle of another window. The *win_poswin()* call
has the futher advantage in that it forces a window to fit entirely within
the display screen. The user-controlled Resize option also does not allow a
window to be placed so that it does not entirely fit on the screen. A window must be redrawn after either function call before it is moved on the
screen.

Figure 2.12—Prototype Definitions for *win_move()*, *win_poswin()*, and *win_attach()*

```
                              /*attach a window to
                                application window*/
void win_attach               /*returns nothing*/
        (ulong winhan,        /*handle of window to attach*/
         int   attach);       /* 1->attach, 0 -> detach*/

                              /*place a window on screen*/
void win_move                 /*returns nothing*/
        (ulong winhan,        /*window to move*/
         int   row,           /*screen row*/
         int   col);          /*screen column*/

                              /*place a window absolute or
                                relative*/
void win_poswin               /*returns nothing*/
        (ulong winhan,        /*window to place*/
         ulong refwin,        /*reference window*/
         int   vertref,       /*row reference:

         int   roffset,       /*row offset*/
         int   horref,        /*column reference:
                                    PSW_SCREEN -> absolute,
                                    PSW_CENTER -> center of refwin
                                    PSW_LEFT   -> bottom of refwin
                                    PSW_RIGHT  -> top of refwin*/
         int   hoffset,       /*column offset*/
         int   redraw);       /* 1->redraw */
```

Programs which have placed windows relatively may not want these windows moved by the user. One way to effect this is to remove the Rearrange command from the DESQview menu when the application is executing. A less severe solution, however, is to attach the two windows together using the *win_attach()* API function call. Two windows that have been attached together move as a unit under the Move command. Windows that have been attached cannot be moved apart by the user.

Note, however, that a window may only be attached to the application's default window—two windows may only be attached together by attaching both to the application window. Also note that the *win_attach()* function has no effect on moves generated from software. Moving the application's window using the *win_move()* or *win_poswin()* API calls does not move any windows that may be attached to it. These must be moved by the application software.

Advanced Windows

Applications are compelled to force their output into windows that fit on a rather small video display. Even in programs that do not utilize windowing, it is often the case that there is more data than room to display it. To address this problem, some windowing systems offer a concept known as logical windowing. The window that the user sees on his display is known as the physical window. Associated with this physical window is a logical window of the same size or larger. The physical window represents a porthole into the logical window, which is also known as the virtual window.

The situation is much the same as with a screen editor. The display of a screen editor, being that which the user sees, forms the physical window. By entering editor commands, this physical window can be made to show different parts of the document being edited. The document is analogous to the logical window since this document contains all of the information that the editor can display.

As is the case with the screen editor, it is often desirable that the logical window be considerably larger than the physical window. When this is the case, the virtual windowing system must be capable of panning and scrolling the logical window behind the confines of the logical window so that the entire logical window may be displayed. This operation is analogous to our screen editor example, which must scroll the target document back and forth across the display to make it visible.

Windowing systems that implement virtual windows can greatly simplify the application software in some operations. One obvious case is that of large menu lists. In a conventional system, the application software must display a portion of the menu and then provide some Up and Down commands to display different sections of the menu. In a virtual windowing system, the user application can simply open up a logical window large enough to hold all of the menu options. This logical window is then assigned to a physical window small enough to fit comfortably within the display. Scrolling of menu choices is no longer an application problem since it is now left up to the virtual windowing system.

DESQview implements such a virtual windowing system. The reader can readily convince himself of this by simply executing a standard DOS application within a window. The application expects to have access to the entire video display. This is its logical window. The part actually being displayed is the physical window. As the application writes to various portions of the screen, DESQview pans the contents of the window back and forth to make the data being written visible.

The sizes specified when a window is created using *win_new()* are actually the logical dimensions of the window. A window is limited to 127 rows and 127 columns. Once a window is opened with *win_new()*, its physical dimensions may be changed using the *win_resize()* API call. In addition, the user may change the size of the physical window using the Resize option of the Rearrange command in the DESQview window. However, the user may not make a window larger than the size specified in the *win_maxsize()* nor smaller than the *win_minsize()* function call. In any case, the physical window may not be made larger than the logical window.

The user cannot affect the size of the logical window, but a window's logical size may be changed using the *win_lsize()* function call. Since a new window node must be allocated, the data within a window is lost if its logical size is changed. (Changing the physical size does not affect the window's contents.) DESQview recommends that the window be erased and the cursor repositioned as the first step after the logical size is changed. The logical dimensions of a window may be deduced from the *win_sizeof()* and *win_len()* API function calls.

Figure 2.13—Prototype Declarations
for Window Sizing Functions

```
                              /*enable/disable justification*/
void api_justify             /*return nothing*/
          (enable);          /* 1 -> enable, 0 -> disable */
                             /*return no. cols in logical window*/
int win_len                  /*return no. cols across*/
          (ulong winhan);    /*handle of window to size*/


                             /*change a window's logical size*/
void win_lsize               /*returns nothing*/
          (ulong winsize;    /*window to resize*/
           int   rows;       /*new number of rows*/
           int   cols);      /*new number of columns*/


                             /*set maximum physical size*/
void win_maxsize             /*returns nothing*/
          (ulong winhan;     /*window to limit*/
           int   rows;       /*new maximum number of rows*/
           int   cols);      /*new maximum number of columns*/


                             /*set minimum physical size*/
void win_minsize             /*returns nothing*/
          (ulong winhan;     /*window to limit*/
           int   rows;       /*new minimum number of rows*/
           int   cols);      /*new minimum number of columns*/


                             /*set origin of physical window
                                within logical window*/
void win_origin              /*returns nothing*/
          (ulong winhan;     /*window to reposition*/
           int   rows;       /*row and column number...*/
           int   cols);      /*...for upper left corner*/


                             /*change a window's physical size*/
void win_resize              /*returns nothing*/
          (ulong winsize;    /*window to resize*/
           int   rows;       /*new number of rows*/
           int   cols);      /*new number of columns*/


                             /*return size of logical window*/
int win_sizeof               /*return no. chars in window*/
          (ulong winhan);    /*window to size*/
```

When the physical dimensions of a window are smaller than its logical dimensions, the problem arises as to which part of the logical window to display. Normally, if justification is enabled via the *api_justify()* API call,

DESQview will attempt to keep the part of the window being updated within the display area; if justification is disabled, it will not. Whether justification is enabled or not, the user may move the logical window behind the physical window to cause different areas to be displayed using the Scroll command in the Rearrange selection of the DESQview menu. Application software may also position the logical window using the *win_origin()* API call. The following program is an example of a panning using *win_origin()*.

```
 1[ 0]: /*****************************************************************
 2[ 0]:     Windowing Program #3 - Open a window which is physically
 3[ 0]:                           smaller than its logical size.
 4[ 0]: *****************************************************************/
 5[ 0]:
 6[ 0]: #include <stdio.h>
 7[ 0]: #include "dvapi.h"
 8[ 0]:
 9[ 0]: /*prototype declarations of user functions*/
10[ 0]: void main (void);
11[ 0]: void program_body (void);
12[ 0]: void display (ulong, int);
13[ 0]:
14[ 0]: /*minimum API version required is DESQview 2.00*/
15[ 0]: #define required 0x200
16[ 0]:
17[ 0]: /*main - standard pattern for DESQview programs*/
18[ 0]: void main (void)
19[ 0]: {
20[ 1]:   int  version;
21[ 1]:
22[ 1]:   version = api_init();
23[ 1]:   if (version < required)
24[ 1]:       printf ("This program requires DESQview %d.%02d or later.\n",
25[ 1]:               required >> 8, required & 0xff);
26[ 1]:   else {
27[ 2]:       /*tell DESQview what extensions to enable
28[ 2]:         and start application*/
29[ 2]:       api_level (required);
30[ 2]:       program_body();
31[ 1]:   }
32[ 1]:   /*if DESQview present (even if wrong version), shut it down*/
33[ 1]:   if (version)
34[ 1]:       api_exit();
35[ 0]: }
36[ 0]:
37[ 0]: /*program_body - open a window which is logically larger than
38[ 0]:                  its physical size.  Write to it, pan it and
39[ 0]:                  then close it*/
40[ 0]: void program_body (void)
41[ 0]: {
42[ 1]:   int i;
```

```
43[ 1]:    ulong win1;
44[ 1]:
45[ 1]:    /*create the menu window and then resize it to be
46[ 1]:       physically smaller*/
47[ 1]:    win1 = win_new ("Big Window", 10, 25, 80);
48[ 1]:    win_move (win1, 1, 1);
49[ 1]:    win_resize (win1, 20, 40);
50[ 1]:    win_unhide (win1);
51[ 1]:    win_top (win1);
52[ 1]:
53[ 1]:    display (win1, 25);              /*write to window*/
54[ 1]:
55[ 1]:    /*now move it right and then back left*/
56[ 1]:    win_origin (win1, 5, 0);
57[ 1]:    for (i = 0; i < 40; i++) {
58[ 2]:        win_origin (win1, 0, i);
59[ 2]:        win_redraw (win1);
60[ 1]:    }
61[ 1]:    for (; i; i--) {
62[ 2]:        win_origin (win1, 0, i);
63[ 2]:        win_redraw (win1);
64[ 1]:    }
65[ 1]:    sleep (2);
66[ 1]:
67[ 1]:    /*finally release them and git*/
68[ 1]:    win_free (win1);
69[ 0]: }
70[ 0]:
71[ 0]: /*display - write some output to the window to allow the
72[ 0]:              user to examine it*/
73[ 0]: void display (winhan, length)
74[ 0]:    ulong winhan;
75[ 0]:    int length;
76[ 0]: {
77[ 1]:    int i,j,k;                      /*use for indexes*/
78[ 1]:
79[ 1]:    k = win_len (winhan) - 5;
80[ 1]:    for (i = 0; i < length; i++) {
81[ 2]:        win_printf (winhan, "%4d:", i);
82[ 2]:        for (j = 0; j < k; j++)
83[ 2]:            win_printf (winhan, "%d", j % 10);
84[ 1]:    }
85[ 0]: }
```

As we noted already, through the use of logical screen attributes, particular sections of the display may be highlighted very rapidly. Windows can also be used to highlight a particular section of the screen such as the correct answer, the field being edited, etc. Particularly useful in this context are windowing systems which allow transparent and translucent fields to be created. As the name implies, a transparent field in a window is a field through which the user can see. Whatever happens to be behind that field appears in that space.

Translucent is similar to transparent, except that some property, usually the color, is taken from the current window. Thus, if a translucent space happened to appear above the letter *a* in a background window, the letter would appear in the space, but it would be the same color as the remainder of the window.

Transparent and translucent characters are extremely useful in highlighting a screen. For example, suppose that the applications programmer wanted to highlight in his program the field currently being entered. The programmer could make each different field a different window and then change the background attribute of the window currently selected so that it stands out. A slightly more clever solution would be to give each field a different logical attribute and then map all of them to the same color, except for the attribute of the currently selected window.

Figure 2.14—Picture of Translucent Overlay

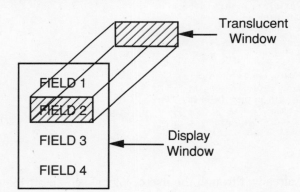

The best solution, however, might be to simply cover the window to be highlighted with a translucent window, which is a highlighted color. The program then simply places the translucent window over the field to be highlighted. The field text continues to show through but the field now appears in the highlighted color of the translucent window. Moving the translucent window to a new field instantly unhighlights the old field and highlights the new field.

DESQview supports both translucent and transparent fields. In the PC's character set there are three ASCII characters which appear as a space. The first is 20 hex, the standard space. The other two are 0 hex (NULL) and FF hex. DESQview uses these two characters for transparent and translucent, respectively.

Remember when building translucent highlight windows that a window may be frameless. A frameless, translucent window does not appear to the user like anything more than a change in the attribute field of the area covered by the window.

```
 1[ 0]: /*******************************************************************
 2[ 0]:    Windowing Program #4 - demonstrate transparent and translucent
 3[ 0]:                            characters.
 4[ 0]: *******************************************************************/
 5[ 0]:
 6[ 0]: #include <stdio.h>
 7[ 0]: #include "dvapi.h"
 8[ 0]:
 9[ 0]: /*prototype declarations for user functions*/
10[ 0]: void main (void);
11[ 0]: void program_body (void);
12[ 0]: void color_thru (ulong);
13[ 0]: void look_thru (ulong);
14[ 0]:
15[ 0]: /*minimum API version required is DESQview 2.00*/
16[ 0]: #define required 0x200
17[ 0]:
18[ 0]: /*main - standard pattern for DESQview programs*/
19[ 0]: void main (void)
20[ 0]: {
21[ 1]:    int  version;
22[ 1]:
23[ 1]:    version = api_init();
24[ 1]:    if (version < required)
25[ 1]:        printf ("This program requires DESQview %d.%02d or later.\n",
26[ 1]:                required >> 8, required & 0xff);
27[ 1]:    else {
28[ 2]:        /*tell DESQview what extensions to enable
29[ 2]:          and start application*/
30[ 2]:        api_level (required);
31[ 2]:        program_body();
32[ 1]:    }
33[ 1]:    /*if DESQview present (even if wrong version), shut it down*/
34[ 1]:    if (version)
35[ 1]:        api_exit();
```

```
36[ 0]: }
37[ 0]:
38[ 0]: /*program_body  -  put a window and another one on top of it.
39[ 0]:                      In the new window, write transparent and
40[ 0]:                      translucent characters */
41[ 0]: void program_body (void)
42[ 0]: {
43[ 1]:    int i,j,k;                     /*use for indexes*/
44[ 1]:    ulong win1, win2;
45[ 1]:
46[ 1]:    /*create the menu window and write to it*/
47[ 1]:    win1 = win_new ("Window #1",9,20,60);
48[ 1]:    win_move (win1,4,19);
49[ 1]:    win_logattr (win1,1);
50[ 1]:    win_attr (win1,1);
51[ 1]:    win_unhide (win1);
52[ 1]:    win_top (win1);
53[ 1]:
54[ 1]:    k = win_len (win1);
55[ 1]:    for (i = 0; i < 20; i++)
56[ 1]:        for (j = 0; j < k; j++)
57[ 1]:            win_printf (win1, "%d", (i+j) % 10);
58[ 1]:
59[ 1]:    /*now open a second window and position it
60[ 1]:      on top of the first*/
61[ 1]:    win2 = win_new ("", 0, 2, 11);
62[ 1]:    win_logattr (win2, 1);
63[ 1]:    win_attr (win2,2);
64[ 1]:    win_unhide (win2);
65[ 1]:    win_top (win2);
66[ 1]:
67[ 1]:    /*first draw transparent characters and pan window right*/
68[ 1]:    look_thru (win2);
69[ 1]:    for (i = -20; i < 20; i++) {
70[ 2]:        win_poswin (win2, win1, PSW_CENTER, 0, PSW_CENTER, i, 1);
71[ 2]:        win_redraw (win2);
72[ 1]:    }
73[ 1]:    sleep (2);
74[ 1]:
75[ 1]:    /*now translucent character (notice color change) and left pan*/
76[ 1]:    color_thru (win2);
77[ 1]:    for (; i > -20; i--) {
78[ 2]:        win_poswin (win2, win1, PSW_CENTER, 0, PSW_CENTER, i, 1);
79[ 2]:        win_redraw (win2);
80[ 1]:    }
81[ 1]:    sleep (2);
82[ 1]:
83[ 1]:    /*finally release them and git*/
84[ 1]:    win_free (win1);
85[ 1]:    win_free (win2);
86[ 0]: }
87[ 0]:
88[ 0]: /*Look-thru - make the current window transparent*/
89[ 0]: void look_thru (winhan)
90[ 0]:    ulong winhan;
91[ 0]: {
```

```
 92[ 1]:    win_title (winhan, "Transparent", 11);
 93[ 1]:    win_open (winhan, 0x00);
 94[ 0]: }
 95[ 0]:
 96[ 0]: /*Color-thru - make the current window translucent*/
 97[ 0]: void color_thru (winhan)
 98[ 0]:    ulong winhan;
 99[ 0]: {
100[ 1]:    win_title (winhan, "Translucent", 11);
101[ 1]:    win_open (winhan, 0xff);
102[ 0]: }
```

In a nonwindowed environment, the currently executing program can always assume that the user can see everything the program writes all of the time. In the event of an error or some condition about which the user should be informed, the program need merely write an error message. If there is any doubt about the matter, using a high contrast color and sending a small "beep" should make sure that the message gets noticed.

In a highly windowed environment, getting the word out to the user in the event of an error is not always so simple. The window to which the current function is writing may be obscured by another window. Even using a bright color will not help if the user cannot see the window.

To make sure that the user sees an error message, the program should open a new, small window, make it the top window in the system and write the error message to it. Once the error is acknowledged, the window may be removed from the screen and freed. Since this is a fairly common occurrence, it is common for an error output function to be available in windowed systems. Such a function outputs the error message in such a way that the user is certain to see it.

DESQview uses the *win_disperor()* API call to alert the user. This function call provides a convenient, single call which is sure to be visible to the user no matter what windows might be covering the application program. In addition, the caller is suspended until the user acknowledges the error by either entering escape or by pointing at the window with the mouse and clicking. Of course, the condition being reported need not actually be an error. As we will see in Chapter 4, *win_disperor()* provides a convenient means for reporting any condition.

Figure 2.15—Function Prototype for *win_disperor()*

```
                        /*display an error message window
                          and wait for user acknowledge*/
int win_disperor        /*returns a 1 if left button pressed
                          to acknowledge message or a 2 if
                          the right button or Escape pressed*/
    (ulong winhan,      /*handle of window sending error*/
     char  *message,    /*message to send*/
     int   msglngth,    /*length of message*/
     int   rows,        /*size of error window*/
     int   cols,        /*(0,0 -> use minimum window to fit
                          message)*/
     int   beep,        /* 1 -> beep when window displayed*/
     int   buttons);    /* 1 -> wait for left button,
                          2 -> wait for right button or ESC,
                          0 -> wait for either button*/
```

Conclusion

The DESQview API provides a powerful and flexible windowing environment of which we will make considerable use throughout this book. Placed strategically at the operating system level, this windowing package is capable of much more than conventional windowing packages.

Multitasking

Background

During the 1950s, computers were quite large, costly, and fairly rare. CPU time was a premium commodity. Almost anything that could be done to better utilize the CPU's time was worth doing. But anyone who examined the way these early beasts operated could see that much time was lost, especially when waiting for input.

A program would often request the computer operator to load a certain tape on the tape drive or a special deck of punch cards into the card reader. Several minutes might elapse while the operator searched for the desired tape or box of cards. During this time the CPU had little choice but to wait by executing some pointless loop. Much computer time was lost that could have been used working on some other problem while the desired input was being prepared.

But CPUs were waiting on more than just the occasional human input. Even after the card deck or tape was loaded, the CPU was required to wait on the relatively slow mechanical devices that read them. To the casual observer it may have seemed that tape drives and card readers operated swiftly, but even compared to the relatively modest CPU performance of the day, these mechanical devices were quite slow. Even slower were output devices such as card punches and printers.

Operating systems were developed that could avoid this needless waste of CPU time by switching an application out of memory when it was waiting on a slow external device (such as an operator), and load in another application that was waiting for its attention. Once the external device was ready, the operating system could switch the earlier application back into memory and continue where it had left off. By better utilizing its time in this fashion, a single CPU could execute two or more applications with little or no increase in the execution time of either application.

This ability became known as "multitasking" since the computer could juggle more than one task (program) at a time. Multitasking is also known as pseudo-parallelism. It is called parallelism because several applications seem to be executing at the same time, or in parallel. Pseudo is used, however, because this is how things appear to be. In fact, a single CPU is only capable of executing a single program at any given instant.

This early form of multitasking led to further developments in computer science far beyond the original problem that it was designed to solve. For example, when people realized that a single computer could handle more than one job at one time, the concept of remote terminals was born. Dozens of users sitting behind computer terminals were connected to a single mainframe computer. Since the majority of terminals were inactive at any one instant while awaiting user input, it appeared that all users had their own computer. This lead to the multiuser megaliths that we still see today.

Although much smaller in both capacity and performance than mainframe computers, personal microcomputers such as 8080-based CPM computers and, later, the IBM PC and Apple Macintosh, achieved rapid popularity. Their low cost allowed anyone to own a computer dedicated to their personal use. Designed for a single user, simplicity was more of a consideration than wasted CPU time, and so these early personal computer operating systems were designed to be single tasking only.

But as the CPUs, internal RAM space, and hard disk drives of these personal computers got faster, cheaper, and denser, people again noticed the advantages of multitasking operating systems. With only one user, CPU time was not a concern. Now the advantage was not the amount of wasted CPU time that could be saved, but rather the amount of time the user could save from watching a slow program monopolize the computer's attention. The programmer could start a compile "in the background," and then proceed to edit another file "in the foreground" at the same time.

In practice, however, this advantage is almost never realized in just the way that it is described. Although occasionally unavoidable, companies do not like to publish software that executes so slowly that the user gets bored and goes to the trouble of bringing up a foreground application. Usually the software is executing slowly only because it is hindered by a relatively slow output device, such as a printer, or by a slow input device, such as a user.

Printers are very slow devices. Even fast printers take a long time to print a multipage document. Nothing is more frustrating than watching your entire personal computer made useless by a "Waiting for Printer" message. It is not surprising that one of the earliest utilities available for both the PC and the Mac was the printer spooler.

The printer spooler accepts output destined to the printer as input on one side and forwards it on to the printer as output on the other side. To the applications program, the printer spooler looks like a very fast printer. The spooler accepts output for printing roughly as fast as the program can offer it, and stores it either into a RAM buffer area or onto the disk. To the printer, the spooler appears to be a patient application. Each time the printer runs out of data to be printed, the spooler reaches into its buffer and pulls out something else.

This crude form of multitasking is very effective. The application program often finishes its part of the printer operation before the printer has finished the first paragraph. So instead of staring blankly at a motionless screen and an unresponsive keyboard while the printer head moves incessantly back and forth over the paper, the user is free to continue to work on another task while printing in the background.

The same principle has recently been applied to modem communications. Even at 2,400 baud, it can take a long time to transmit a file of any size over a serial communications link. More recent communications programs offer a mode called background communications. In this mode, the program can send or receive files from the modem in the background, while allowing the user to execute any other program desired at the same time.

Generalizing from these two examples, programs known as switchers were developed to allow the user to leave any application in memory while temporarily executing another. Occasionally the first application is still capable of servicing interrupts (which is all that is required to send spooled data to a printer or to service a modem), but otherwise it lies completely dormant until it is again made the foreground application.

Switcher programs have proven very popular, especially for the Macintosh. It is common for a user to be in the middle of an application when the need arises to execute another, unrelated program. The phone rings and a colleague needs some information, or perhaps the user comes to some long forgotten number in the middle of his report that must be looked up in another program. It is very clumsy for users to exit the current application—a process that might take many steps and several disk accesses—to bring up a new application, and look up a single number only to re-execute the former program and find where they left off.

With a switcher, the user simply executes the new program over the old one. The interrupted program sits patiently in the background until the user has the desired information. Closing the foreground application resumes operation of the background program exactly where it was interrupted. Although extremely useful, this is not true multitasking. The foreground application gets all of the CPU's attention and any applications in the background must wait.

The DESQview multitasking operating system has this switching capacity as a natural outgrowth. An application currently executing in the foreground can be relegated to background status while the user searches for information in another program. To return to the interrupted application, the user simply selects Switch Windows from the DESQview window. The fact that background applications continue to receive some CPU time means that they may continue communicating with modems, printers, or anything else. Spoolers and special background communicators are no longer required.

Software Modularity

Multitasking brings more than just advanced switching or spooling ability, however. Multitasking operating systems carry with them a tremendous advantage for the software developer that is often overlooked: program modularity.

As we have noted, several programs may be executing at the same time under a multitasking environment. Up until now however, we have assumed that these programs are completely unrelated, but this need not be the case. The programs that are executing may actually be parts of a greater whole.

Take the example of the Integrated Environments, such as Lotus's Symphony and Ashton-Tate's Framework. An Integrated Environment is a single program that contains all of the functions a user commonly requires. It usually contains a word processor, a spreadsheet, a database, and a terminal emulation program. It may include other features such as a datebook, an ASCII look-up table, a calculator, etc. All of these features are built into a single program. By being able to move rapidly from one area to another, the Integrated Environment effectively takes the place of the switcher mentioned earlier. By being designed to work with each other, the applications of an Integrated Environment can exchange data as well.

But Integrated Environments run into several problems that greatly reduce their attractiveness. First, Integrated Environments are an all or nothing proposition. The user may be perfectly happy with the word processor and database, but if the spreadsheet is lacking, the user will be dissatisfied. Besides that, Integrated Environments are very large. Large amounts of RAM are required just to hold the code. Even if the user only intends to utilize the word processor, room must still be found to hold the code to support the other features of the Integrated Environment. Finally, switching is only supported between parts of the Integrated Environment and not with other programs.

But what if the Integrated Environment was implemented as a series of separate programs under a multitasking environment? If the programs can agree on how communication should be handled between them, several distinct advantages appear. Users are free to choose the individual applications they desire. As long as the new application agrees to communicate the same as the other programs, users can execute whichever spreadsheet they find most suitable. In addition, this approach does not require as much memory as the Integrated Environment approach. In the modular program approach, users only execute the programs in which they are interested. If all they want to do is word processing, the database and spreadsheet can remain on the disk where they belong.

The benefits of such a multitasking approach are fairly obvious in such a case. Perhaps less obvious is that the same advantages apply to other, more conventional applications as well. Take, for instance, a simple spreadsheet. Such a program could logically be divided into four parts: the input program, the calculator program, the tabular output program, and the graphics output program (one could envision other, equally logical divisions). The input program accepts input to the spreadsheet and feeds it to the calculator program that processes it. Output from the calculator program is displayed in tabular form by the tabular output program, and in graphic form by the graphics output program.

Anyone familiar with the concepts of modular programming might come to the same conclusion and, having done so, set off to program these four parts as four separate modules within a single program. This is undoubtedly the way all major spreadsheets are written. Dividing the application into four separate programs, however, leads to the same advantages mentioned above. Not all of the programs must be in memory at any given time. The graphics program is not loaded until it is actually needed. If the tabular output program must be unloaded from memory for the graphics program to be loaded, then so be it. Using separate programs divides the problem into pieces that the operating system can deal with, rather than a monolithic whole. This allows the operating system to make better use of existing RAM. It is even possible to execute a 1 MB spreadsheet program on a machine equipped with less than 1 MB of memory as long as each of the individual programs fits within existing memory. (There is, of course, a performance penalty as the different programs are paged back and forth to disk.)

Even more important is that individual parts can be replaced as necessary. Several graphics standards exist for the PC today. Each of these graphics cards must be accessed in slightly different ways. Today, device drivers that are designed to handle the different adapters and yet present a common interface to the program software are used to handle this problem. In this approach, the details of the graphics card are hidden from the graphing routines.

Using the modular program approach, however, the user could select a completely different graphics program, depending on the video display adapter. The image displayed can be varied. Rather than making all video displays appear identical to the software, custom graphics programs can be customized to better utilize the features available in each display. For example, you could display a larger, simpler graphic image on low resolution displays and a more detailed graph on higher resolution displays.

Similarly, the default input program looks at the keyboard for input. However, a replacement input program might actually accept input from a database file in dBase format or from a modem connected to a remote site. As long as the input program sent the same messages in the same format, the other programs of the application are blissfully ignorant of the slight of hand being performed. In fact, if built properly, both input programs may be executing at the same time, generating input to the remainder of the program.

Again, proponents of modular programming might maintain that their programming techniques offer the same advantages. A module can be designed to take keyboard input and reformat it for the remainder of the program in such a way that the program's core is unaware (and uncaring) of how the data was obtained, whether from the keyboard or from a dial-up log-on service.

The difference is that with the modular programming solution, the programmer must decide which modules and capabilities to include when linking the program. With multitasking, that decision can be made at execution time when the user decides which programs to execute. This is a powerful paradigm which the reader should keep in mind as we will revisit it several times in the next few chapters.

Context Switching

When the operating system decides that it is time to suspend execution of one application so that execution of another application may begin, it must go through a process known as a context switch. The execution thread that is switched in or out by the operating system is known as a task. In the context switch, the CPU must save every piece of information necessary to restore the suspended task when it comes time. The vast majority of information is already saved in memory anyway: the machine code being executed, the data space, and the current stack. These memory areas are known as the code segment, data segment, and stack segment, respectively. The operating system must also save the CPU's registers, including the Instruction Pointer, which points to the next instruction to be executed, and the status flags as well as the state of the surrounding hardware, such as the display mode.

Since the memory areas used by the task must not be overwritten by other tasks, the address and length of these areas must also be recorded. Generally, the operating system maintains a structure, known as a Task Descriptor, for each task that is currently executing. In reality, the Task Descriptor plus the memory areas to which it points are the task to the operating system since they contain all of the information necessary to resuscitate it. The Task Descriptor and its associated memory are also known as an execution thread. A thread begins when the Task Descriptor is created, and dies with the return of the Task Descriptor and its associated memory to the available memory pool.

At any given instant, a task may be in one of several states. For example, a task may be waiting for some event such as a key from the keyboard or for a given amount of time to transpire. It would be pointless to give control to such a task until the event occurs since it is not prepared to continue execution. Such a task is said to be in the "Blocked" state. A task that is not waiting for an event is said to be in the "Ready" state. At any given time one of the Ready tasks may be executing. This task is said to be in the "Executing" state. A context switch takes a task which is in state Executing and places it in state Ready and then takes another task in state Ready and transitions it into state Executing. This is described in the picture below.

There are two approaches to deciding when it is time to perform a context switch. The first approach is to wait for the application program to give up control voluntarily via a system call. This is known as nonpreemptive scheduling. The second approach is to give each task a fixed amount of time that is measured by the hardware clock. Once that time has expired, the task is interrupted and a context switch is performed to the next task waiting in the queue. This is known as preemptive scheduling.

Figure 3.1—Task State Transitions

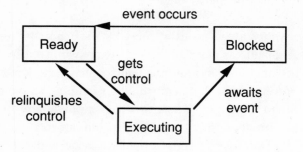

Nonpreemptive scheduling has its advantages. It is generally the easiest to implement. The task knows when it is in position to accept being put to sleep for a while. It is usually the most efficient in terms of overall throughput, if not in response time, since there is generally no advantage to switch out a task that is still performing useful work until it has finished. The voluntary nature of nonpreemptive scheduling that gives it its efficiency advantage is also its most serious drawback. The responsibility for switching tasks lies with the application task. If the task decides to go into an infinite loop without ever giving up control, the entire system quits working.

Preemptive scheduling avoids the drawback of stingy tasks. By using an impartial judge such as a hardware clock, preemptive schedulers remove the responsibility from the application task and place it back in the operating system where it belongs. Even tasks in infinite loops are occasionally interrupted and switched out, and other tasks are allowed to execute.

A properly designed operating system protected by the proper hardware support such as memory protection cannot be crashed by an errant application task. Any user of multiuser systems knows that this is never completely the case, but it is nonetheless amazing the number and variety of programming errors I have made, and I have never knowingly crashed a multiuser operating system.

For this advantage there is a price. The most serious is that every task must be prepared to give up control to another task at any instant. Programs must be built completely interruptible, since the programmer can never know when the hardware clock's alarm might go off.

The same problem arises in a slightly different context when functions are accessible from more than one task, as is the case with most functions in the operating system. Such a function must be written reentrantly; that is, it may only write to locations that are unique to a task, such as the stack area. (As we will see later, code and data areas may be shared between tasks, but the stack is *always* unique.) Otherwise, task A calls a function that saves variables into a shared space. While executing the function, task A is interrupted and task B is selected to run.

Task B calls the same function that again stores information into the same shared space, overwriting the data written there by task A. When task A again gets control, it resumes execution in the function, but now all of the data previously written there has been overwritten and the function generates unpredictable results. Both the DOS operating system for the PC and the Finder operating system for the Macintosh are non-reentrant.

There are several algorithms for deciding which Ready task to execute next, once the Executing task is returned to the Ready state. No scheduling algorithm is best all of the time, but the scheduling algorithm can have a profound effect on performance. The democratic approach is to cycle in circular fashion between all tasks that are currently Ready. Each task gets 1/Nth of the CPU's attention, where N is the number of currently ready tasks. This Round Robin algorithm is certainly the fairest approach, but has some drawbacks.

The problem is that not all tasks are equally important. Some tasks are not time critical and can wait as long as necessary for the CPU's attention. Some tasks are time critical, however, including tasks that perform any type of communications. To address this issue many systems assign priorities to tasks. Higher priority tasks are scheduled ahead of lower priority ones.

Here again there is disagreement as to the best method. In a simple priority scheme, higher priority tasks run to the exclusion of lower priority ones. If only one high priority task is ready, it will run until it either completes or blocks on an event, irrespective of how many low priority tasks might be waiting. Among tasks of the same priority, a Round Robin approach is assumed. In more complex-weighted algorithms, the high priority tasks get more time than lower priority ones, but all tasks get some time.

DESQview takes a preemptive scheduling approach using the PC's hardware clock that ticks 18.2 times per second. DESQview does not assign priorities to tasks except that the currently active application is known as the foreground application. All others are known as the background applications.

DESQview assigns a certain number of time slices to the foreground application and a certain number to each of the background applications. The default is 9 for the foreground and 3 for each of the background applications, but this can be changed in the DESQview SetUp. In addition, the user can change the current mix by selecting the Tune Performance option under Rearrange on the DESQview window.

Consider the following case where the user has 4 applications currently active: a spreadsheet in the foreground with a word processor which is printing, a half-played chess game which is calculating the next move, and the DESQview Notepad which is waiting for input in the background. In this case there is one foreground application (the spreadsheet), one background application which is blocked (the notepad waiting for keyboard input), and two background applications vying for CPU time (the word processor and the chess game). Using the example time slice values of 6 and 3 and a rough value of 18 time slices per second, the timing resembles the following:

```
total time for one cycle = 12 clock ticks (= 6 + 2*3)
                         = 12/18 = 2/3 second each cycle
foreground               = 6/12  = 1/2 of the time
                         = 6/18  = 1/3rd second each cycle
two "Ready" backgrounds  = 3/12  = 1/4th of the time
                           3/18  = 1/6th second each cycle
one "Blocked" background = no time
```

Making the foreground number large in relation to the background numbers will cause the currently active application to execute as if there were no background applications at all. Making the number small will speed up the background applications at the expense of the current application.

It should be noted that typing a key automatically restarts the foreground application when it is reading a character from the keyboard. This gives more time to an application that is currently interacting with the user. This, in turn, shortens response time and gives the system a more lively feel.

Multitasking Models

There are essentially three ways in which a program can use a multitasking system. Conventional programs simply ignore the fact that multitasking is going on at all. This is the mode in which the vast majority of programs built for multiuser systems, and essentially all personal computer software executes. Such programs are inflexible in their design—the user cannot customize them except in ways for which the designer specifically provides.

The simplest multitasking model is that of simple tasks, also known as threads. In this model, several tasks execute within the same module. These tasks share code and data segments (although not stack segments). Communications between tasks is only slightly more difficult than between modules of a conventional program. Programs using this model are often easier to write than conventional programs but no more customizable.

The third model is the multiprocessing module. Under multiprocessing, tasks execute independently of each other, sharing neither code, data, or stack segments. Communication between processes is somewhat more difficult but more controlled than in the previous two models. Programs written using the multiprocessing model are easy to write and integrate, and are customizable by the end user. These models are not mutually exclusive. A process may itself consist of multiple tasks, as we shall see.

DESQview supports all three multitasking models. Written to support conventional DOS applications, the vast majority of programs executing under DESQview know nothing of the multitasking capabilities available with DESQview. Of course, the DESQview API also supports multitasking and multiprocessing. With DESQview, tasks and processes have the additional distinction that processes are independently controllable from within the DESQview menu. Processes may be Selected, Frozen, and be PutAside from within the DESQview window. Tasks may not.

In addition, DESQview introduces a third multitasking model called multi-application. An application lies somewhere between a task and a process. Applications share code and data segments, like tasks, but can be controlled from the DESQview window, like processes. We will examine all three in detail in the following chapters.

Tasks

Tasks, or threads, are conceptually the simplest form of multitasking and are a good place to start. Tasks resemble simple functions except that the caller and the function execute simultaneously. In a normal function call, the caller is effectively suspended while the function executes. In multitasking parlance, the execution thread passes from the caller to the function and is not returned until the function completes. Since there is only one execution thread, the call cannot continue until the function returns it.

In a task call by comparison, the function begins execution just like before, but the caller retains his execution thread. A new thread is created for the function, and they both execute in parallel. When the sub-task completes, either via a system call or by returning, its execution thread is terminated.

Let's take our venerable spreadsheet example by way of explanation. In a conventional spreadsheet, when the user hits the ReCalc key a recalculate function is invoked somewhere deep within the program. While this function is working (which could be a considerable length of time), the program appears to "go away." Once this function is completed, control is returned to the main body and the program is ready to accept keyboard input.

If the recalculate function was executed as a separate task, the results would be quite different. Depressing the ReCalc key causes the spreadsheet program to start the recalculate task. The operating system creates a Task Control block and starts a new execution thread with the function. Control returns to the calling function, which continues on to await further user commands. The recalculate task begins to execute. As soon as the recalculate completes, the recalculate function terminates. A multitasking spreadsheet responds very rapidly to user input. As soon as the ReCalc function is started the program is ready to accept further input. There is no "going away" for large periods of time. (Of course, the user may be precluded from executing certain operations during the ReCalc.)

This level of multitasking is fairly simple to implement. It is unfortunate that DOS did not include this rudimentary multitasking ability. If it had, the face of software for the PC and its clones would look much different today.

The only hardship independent tasks place on the user software is reentrancy. A task may be interrupted at any time. It is therefore important that any function which may be called by more than one task be completely interruptible. For example, assume that our example spreadsheet used a common function for outputting characters to the display. The recalculate task uses this function to update the value of cells that change during recalculation at the same time the main program uses that same function to display menu choices. No problem will arise as long as this output function is careful to only save variables on the stack and not in local memory.

Interestingly, DOS is not reentrant and cannot be made so. DESQview must make special provisions to avoid two tasks from executing a DOS call at the same time. If a task is interrupted in the middle of a DOS call, all other tasks are prevented from making a DOS call by being blocked until the first task's call finishes.

Creating a task is hardly more difficult than a simple system call. Contained in the call is the address of the task function to start. Returned is a status code indicating whether the task was started or not and, often, some task identification handle.

DESQview uses a series of API calls to deal with tasks. All of the calls begin with the letters *tsk_*. The function *tsk_new()* is used to create tasks. This function returns the handle of the new task as shown in Figure 3.2.

Figure 3.2—Prototype Declaration of *tsk_new()*

```
                                /*start a new task*/
    ulong tsk_new               /*return task handle*/
            (int (*entryp)(), /*address of task*/
            char *stack,        /*address of stack*/
            int  lstack,        /*length of stack*/
            char *title,        /*title of new window*/
            int  ltitle,        /*length of title*/
            int  rows,          /*height of window*/
            int  cols);         /*width*/
```

The following is an excerpt showing the function *subtask()* as a separate task using the function *tsk_new()*.

```
#define STACKSIZE 1000
#define NUMROWS      10
#define NUMCOLS      25

ulong tskhan;
int subtask();
char stack [STACKSIZE];
char titlebuf [80];
int taskcount, titlesize;

titlesize = sprintf (titlebuf, "Task #%d", ++taskcount);
tskhan = tsk_new (subtask, stack, STACKSIZE,
                  titlebuf, titlesize, NUMROWS, NUMCOLS);
```

The first argument is the address of the function to start as a separate task. In the above example this function has been declared to be of type *INT* to agree with the description in the DESQview API manual, but it could just as well be of type *VOID* as this function will not return anything.

The second argument is a pointer to the memory area that the new task will use as a stack. In this example, I have merely declared an array of sufficient size and passed that. It is important that this array be declared on the parent task's stack. (Some compilers get confused when these stack areas are declared globally.) Also, knowing how much stack to declare is difficult. Every time a function is called, room is allocated on the stack for the return address, plus any local variables declared within the function. This space is returned to the stack when the function returns.

If the programmer diagrams the amount of stack required by the calls each function makes, and the calls these functions make, and so on, the results resemble a tree. Each branch reaches further up into the stack as calls are made and retreats back towards earth as returns are executed. The stack space allocated to a task must be larger than the tallest branch of this tree if this branch is not to reach out and overwrite some other task's memory area.

Although not very satisfying, the amount of stack to allocate may be determined empirically by allocating the maximum amount of space possible during debug and then shrinking it back after everything works (until problems begin to arise or a sufficiently small number is achieved).

The third argument to *tsk_new()* is simply the name of the task. In this case, the variable *TASKCOUNT* is simply the number of the current task that is used to build a name of the form *Task* #, where # is the task number.

The final argument is the logical and physical size of the window created for this task. Every task has a window associated with it. When created, the task adopts the same color scheme as the parent, at screen location 0,0, and is hidden. If the task has no visual output, the window may remain hidden and it may be of size 0,0.

The function *tsk_new()* returns the task handle of the task created. A pointer to where window information is stored is much like the window handler. The task handle is the address of the Task Descriptor where the task's critical information is stored, but in DESQview it is equivalent to the name of the task. The task handle must be presented to other *tsk_* function calls to indicate which task the function is to operate on.

Once a task's job is completed, it must give control back to the system. If it has merely reached a nice place to pause, a task may simply pass temporary control back to the operating system, relinquishing the remainder of its time slice. If the task is finished, it may kill itself via a system call or simply return from the highest level function. This is completely equivalent to a C program that can either call the C function *exit()* or return from the *main()* function to terminate. A task may also be killed by another task, if desired.

The API function *api_pause()* releases control back to DESQview. The task is left in the Ready state, so the task regains control when it is again its turn. *api_pause()* returns to the calling task as if there had been no interruption. Certain other API calls automatically invoke *api_pause()* to improve multitasking performance.

Figure 3.3—Prototype Declarations of Some Simple Task Calls

```
                        /*release control*/
void api_pause (void);   /*no arguments*/

                        /*return calling task's handle*/
ulong tsk_me (void);     /*no arguments*/

                        /*kill task and free its handle*/
void  tsk_free            /*returns nothing*/
        (ulong tskhan); /*handle of task to kill*/

                        /*restart a stopped task*/
void  tsk_start           /*returns nothing*/
        (ulong tskhan); /*handle of task to restart*/

                        /*stop a task until restarted*/
void  tsk_stop            /*returns nothing*/
        (ulong tskhan); /*handle of task to stop*/
```

The function *tsk_free()* is used to kill tasks in DESQview. *tsk_free* takes one argument; the handle for the task to be killed. A task's parent receives the task handle from the *tsk_new()* call. The task itself may know its own handle by calling *tsk_me()*. The code sequence:

```
tsk_free (tsk_me ())     /*free self*/
```

will always free the calling task.

Freeing a task returns its Task Descriptor for use by other tasks, and frees up its stack space and any windows that it may have allocated. If a task has spawned other tasks, they are also freed. A task handle must not be used again after the task has been freed.

A task may also be stopped and restarted using the *tsk_stop()* and *tsk_start()* calls. A task that is stopped is left intact but it does not receive any execution time as it is in a Blocked state until it is restarted. Once restarted, the task does not begin execution immediately, but only when its turn comes around again.

The concepts of windows and tasks are not unrelated. Most tasks have some sort of output. This output is the most obvious physical evidence that a task exists. In addition, a task should not use the windows created by the parent task. The child task should be built to execute as an autonomous unit. As we discussed in Chapter 3, software functional groups are easier to develop if their output is independent of other functional groups. Such software need not rely on knowing the condition of the screen nor any existing windows when it executes. Each task should open its own windows for output as necessary and let the operating system merge them into a coherent screen.

In DESQview, the concepts of tasks and windows are so tightly bound that the Task Descriptor and Window Descriptor are, in fact, one and the same. This is one reason the API call *tsk_new()* creates a window automatically when the task is created. The *win_new()* API call simply creates a window with no task attached. The *tsk_new()* call creates a window and attaches a new task to it.

A task may know its default window via the *win_me()* call, which returns its handle. With this handle, a task may manipulate its default window using the *win_* API calls discussed in Chapter 3. If a task has no visual output, it does not have to unhide it's window or otherwise make it visible on the screen. Interestingly, since the Window and Task Descriptors are the same entities, so are the window and task handles. The task handle returned by *tsk_me()* is exactly the same as the default window handle returned by *win_me()*, the two functions being merely pseudonyms for each other.

Communicating with a task is not too much different than communicating with a conventional function. In some environments the creating task is allowed to pass arguments to the starting function (this is generally only the case with programming languages in which multitasking is built in). Even when arguments may not be passed, child tasks have access to the same global variables as the parent task. This is a result of the fact that both the parent and child tasks data segments are compiled and linked together. For example, in the code segment below:

```
int assign_no;

void parenttask()
{
    /*parent task body here*/
}

void childtask ()
{
    /*child task body here*/
}
```

both tasks have access to the global variable *ASSIGN_NO*. If the parent task saves a value there, the child task can read the data back out of it, or vice versa.

```
int assign_no = 0;

void parenttask()
{
    /*parent task can save data into ASSIGN_NO*/
    assign_no = 1;
}

void childtask ()
{
    int local;

    /*child task must wait for ASSIGN_NO to be set*/
    while (assign_no == 0)
        api_pause();

    /*child task may now read ASSIGN_NO*/
    local = assign_no;
```

If this means of access seems a bit too uncontrolled, tasks can also communicate via functions. Two functions in the above example, *get_assign_no()* and *put_assign_no()*, could be written to retrieve and store the value of *ASSIGN_NO* respectively. Since tasks share code segments, these two functions are accessible to both the parent task and the child task.

```
int assign_no = 0;

void parenttask()
{
```

```
    /*parent task can save data using a function*/
    put_assign_no (1);
}

void childtask ()
{
    int local;

    /*child task may now read data with a function*/
    local = get_assign_no ();
}

/*define functions to access ASSIGN_NO*/
int get_assign_no ()
{
    while (assign_no == 0)
        api_pause();
    return assign_no;
}

void put_assign_no (new_value)
    int new_value;
{
    assign_no = new_value;
```

The programmer must be careful here, however. As mentioned above, a task must be interruptible at any point during its execution. Any function that is to be executed by more than one task must be reentrant. The operating system may interrupt the execution of one task while in a given function only to pass control to another task that is executing the exact same function.

Similar problems can arise with tasks that share data. In our above example, assume that both *parenttask()* and *childtask()* could increment *ASSIGN_NO*. Now suppose *parenttask()* reads the value of *ASSIGN_NO* into a register and increments it, but before it can write the value back out to memory, its time slice expires and it is suspended. If *childtask()* attempts to increment *ASSIGN_NO* during its time slice, it will be working on the old value as *parenttask()* had not completed its write. When the *parenttask()* does eventually regain control, it will continue with the interrupted write operation, overwriting the now incremented value placed there by *childtask()*.

Such an event is known as a collision. The sequence of code in which a collision is possible is known as a critical region. The above example may seem extremely contrived. One might argue that the chances of events occurring exactly as described are quite small. It is true that this *particular* data collision is unlikely, as the critical region is only a few instructions long. However, there are many ways in which collisions occur and many critical regions are much larger. All data collisions result in the same thing: lost or corrupted data. Due to the chance timing involved in their occurrence, data collisions are extremely difficult to track down and correct.

Figure 3.4—Example Data Collision

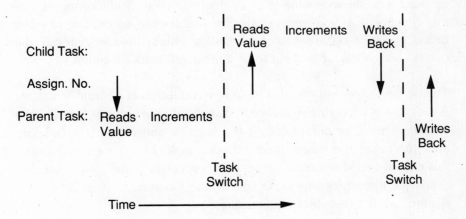

Data collisions over a given location in memory are avoided if only one task is allowed to write that location at a time, even if many tasks are allowed to read it. The easiest way to insure this is to only allow one task ever to write each location. For example, two tasks might use a global variable like a two-way communications street. Doing so, however, runs the risk of data collisions as the two tasks both write the global variable. The problem is easily solved by dividing the single two-way street into two one-way streets. That is, assign each task a separate variable that it is allowed to write. Both tasks can read both global variables, but each task is allowed to write only one of them. In this way, no collision can occur from two tasks writing to the same location.

If it is not possible to keep multiple tasks from ever writing a given memory location, then the programmer must insure only single-task access. This is often the case merely due to the logic of the program. A parent task might load a variable with a value to be communicated to a child task. The child task acknowledges receipt of the value by zeroing the location. The parent task will never write new data into the variable until the old value has been zeroed out. The child task will never zero out the location until a new value has been placed there. Data collisions have been avoided programmatically.

When neither of these approaches are possible, the programmer must make sure that a task is not interrupted while it is manipulating a memory location accessible to more than one task. Multitasking operating systems provide a system call that disables the scheduling of other tasks. Until the task reenables scheduling with another system call, the current task is guaranteed not to be interrupted in its execution.

This same system call can also be used to protect nonreentrant functions. A task that is preparing to invoke a shared but nonreentrant function can disable scheduling before calling the function and reenable scheduling once the function returns. Since no other tasks can gain control during this critical period between system calls, execution of the unsafe function cannot be disturbed (unless, of course, the function itself invokes some system call that reenables multitasking).

The entire subject of collisions will be revisited in detail in Chapter 7.

In DESQview, the system call that disables multitasking is known as *api_beginc()*, which stands for "begin critical." Once a task calls *api_beginc()*, it retains control of the system without interruption until it calls *api_endc()* or until it suspends itself. As this call can profoundly degrade multitasking performance, this call should only be used when data collisions cannot be avoided in the other two ways mentioned. Even then, the number of instructions executed between the *api_beginc()* and *api_endc()* calls should be kept small.

The program *TSKTEST.C* shows an example of a task that starts other tasks. The main function does nothing more than start up several tasks and wait for them to finish. While waiting, the main task prints out a message, each time indicating the number of messages it has printed while waiting and the number of child tasks which it thinks are active. As soon as all the child tasks have been freed, the main task quits.

Figure 3.5—Prototype Declarations for *api_beginc()* and *api_endc()*

```
                              /*begin a critical on*/
     void  api_begin(void);   /*no arguments*/

                              /*end a critical region*/
     void  api_endc (void);   /*no arguments*/
```

Each of the child tasks start by positioning its windows, setting the proper color and then redrawing it to the screen. It is interesting to note that each of the child tasks executes the same code, namely the function *subtask()*. Each child task counts down a variable towards zero. With each count, the child task outputs a short message in its window. Once the count reaches zero, the child task uses the *win_disperor()* API call to display a message. Once the user acknowledges receipt of the message by depressing the ESCAPE key or by clicking the mouse on the error message, the task terminates itself by returning. As simple as it is, there are several interesting points to note about this program.

Figure 3.6—Prototype Declaration for *win_disperor()*

```
                        /*display message and wait for mouse
                          button to acknowledge*/
int win_disperor        /*indicates button depressed*/
        (ulong winhan,  /*window in which to place msg*/
         char *message, /*message to output*/
         int  msglngth, /*length of message*/
         int  rows,     /*size of ...*/
         int  cols,     /*   ... message window*/
         int  beep,     /* 1-> beep and make topsys, else 0*/
         int  buttons); /* 1->left button, 2->right, 0->both*/
```

Execute the example program. Notice how the child tasks rapidly take their places and begin counting down. Multitasking is very smooth in the example as each task is careful to surrender control back to DESQview immediately after writing to the screen via calls to *api_pause()*. DESQview with its preemptive scheduling only allows each task a set amount of time anyway, so removing the *api_pause()* calls has little effect in this example, but the reader should quickly get into the habit of placing *api_pause()* calls within execution loops of any duration.

Communication between the parent and the children tasks is via global variables. All three of the methods mentioned for avoiding data collisions have been used. The variables *XLOC* and *YLOC*, which are used to instruct *subtask()* where to place its window on the screen, are only written by the parent task and are only read by the child task.

The variable *ACK* is used as an acknowledgement for the location variables. The main task sets *ACK* to 1 and waits for *subtask()* to zero it once it has read the values out of *XLOC* and *YLOC*. Due to the logic of the program, this variable is never written by more than one task at a time.

The global variable *TCOUNT* contains a count of the number of child tasks currently executing. *TCOUNT* is incremented by the parent task whenever it starts a task and decremented by the tasks when they have finished counting down and are preparing to exit. Since two or more subtasks could exit at the same time, there is no way of assuring that two of them would not attempt to write the variable at the same time. Thus, access to *TCOUNT* has been protected by calls to *api_beginc()* and *api_endc()*. To make sure that all accesses to *TCOUNT* are properly controlled, functions are used (*taskinc()* to increment *TCOUNT*, *taskdec()* to decrement it, and *taskcount()* to simply read it). Notice how the task count in the parent task's window decrements as each task's error-terminate message is acknowledged. (The proper use of API calls to avoid data collisions will be examined again in the discussion of semaphores in Chapter 7.) Once again, for some compilers, it is important that the matrix *STACKS*, from which each of the subtasks takes its stack, be declared locally to the function *program_body()*. Doing so places it on the main

task's stack. It may not be declared within the function *fork()*, as this
function returns its stack when it completes, long before the subtask terminates.

```
 1[ 0]: /**********************************************************
 2[ 0]:    Task Test - create several visible tasks and
 3[ 0]:                   communicate between them.
 4[ 0]: **********************************************************/
 5[ 0]:
 6[ 0]: #include <stdio.h>
 7[ 0]: #include "dvapi.h"
 8[ 0]:
 9[ 0]: /*locally declared programs*/
10[ 0]: void main (void);
11[ 0]: void program_body (void);
12[ 0]: ulong fork (int, int, char *, int);
13[ 0]: int subtask (void);
14[ 0]: int taskcount (void);
15[ 0]: void taskinc (void);
16[ 0]: void taskdec (void);
17[ 0]:
18[ 0]: /*minimum API version required is DESQview 2.00*/
19[ 0]: #define required 0x200
20[ 0]:
21[ 0]: /*main - standard pattern for DESQview programs*/
22[ 0]: void main (void)
23[ 0]: {
24[ 1]:    int  version;
25[ 1]:
26[ 1]:    version = api_init();
27[ 1]:    if (version < required)
28[ 1]:        printf ("This program requires DESQview %d.%02d or later.\n",
29[ 1]:                required >> 8, required & 0xff);
30[ 1]:    else {
31[ 2]:        /*tell DESQview what extensions to enable
32[ 2]:          and start application*/
33[ 2]:        api_level (required);
34[ 2]:        program_body();
35[ 1]:    }
36[ 1]:    /*if DESQview present (even if wrong version), shut it down*/
37[ 1]:    if (version)
38[ 1]:        api_exit();
39[ 0]: }
40[ 0]:
41[ 0]: /*program body - start up 5 tasks and wait for them to quit*/
42[ 0]:
43[ 0]: #define NUMROWS     10
44[ 0]: #define NUMCOLS     25
45[ 0]:
46[ 0]: #define NUMTASKS     5  /*start up 5 subtasks*/
47[ 0]: int X[NUMTASKS] = {60, 40, 20,  1, 30},
48[ 0]:     Y[NUMTASKS] = { 1,  5, 10, 15, 20};
49[ 0]:
50[ 0]: void program_body (void)
```

```
51[ 0]: {
52[ 1]:    int i,j;                            /*use for indexes*/
53[ 1]:    ulong winhan;
54[ 1]:    #define STACKSIZE 1000          /*allocate some stack space for each*/
55[ 1]:    char stacks [NUMTASKS][STACKSIZE];
56[ 1]:
57[ 1]:    winhan = win_new ("Main Program", 12, 10, 38);
58[ 1]:    win_move (winhan, 1, 1);
59[ 1]:    win_logattr (winhan, 1);
60[ 1]:    win_attr (winhan, 1);
61[ 1]:    win_unhide (winhan);
62[ 1]:    win_top (winhan);
63[ 1]:
64[ 1]:    /*now start subtask NUMTASKS number of times*/
65[ 1]:    for (i = 0; i < NUMTASKS; i++)
66[ 1]:        fork (X[i], Y[i], stacks [i], STACKSIZE);
67[ 1]:
68[ 1]:    /*wait for them all to quit - show we are alive in the mean time*/
69[ 1]:    i = 0;
70[ 1]:    while (j = taskcount()) {
71[ 2]:        win_printf (winhan, "Waiting; taskcount = %d, count = %d\n",
72[ 2]:                            j, i++);
73[ 2]:        api_pause ();
74[ 1]:    }
75[ 1]:
76[ 1]:    /*now put the window away*/
77[ 1]:    win_free (winhan);
78[ 0]: }
79[ 0]:
80[ 0]: /*global variables used for inter-task communication*/
81[ 0]: int tcount;                        /*number of sub-tasks executing*/
82[ 0]: int xloc, yloc;                    /*location of next window*/
83[ 0]: int ack;                           /*hand shake for window location*/
84[ 0]:
85[ 0]: /*fork - fork a new task*/
86[ 0]: ulong fork (x, y, stack, stacksize)
87[ 0]:    int x, y;
88[ 0]:    char *stack;
89[ 0]:    int stacksize;
90[ 0]: {
91[ 1]:    char titlebuf [80], titlesize;
92[ 1]:    ulong tskhan;
93[ 1]:
94[ 1]:    /*store off the window location*/
95[ 1]:    ack = 1;
96[ 1]:    xloc = x;
97[ 1]:    yloc = y;
98[ 1]:
99[ 1]:    /*now start the subtask*/
100[ 1]:    titlesize = sprintf (titlebuf, "Task #%d", taskcount());
101[ 1]:    tskhan = tsk_new (subtask, stack, stacksize, titlebuf, titlesize,
102[ 1]:                      NUMROWS, NUMCOLS);
103[ 1]:
104[ 1]:    /*wait until subtask has acknowledge reading window location
105[ 1]:      before continuing*/
106[ 1]:    while (ack)
```

```
107[ 1]:        api_pause ();
108[ 1]:    taskinc ();                     /*count it*/
109[ 1]:    return tskhan;
110[ 0]: }
111[ 0]:
112[ 0]: /*access the task count field - must be protected*/
113[ 0]: int taskcount (void)
114[ 0]: {
115[ 1]:    return tcount;
116[ 0]: }
117[ 0]: void taskdec (void)
118[ 0]: {
119[ 1]:    api_beginc ();
120[ 1]:    tcount--;
121[ 1]:    api_endc ();
122[ 0]: }
123[ 0]: void taskinc (void)
124[ 0]: {
125[ 1]:    api_beginc ();
126[ 1]:    tcount++;
127[ 1]:    api_endc ();
128[ 0]: }
129[ 0]:
130[ 0]: /*subtask - an example subtask which opens a window, counts down
131[ 0]:             and then removes itself*/
132[ 0]: int subtask (void)
133[ 0]: {
134[ 1]:    int i;
135[ 1]:    ulong winhan;
136[ 1]:
137[ 1]:    /*set up window and then acknowledge to parent*/
138[ 1]:    winhan = win_me ();
139[ 1]:    win_move (winhan, yloc, xloc);
140[ 1]:    win_logattr (winhan, 1);
141[ 1]:    win_attr (winhan, taskcount()+2);
142[ 1]:    win_unhide (winhan);
143[ 1]:    win_top (winhan);
144[ 1]:
145[ 1]:    ack = 0;                         /*ackowlege that we read location*/
146[ 1]:
147[ 1]:    /*now print out, politely giving up control after each round*/
148[ 1]:    for (i = 200; i; i--) {
149[ 2]:      win_printf (winhan, "I'm counting down %d\n", i);
150[ 2]:      api_pause ();
151[ 1]:    }
152[ 1]:
153[ 1]:    /*acknowlege task over*/
154[ 1]:    win_disperor (winhan, "Finished", 8, 1, 10, 1, 0);
155[ 1]:    taskdec ();                      /*remove self from list*/
156[ 0]: }
```

Applications

As noted earlier, DESQview supports a level of multitasking between tasks and processes. It calls this level "applications." Applications share code and data segments like tasks, but they are independently known to the operating system, like processes. An application may, itself, have several tasks.

Applications are handled in DESQview with the *app_* API calls. The *app_new()* call, which is used to create an application, has exactly the same arguments as the *tsk_new()* call described earlier. Although the Quarterdeck documentation explains that *app_new()* returns an application handle, there is little difference between an application handle and a task handle. In fact, there is not even an *app_me()* in the API library. Applications use the *tsk_me()* call instead to find out their own handle.

Figure 3.7—Prototype Declaration for app_new() and win_topsys()

```
                              /*start a new application*/
ulong app_new                 /*return application handle*/
         (int (*ap)(),        /*address of application*/
         char *stack,         /*address of stack for app*/
         int  lstack,         /*length of stack*/
         char *title,         /*application name*/
         int  ltitle,         /*length of name*/
         int  rows,           /*size of ...*/
         int  cols);          /*  ... application window*/
                              /*make window topmost in system*/
void win_topsys               /*returns nothing*/
         (ulong winhan);      /*handle of window to bring to top*/
```

An application is terminated either by invoking the *app_free()* call or by returning from the highest-level function, much as with tasks described earlier. Since applications share data segments, applications are free to communicate through global variables exactly like tasks.

Because of these similarities, the example application program, *APPTEST*, appears virtually identical to its single application, multiple tasked cousin, *TSKTEST*. Executing *APPTEST* reveals some subtle but important differences, however.

It is no longer sufficient to *win_top()* the child application's window within *subapp()* to make it visible. The API call *win_top()* merely makes a window the top-most window within its application. Each child application must now use the API call *win_topsys()* to bring its window above the parent application's window. (Alternatively, each application could use the API call *api_gofore()* to become the currently selected application, since the currently selected application's windows are always on top.)

Execute the example program again. While the child applications are counting down, bring up the DESQview window and select the Switch command. Notice how each of the applications now appears in the Switch window. Look carefully at the windows on the display. The parent application's window appears with a double-lined border because it remains the foreground application. The windows of the child applications, by comparison, appear with single-lined borders as they are not in the foreground. If you select one of the child applications (either from the switch window or by clicking on it with a mouse) you will notice that the parent's window is now single-lined and the selected application gets double lines, but little else changes.

```
 1[ 0]: /**********************************************************
 2[ 0]:    App Test - create several visible applications and
 3[ 0]:               communicate between them; compare with task
 4[ 0]:               test earlier.
 5[ 0]: **********************************************************/
 6[ 0]:
 7[ 0]: #include <stdio.h>
 8[ 0]: #include "dvapi.h"
 9[ 0]:
10[ 0]: /*locally declared programs*/
11[ 0]: void main (void);
12[ 0]: void program_body (void);
13[ 0]: ulong fork (int, int, char *, int);
14[ 0]: int subapp (void);
15[ 0]: int taskcount (void);
16[ 0]: void taskinc (void);
17[ 0]: void taskdec (void);
18[ 0]:
```

```
19[ 0]: /*minimum API version required is DESQview 2.00*/
20[ 0]: #define required 0x200
21[ 0]:
22[ 0]: /*main - standard pattern for DESQview programs*/
23[ 0]: void main (void)
24[ 0]: {
25[ 1]:   int  version;
26[ 1]:
27[ 1]:   version = api_init();
28[ 1]:   if (version < required)
29[ 1]:       printf ("This program requires DESQview %d.%02d or later.\n",
30[ 1]:                  required >> 8, required & 0xff);
31[ 1]:   else {
32[ 2]:       /*tell DESQview what extensions to enable
33[ 2]:          and start application*/
34[ 2]:       api_level (required);
35[ 2]:       program_body();
36[ 1]:   }
37[ 1]:   /*if DESQview present (even if wrong version), shut it down*/
38[ 1]:   if (version)
39[ 1]:       api_exit();
40[ 0]: }
41[ 0]:
42[ 0]: /*program body - start up 5 apps and wait for them to quit*/
43[ 0]:
44[ 0]: #define NUMTASKS    5          /*start up 5 subtasks*/
45[ 0]: #define NUMROWS    10
46[ 0]: #define NUMCOLS    25
47[ 0]:
48[ 0]: int X[NUMTASKS] = {60, 40, 20,  1, 30},
49[ 0]:     Y[NUMTASKS] = { 1,  5, 10, 15, 20};
50[ 0]:
51[ 0]: void program_body (void)
52[ 0]: {
53[ 1]:   int i,j;                     /*use for indexes*/
54[ 1]:   ulong winhan;
55[ 1]:   #define STACKSIZE 1000        /*allocate some stack space for each*/
56[ 1]:   char stacks [NUMTASKS][STACKSIZE];
57[ 1]:
58[ 1]:   /* hide starting window so application windows can be seen*/
59[ 1]:   win_hide (win_me());
60[ 1]:   win_redraw (win_me());
61[ 1]:
62[ 1]:   winhan = win_new ("Main Program", 12, 10, 38);
63[ 1]:   win_move (winhan, 1, 1);
64[ 1]:   win_logattr (winhan, 1);
65[ 1]:   win_attr (winhan, 1);
66[ 1]:   win_unhide (winhan);
67[ 1]:   win_top (winhan);
68[ 1]:
69[ 1]:   /*now start subtask NUMTASKS number of times*/
70[ 1]:   for (i = 0; i < NUMTASKS; i++)
71[ 1]:       fork (X[i], Y[i], stacks [i], STACKSIZE);
72[ 1]:
73[ 1]:   /*wait for them all to quit - show we are still alive in mean time*/
74[ 1]:   i = 0;
```

```
75[ 1]:    while (j = taskcount()) {
76[ 2]:        win_printf (winhan, "Waiting; taskcount = %d, count = %d\n",
77[ 2]:                                        j, i++);
78[ 2]:        api_pause ();
79[ 1]:    }
80[ 1]:
81[ 1]:    /*now put the window away*/
82[ 1]:    win_free (winhan);
83[ 1]:
84[ 1]:    /* un-hide starting window or else all will simply go dark*/
85[ 1]:    win_unhide (win_me());
86[ 1]:    win_redraw (win_me());
87[ 0]: }
88[ 0]:
89[ 0]: /*global variables used for inter-task communication*/
90[ 0]: int tcount;                      /*number of sub-tasks executing*/
91[ 0]: int xloc, yloc;                  /*location of next window*/
92[ 0]: int ack;                         /*hand shake for window location*/
93[ 0]:
94[ 0]: /*fork - fork a new task*/
95[ 0]: ulong fork (x, y, stack, stacksize)
96[ 0]:    int x, y;
97[ 0]:    char *stack;
98[ 0]:    int stacksize;
99[ 0]: {
100[ 1]:    char titlebuf [80], titlesize;
101[ 1]:    ulong apphan;
102[ 1]:
103[ 1]:    /*store off the window location*/
104[ 1]:    ack = 1;
105[ 1]:    xloc = x;
106[ 1]:    yloc = y;
107[ 1]:
108[ 1]:    /*now start the application*/
109[ 1]:    titlesize = sprintf (titlebuf, "Application #%d", taskcount());
110[ 1]:    apphan = app_new (subapp, stack, stacksize, titlebuf, titlesize,
111[ 1]:                    NUMROWS, NUMCOLS);
112[ 1]:
113[ 1]:    /*wait until subtask has acknowledge reading window location
114[ 1]:      before continuing*/
115[ 1]:    while (ack)
116[ 1]:        api_pause ();
117[ 1]:    taskinc ();                      /*count it*/
118[ 1]:    return apphan;
119[ 0]: }
120[ 0]:
121[ 0]: /*access the task count field - must be protected*/
122[ 0]: int taskcount (void)
123[ 0]: {
124[ 1]:    return tcount;
125[ 0]: }
126[ 0]: void taskdec (void)
127[ 0]: {
128[ 1]:    api_beginc ();
129[ 1]:    tcount--;
130[ 1]:    api_endc ();
```

```
131[ 0]: }
132[ 0]: void taskinc (void)
133[ 0]: {
134[ 1]:    api_beginc ();
135[ 1]:    tcount++;
136[ 1]:    api_endc ();
137[ 0]: }
138[ 0]:
139[ 0]: /*subapp - an example application which opens a window, counts down
140[ 0]:              and then removes itself*/
141[ 0]: int subapp (void)
142[ 0]: {
143[ 1]:    int i;
144[ 1]:    ulong winhan;
145[ 1]:
146[ 1]:    /*set up window and then acknowledge to parent*/
147[ 1]:    winhan = win_me ();
148[ 1]:    win_move (winhan, yloc, xloc);
149[ 1]:    win_logattr (winhan, 1);
150[ 1]:    win_attr (winhan, taskcount()+2);
151[ 1]:    win_unhide (winhan);
152[ 1]:    win_topsys (winhan);
153[ 1]:
154[ 1]:    ack = 0;                       /*ackowlege that we read location*/
155[ 1]:
156[ 1]:    /*now print out, politely giving up control after each round*/
157[ 1]:    for (i = 200; i; i--) {
158[ 2]:      win_printf (winhan, "I'm counting down %d\n", i);
159[ 2]:      api_pause ();
160[ 1]:    }
161[ 1]:
162[ 1]:    /*acknowlege task over*/
163[ 1]:    win_disperor (winhan, "Finished", 8, 1, 10, 1, 0);
164[ 1]:    taskdec ();                    /*remove self from list*/
165[ 0]: }
```

As we noted in Chapter 2, the foreground application is a special animal in DESQview. First, its time slice is usually longer than those of background applications. Second, it is the only application that gets keystrokes entered at the keyboard. To indicate to the user which application is in the foreground, any windows belonging to that application are drawn with a double-lined border.

Look again at *TSKTEST*. When it is executed, all of the task windows appear with double-lined borders. This is because they all belong to the parent application and therefore are all foreground tasks. Opening the switch window when these tasks are executing reveals *TSKTEST* as the only application running. Selecting another application while *TSK-TEST* is executing deselects all of the tasks as a unit.

If we look even more carefully we will notice that each of the child application windows carries a number that the parent program did not place there. This is the same number that appears in the DESQview switch window. Applications in DESQview are numbered roughly in sequential order of creation. Although this number has no particular significance (other than identification to the user), an application may know its identification number via the *app_number()* API call.

Our example applications are not as independent as the Switch window might make them appear. During the execution of *APPTEST*, if you select any one of the applications and select Put Aside from within the Rearrange command of the DESQview window, all of the windows disappear. Putting an application aside forces it to be unloaded from memory and written to disk, thereby freeing up memory for other uses. Putting a normal application aside removes its window from the display because it can no longer execute. Selecting the application restores it from disk and restores its windows to the screen.

However, our test applications all share the same code and data segments. Forcing any one of them to disk forces them all to disk, and they all disappear. Selecting any one of the test applications again restores them all. (You may even select a different application than was put aside—as they share memory, it makes no difference.)

There are a few other operations that can be performed on applications. An application may specify that it only wishes to execute when it is in the foreground using the *app_foreonly()* API call. This is useful for applications that interact with the user. When they are not the foreground application, it might be a waste of CPU time for them to gain control. Add the sequence:

```
app_foreonly (tsk_me (), 1);
```

to the function *subapp()* in *APPTEST* and notice that the child applications count down in single file rather than simultaneously as they did before.

An application may hide itself using the *app_hide()* API call. Doing so hides any windows belonging to the application until the application is later unhidden via the *app_show()* call. A hidden application continues to get CPU time. An application that has been suspended via the *app_suspend()* API call is also hidden, but it no longer receives CPU time until it is made the foreground application.

Figure 3.8—Prototype Declarations for *app_number()*, *app_foreonly()*, *app_gofore()*, and *app_goback()*

```
                               /*return number of current
                                  application*/
int app_number                 /*return app number*/
         (void);               /*takes no arguments*/

                               /*specify whether app can run in
                                  background*/
void app_foreonly              /*returns nothing*/
         (ulong apphan,        /*application handle*/
          int flag);           /* 1->foreground only,
                                  0->background also*/

                               /*bring app to the foreground*/
void app_gofore                /*returns nothing*/
         (ulong apphan);       /*application to bring up*/

                               /*put app into background*/
void app_goback                /*returns nothing*/
         (ulong apphan);       /*application to put back*/
```

Finally, an application may bring itself into the foreground with the *app_gofore()* API call or force itself into the background with the *app_goback()* call. Bringing the application into the foreground is useful when an error or special event occurs, as the foreground application is always assured of being visible.

Processes

Processes have the highest level of independence between programs in a multitasking operating system. Not only do processes execute simultaneously, as do tasks, but they execute with different code and data segments. Where tasks are bound to run as a single executable file, processes are not. This gives processes some very distinct advantages over simple tasks or single-task applications.

Not all of the processes that are currently active need be in memory at the same time. A program that has been carefully divided into multiple processes may be larger than the 640K limit placed on most DOS programs. In fact, the total size of all processes that are currently active may be larger than the amount of RAM installed in the host computer.

Processes may be invoked independently, either from software or by the user. This gives the user a considerable amount of control over the program at execution time. For example, suppose that a company generates a new database program consisting of multiple processes. An I/O process interacts with the user and a second acts as the database engine. Pictorially such a configuration resembles that in Figure 3.9.

If users decided to use this program as a database server, all they need do is provide a new I/O process designed to interface with the LAN rather than with a single user. The database engine process remains the same. Suppose the end user is provided with several I/O processes, each designed for a different type of physical connection. Because the physical setup is known, the decision regarding which processes are required can be made at execution time. If the host computer has no LAN, there is no need to load the LAN interface process. But if the host has both a keyboard and a modem, both interface processes may be loaded to simultaneously access the single-database engine.

This is a powerful paradigm for the computer user. It is an equally powerful model for the software developer. Assume that our database program was developed and delivered without support for the newly introduced LAN of Promise. All that is required to bring the application up to speed is to develop and distribute a new I/O process to handle the new LAN. No changes are required to any of the existing processes.

Figure 3.9—Representation of Multiprocess Database Program

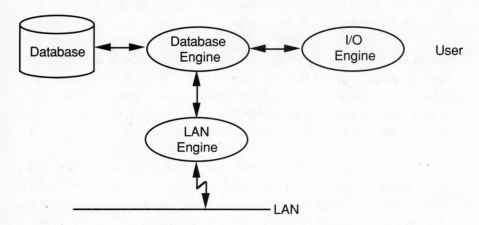

Perhaps even more promising, the I/O process need not be a simple keyboard handler at all. It could just as well be another program. A point-of-sale program, for example, might access our original database process to fetch product prices and record purchases just as easily as a human operator might. The resulting situation is pictured in Figure 3.10.

Figure 3.10—Cooperative Processes

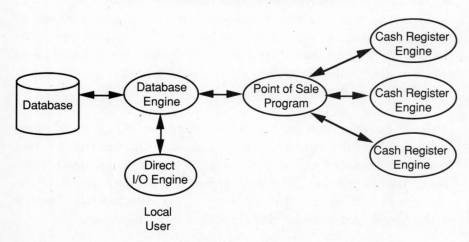

Processes are also controlled using the API function calls beginning with *app_*. In general, the *app_* function calls have the same effect on processes as they do on applications. In fact, in the DESQview world a process is hardly more than an application with a separate source file.

Processes are not started using *app_new()*, however, as *app_new()* expects the address of a function. Instead, the API function *app_start()* is used to start a process. *app_start()* accepts the address of a memory resident *.DVP* (or *.PIF*) file as its argument.

Figure 3.11—Prototype Declaration for Function *app_start().*

```
                                /*start a new process*/
ulong app_start                 /*return process handle*/
        (char *dvpbuf,          /*address of .DVP file in memory*/
         int size);             /*size of buffer*/
```

A *.DVP* file is the file that is created by the "Add a Program" command under the Open selection of the DESQview window. Multitasking operating systems need more information about an executable file than do single-tasking systems such as DOS. For this reason, DOS's *.EXE* files simply do not contain enough information for DESQview to know how to properly execute a program. Every program that appears in DESQview's Open Window has a *.DVP* file for it that tells DESQview such things as how much memory the application requires, whether it can execute in the background, etc. The *.PIF* file is an earlier and smaller version of the same thing. The exact format of the these files is given in Table 3.12 below.

Figure 3.12—Format of .DVP File

offset	length	meaning
0	2	reserved
2	30	program title (blank filled)
32	2	maximum memory required [kbytes]
34	2	minimum memory required [kbytes]
36	64	command to start program [ASCIIZ]
100	1	default drive (A, B, C, etc)
101	64	default directory name [ASCIIZ]
165	64	program parameters [ASCIIZ]

229	1	initial screen mode
230	1	# of text pages used by application
231	1	# of first interrupt to be saved on task switch
232	1	# of last interrupt to be saved on task switch
233	1	# rows in logical window
234	1	# columns in logical window
235	1	initial row location
236	1	initial column location
237	2	system memory size [kbytes]
239	64	shared program file name [ASCIIZ]
303	64	shard program data name [ASCIIZ]
367	1	control byte 1 :
		0x80 - writes directly to screen
		0x40 - executes in foreground only
		0x20 - uses math coprocessor
		0x10 - accesses keyboard buffer
		0x01 - swappable
368	1	control byte 2 :
		0x40 - uses command line parameters
		0x20 - swaps interrupt vectors

beginning of DESQview .DVP

369	2	keys to use in Open Window menu
371	2	size of script file [bytes]
373	2	automatically execute api_pause() after this many keyboard polls in one clock tick
375	1	TRUE -> disable automatic color mapping
376	1	TRUE -> application is swappable
377	3	equal to 0
380	1	TRUE -> automatically close application on exit
381	1	TRUE -> copy-protect disk required

beginning of extended .DVP (DESQview 2.00 or greater)

382	1	equal to 1
383	1	TRUE -> program shares system memory
384	1	initial # rows in physical window
385	1	initial # columns in physical window
386	2	maximum expanded memory available [kbytes]
388	1	control byte 3:
		0x80 - automatically assign position
		0x20 - honor maximum memory value
		0x10 - disallow Close command
		0x08 - foreground only when doing graphics
		0x04 - don't virtualize
389	1	keyboard conflict level [0 through 4]
390	1	# graphics pages used by program
391	2	system memory size [kbytes]
393	1	initial screen mode
394	22	reserved

The following excerpt shows how a *.DVP* file is loaded and how the associated process is started (notice that error returns are not checked here for clarity):

```
FILE *handle;
char buffer [416];
ulong prchan;

/*read the .DVP file into memory*/
handle = fopen ("C:\\DVP\\PRCTEST.DVP", "rb");
fread (buffer, 416, 1, handle);
fclose (handle);

/*now start the application*/
prchan = app_start (buffer, 416);
```

The file *PRCTEST.DVP* is read from the directory *DVP* on disk drive C. Notice how the directory divider \ must be doubled when specified within a C character string, since the backslash is also used to introduce other control characters. Once opened, the file is simply read into a buffer and closed, and the buffer is handed over to *app_start()* which starts the process.

Our example test program, rewritten to run as separate processes rather than tasks or applications, is shown below. Notice that it now appears as two separate listings with the parent code in *PRCTST1* and the child code in *PRCTST2*. These two source files are compiled and linked separately to create the one "process test" program.

```
 1[ 0]: /***********************************************************
 2[ 0]:    Process Test  - create several children processes and wait for
 3[ 0]:                    them to finish.  Use some unused memory in the
 4[ 0]:                    video adapter to communicate (this is quite
 5[ 0]:                    kludgy, so it may not work...wait for Chap 4
 6[ 0]:                    for "real" interprocess communication).
 7[ 0]: ***********************************************************/
 8[ 0]:
 9[ 0]: #include <stdio.h>
10[ 0]: #include "dvapi.h"
11[ 0]:
12[ 0]: /*locally declared programs*/
13[ 0]: void main (void);
14[ 0]: void program_body (void);
15[ 0]: ulong fork (int, int);
16[ 0]: int taskcount (void);
17[ 0]: void taskinc (void);
```

```
18[ 0]: void taskdec (void);
19[ 0]: int readpif (char *, char *, unsigned);
20[ 0]:
21[ 0]: /*minimum API version required is DESQview 2.00*/
22[ 0]: #define required 0x200
23[ 0]:
24[ 0]: /*main - standard pattern for DESQview programs*/
25[ 0]: void main (void)
26[ 0]: {
27[ 1]:    int  version;
28[ 1]:
29[ 1]:    version = api_init();
30[ 1]:    if (version < required)
31[ 1]:        printf ("This program requires DESQview %d.%02d or later.\n",
32[ 1]:                 required >> 8, required & 0xff);
33[ 1]:    else {
34[ 2]:        /*tell DESQview what extensions to enable
35[ 2]:          and start application*/
36[ 2]:        api_level (required);
37[ 2]:        program_body();
38[ 1]:    }
39[ 1]:    /*if DESQview present (even if wrong version), shut it down*/
40[ 1]:    if (version)
41[ 1]:        api_exit();
42[ 0]: }
43[ 0]:
44[ 0]: /*global variables used for inter-task communication -
45[ 0]:   use a very small section of unused memory in the video
46[ 0]:   adapter (use 0xB0000FF0 for monochrome adapters)*/
47[ 0]: struct INTER_PROCESS {
48[ 1]:    int tcount;                    /*number of sub-tasks executing*/
49[ 1]:    int xloc, yloc;                /*location of next window*/
50[ 1]:    int ack;                       /*hand shake for window location*/
51[ 0]: } *ptr = 0xB8000FF0L;
52[ 0]:
53[ 0]: /*program body - start up 5 processes and wait for them to quit*/
54[ 0]:
55[ 0]: #define NUMTASKS     5           /*start up 5 child processes*/
56[ 0]:
57[ 0]: int X[NUMTASKS] = {60, 40, 20,  1, 30},
58[ 0]:     Y[NUMTASKS] = { 1,  5, 10, 15, 20};
59[ 0]:
60[ 0]: void program_body (void)
61[ 0]: {
62[ 1]:    int i,j;                       /*use for indexes*/
63[ 1]:    ulong winhan;
64[ 1]:
65[ 1]:    /* hide starting window so application windows can be seen*/
66[ 1]:    win_hide (win_me());
67[ 1]:    win_redraw (win_me());
68[ 1]:
69[ 1]:    winhan = win_new ("Main Process", 12, 10, 38);
70[ 1]:    win_move (winhan, 1, 1);
71[ 1]:    win_logattr (winhan, 1);
72[ 1]:    win_attr (winhan, 1);
73[ 1]:    win_unhide (winhan);
```

```
 74[ 1]:   win_top (winhan);
 75[ 1]:
 76[ 1]:   /*zero the process count*/
 77[ 1]:   ptr -> tcount = 0;
 78[ 1]:
 79[ 1]:   /*now start subtask NUMTASKS number of times*/
 80[ 1]:   for (i = 0; i < NUMTASKS; i++)
 81[ 1]:       fork (X[i], Y[i]);
 82[ 1]:
 83[ 1]:   /*wait for them all to quit - show we are still alive in mean time*/
 84[ 1]:   i = 0;
 85[ 1]:   while (j = taskcount()) {
 86[ 2]:       win_printf (winhan, "Waiting; taskcount = %d, count = %d\n",
 87[ 2]:                             j, i++);
 88[ 2]:       api_pause ();
 89[ 1]:   }
 90[ 1]:
 91[ 1]:   /*now put the window away*/
 92[ 1]:   win_free (winhan);
 93[ 1]:
 94[ 1]:   /* un-hide starting window or else all will simply go dark*/
 95[ 1]:   win_unhide (win_me());
 96[ 1]:   win_redraw (win_me());
 97[ 0]: }
 98[ 0]:
 99[ 0]:
100[ 0]: /*fork - fork a new process*/
101[ 0]: ulong fork (int x, int y)
102[ 0]: {
103[ 1]:   ulong prchan;
104[ 1]:   char buffer [500];
105[ 1]:
106[ 1]:   /*read the PIF file into local buffer - if unsuccessful, forget
107[ 1]:     about starting process*/
108[ 1]:   prchan = 0;
109[ 1]:   if (readpif ("prctst2.dvp", buffer, 416)) {
110[ 2]:
111[ 2]:     /*store off the window location*/
112[ 2]:     ptr -> ack = 1;
113[ 2]:     ptr -> xloc = x;
114[ 2]:     ptr -> yloc = y;
115[ 2]:
116[ 2]:     /*now start the application*/
117[ 2]:     prchan = app_start (buffer, 416);
118[ 2]:
119[ 2]:     /*wait until subtask has acknowledge reading window location
120[ 2]:       before continuing*/
121[ 2]:     while (ptr -> ack)
122[ 2]:       api_pause ();
123[ 2]:     taskinc ();                          /*count it*/
124[ 1]:   }
125[ 1]:   return prchan;
126[ 0]: }
127[ 0]:
128[ 0]: /*access the task count field - must be protected*/
129[ 0]: int taskcount (void)
```

```
130[ 0]: {
131[ 1]:   return ptr -> tcount;
132[ 0]: }
133[ 0]: void taskdec (void)
134[ 0]: {
135[ 1]:   api_beginc ();
136[ 1]:   ptr -> tcount--;
137[ 1]:   api_endc ();
138[ 0]: }
139[ 0]: void taskinc (void)
140[ 0]: {
141[ 1]:   api_beginc ();
142[ 1]:   ptr -> tcount++;
143[ 1]:   api_endc ();
144[ 0]: }
145[ 0]:
146[ 0]: /*readpif - read a .DVP file off of disk into a buffer*/
147[ 0]: int readpif (fname, buffer, size)
148[ 0]:   char *fname, *buffer;
149[ 0]:   unsigned size;
150[ 0]: {
151[ 1]:   FILE *handle;
152[ 1]:
153[ 1]:   if (!(handle = fopen (fname, "rb")))
154[ 1]:     return 0;
155[ 1]:
156[ 1]:   if (fread (buffer, size, 1, handle) != 1)
157[ 1]:     return 0;
158[ 1]:
159[ 1]:   fclose (handle);
160[ 1]:   return 1;
161[ 0]: }



  1[ 0]: /***************************************************************
  2[ 0]:   Process Test SubProc - this is the subprocess which goes
  3[ 0]:                          with PRCTST1.C.  Otherwise,
  4[ 0]:                          identical to the subtask and subapp
  5[ 0]:                          presented in TSKTST1.C and APPTST1.C.
  6[ 0]: ***************************************************************/
  7[ 0]:
  8[ 0]: #include <stdio.h>
  9[ 0]: #include "dvapi.h"
 10[ 0]:
 11[ 0]: /*locally declared programs*/
 12[ 0]: void main (void);
 13[ 0]: void program_body (void);
 14[ 0]: void subprc (void);
 15[ 0]: int taskcount (void);
 16[ 0]: void taskinc (void);
 17[ 0]: void taskdec (void);
 18[ 0]:
 19[ 0]: /*minimum API version required is DESQview 2.00*/
 20[ 0]: #define required 0x200
 21[ 0]:
```

```
22[ 0]: /*main - standard pattern for DESQview programs*/
23[ 0]: void main (void)
24[ 0]: {
25[ 1]:    int  version;
26[ 1]:
27[ 1]:    version = api_init();
28[ 1]:    if (version < required)
29[ 1]:        printf ("This program requires DESQview %d.%02d or later.\n",
30[ 1]:                    required >> 8, required & 0xff);
31[ 1]:    else {
32[ 2]:        /*tell DESQview what extensions to enable
33[ 2]:          and start application*/
34[ 2]:        api_level (required);
35[ 2]:        program_body();
36[ 1]:    }
37[ 1]:    /*if DESQview present (even if wrong version), shut it down*/
38[ 1]:    if (version)
39[ 1]:        api_exit();
40[ 0]: }
41[ 0]:
42[ 0]: /*global variables used for inter-task communication -
43[ 0]:    stash them away in a very small area of extra memory in the
44[ 0]:    video display*/
45[ 0]: struct INTER_PROCESS {
46[ 1]:    int tcount;                      /*number of sub-tasks executing*/
47[ 1]:    int xloc, yloc;                  /*location of next window*/
48[ 1]:    int ack;                         /*hand shake for window location*/
49[ 0]: } *ptr = 0xB8000FF0L;
50[ 0]:
51[ 0]: /*program body - simply execute the subprc function*/
52[ 0]: void program_body (void)
53[ 0]: {
54[ 1]:    subprc ();
55[ 0]: }
56[ 0]:
57[ 0]: /*access the task count field - must be protected*/
58[ 0]: int taskcount (void)
59[ 0]: {
60[ 1]:    return ptr -> tcount;
61[ 0]: }
62[ 0]: void taskdec (void)
63[ 0]: {
64[ 1]:    api_beginc ();
65[ 1]:    ptr -> tcount--;
66[ 1]:    api_endc ();
67[ 0]: }
68[ 0]: void taskinc (void)
69[ 0]: {
70[ 1]:    api_beginc ();
71[ 1]:    ptr -> tcount++;
72[ 1]:    api_endc ();
73[ 0]: }
74[ 0]:
75[ 0]: /*subprc - an example child process which opens a window,
76[ 0]:             counts down and then removes itself*/
77[ 0]: void subprc (void)
```

```
78[ 0]: {
79[ 1]:   int i;
80[ 1]:   ulong winhan;
81[ 1]:
82[ 1]:   /*set up window and then acknowledge to parent*/
83[ 1]:   winhan = win_me();
84[ 1]:   win_move (winhan, ptr -> yloc, ptr -> xloc);
85[ 1]:   win_logattr (winhan, 1);
86[ 1]:   win_attr (winhan, taskcount()+2);
87[ 1]:   win_unhide (winhan);
88[ 1]:   win_topsys (winhan);
89[ 1]:
90[ 1]:   ptr -> ack = 0;                  /*ackowlege that we read location*/
91[ 1]:
92[ 1]:   /*now print out, politely giving up control after each round*/
93[ 1]:   for (i = 500; i; i--) {
94[ 2]:     win_printf (winhan, "I'm counting down %d\n", i);
95[ 2]:     api_pause ();
96[ 1]:   }
97[ 1]:
98[ 1]:   /*acknowlege task over*/
99[ 1]:   win_disperor (winhan, "Finished", 8, 1, 10, 1, 0);
100[ 1]:   taskdec ();                     /*remove self from list*/
101[ 0]: }
```

Since processes do not share data segments, our example test program had to be changed slightly to produce this process version. It is no longer sufficient to define a global variables *TCOUNT, XLOC,* or *YLOC* in the parent process. Even if the child process knew where these variables were, it would not necessarily be able to access them.

We will cover the entire subject of interprocess communication in Chapter 4, but for now we need a trick to get our process test program up and running. It turns out that there is a small area of memory, otherwise unused, that any process can access. A video adapter contains sufficient memory to save a page of video characters. Actually most adapters contain considerably more, but all contain at least 4096 bytes of video memory. If you work out the actual requirements of an 80x25 page of characters you find that only 4000 bytes are required, leaving some 96 bytes left over at the end.

This memory is not truly safe, as DESQview does not expect anyone to save data in this area. Using the edit command within DOS's DEBUG, you can quickly convince yourself that this memory is occasionally cleared by DESQview. Under a DOS window in DESQview, execute the

DOS DEBUG command. Edit memory above the first page by entering the command:

```
- E B800:0FF0 (use B000:0000 for monochrome and Herculese monitors)
```

Place any values you like there. Using the same command, you may then return and inspect these locations. You will find that they retain their value. Now open and close other applications including the window you are in. After each operation, reopen a DEBUG window and examine the same location and you will quickly find which operations clear this location.

However, it is sufficiently safe to use as our communications area for *PRCTST*. *PRCTST1* defines a pointer to a structure that it places at 0xB8000FF0 (use 0xB0000FF0 for monochrome monitors). In this structure it stores the *TCOUNT, XLOC, YLOC,* and *ACK* variables so that when *PRCTST2* looks, it finds their values still there. In Chapter 4, we will examine some safer means of interprocess communication.

It may have seemed odd that *app_start()* requires users to read the *.DVP* file themselves. Why doesn't *app_start()* merely accept the name of the *.DVP* file and read the file itself? Since the format of the *.DVP* file is known, it does not always have to be read from disk. It can be defined within the code. The easiest way to go about this is to develop the *.DVP* using Add a Program and then examine its contents using a debugger. Doing so reduces some flexibility at execution time, but it also reduces the number of files that the program requires to execute.

Furthermore, since we know the format of the *.DVP* file, it is even possible to edit critical fields between the time it is read into memory and the call to *app_start()*. For example, the program title field is given at offset 2 through 31. The invoking process may want the subprocess to carry the same name as the program, irrespective of what name is specified in the *.DVP* file (the name field is only used to identify the process to the user). The name field is a rather trivial example; however, some of the other fields can have a profound effect on process performance.

For example, *PRCTST3.C* reads in a *.DVP* file and then goes back and fills in the name of the process to execute after the fact. If necessary, other fields can be filled in as well.

```
 1[ 0]: /*****************************************************************
 2[ 0]:    Process Test #2  - allow the user to specify the pathname
 3[ 0]:                        of the process to load and execute.
 4[ 0]:                        Execute specified program as a separate
 5[ 0]:                        process in a background window.
 6[ 0]: *****************************************************************/
 7[ 0]:
 8[ 0]: #include <stdio.h>
 9[ 0]: #include <string.h>
10[ 0]: #include "dvapi.h"
11[ 0]:
12[ 0]: /*locally declared programs*/
13[ 0]: void main (void);
14[ 0]: void program_body (void);
15[ 0]: int readpif (char *);
16[ 0]: void parse (char *, char *, char *, char *, char *);
17[ 0]:
18[ 0]: /*minimum API version required is DESQview 2.00*/
19[ 0]: #define required 0x200
20[ 0]:
21[ 0]: /*main - standard pattern for DESQview programs*/
22[ 0]: void main (void)
23[ 0]: {
24[ 1]:   int  version;
25[ 1]:
26[ 1]:   version = api_init();
27[ 1]:   if (version < required)
28[ 1]:       printf ("This program requires DESQview %d.%02d or later.\n",
29[ 1]:               required >> 8, required & 0xff);
30[ 1]:   else {
31[ 2]:       /*tell DESQview what extensions to enable
32[ 2]:         and start application*/
33[ 2]:       api_level (required);
34[ 2]:       program_body();
35[ 1]:   }
36[ 1]:   /*if DESQview present (even if wrong version), shut it down*/
37[ 1]:   if (version)
38[ 1]:       api_exit();
39[ 0]: }
40[ 0]:
41[ 0]: /*a structure containing the format of the extended .DVP*/
42[ 0]: struct DVP {
43[ 1]:   unsigned reserved1;            /*set to 0x0097*/
44[ 1]:   char title [30];              /*program title - pad with blanks*/
45[ 1]:   unsigned maxmem;              /*maximum memory required [kbytes]*/
46[ 1]:   unsigned minmem;              /*minimum memory required [kbytes]*/
47[ 1]:   char command  [64];          /*start command [ASCIIZ]*/
48[ 1]:   char drive;                  /*default drive in ASCII
49[ 1]:                                    (blank for none)*/
50[ 1]:   char directory [64];         /*default directory [ASCIIZ]*/
```

```
51[ 1]:   char params    [64];        /*parameters to command [ASCIIZ]*/
52[ 1]:   char screenmode;           /*initial screen mode*/
53[ 1]:   char numpages;             /*number of video pages*/
54[ 1]:   char firstvect;            /*first interrupt vector to be saved*/
55[ 1]:   char lastvect;             /*last interrupt vector to be saved*/
56[ 1]:   char rows;                 /*no. rows in default window*/
57[ 1]:   char cols;                 /*no. columns in default window*/
58[ 1]:   char yloc;                 /*initial row position*/
59[ 1]:   char xloc;                 /*initial column position*/
60[ 1]:   unsigned reserved2;        /*system memory - overridden later*/
61[ 1]:   char sharedprog [64];      /*name of shared program [ASCIIZ]*/
62[ 1]:   char sharedata  [64];      /*name of shared data*/
63[ 1]:   char controlbyte1;         /*control byte 1 -
64[ 1]:                                   0x80 - writes directly to screen
65[ 1]:                                   0x40 - foreground only
66[ 1]:                                   0x20 - uses 8087
67[ 1]:                                   0x10 - accesses keyboard buffer
68[ 1]:                                   0x01 - swappable*/
69[ 1]:   char controlbyte2;         /*control byte 2 -
70[ 1]:                                   0x40 - uses command line params
71[ 1]:                                   0x20 - swaps interrupt vectors*/
72[ 1]:   char startkeys [2];        /*starting keys from menu*/
73[ 1]:   char scriptsize [2];       /*size of script file [bytes]*/
74[ 1]:   unsigned autopause;        /*pause after this many keyboard
75[ 1]:                                  requests*/
76[ 1]:   char disablecolormap;      /*1 -> disable color mapping*/
77[ 1]:   char swappable;            /*1 -> application is swappable*/
78[ 1]:   char reserved3 [3];
79[ 1]:   char closeonexit;          /*1 -> close on exit*/
80[ 1]:   char keyfloppy;            /*1 -> key floppy required*/
81[ 1]:   char reserved4;
82[ 1]:   char sharesmem;            /*1 -> uses shared memory*/
83[ 1]:   char physrows;             /*no. physical rows in initial window*
84[ 1]:   char physcols;             /*no. physical cols in initial window*
85[ 1]:   unsigned expandedmem;      /*amount of avail EMS [kbytes]*/
86[ 1]:   char controlbyte3;         /*control byte 3 -
87[ 1]:                                   0x80 - automatically assign pos
88[ 1]:                                   0x20 - honor max memory value
89[ 1]:                                   0x10 - disallow close command
90[ 1]:                                   0x08 - foreground only when graphic
91[ 1]:                                   0x04 - don't virtualize*/
92[ 1]:   char kbdconflict;          /*keyboard conflict*/
93[ 1]:   char graphicspages;        /*no. of graphics pages*/
94[ 1]:   unsigned systemmem;        /*system memory size*/
95[ 1]:   char initmode;             /*initial video mode - default 0xff*/
96[ 1]:   char reserved5 [22];
97[ 0]: } dvpbuff;
98[ 0]:
99[ 0]: /*Program_body - load a .DVP from disk into memory.  Request the name
100[ 0]:                    of a program to execute.  Copy its name, directory
101[ 0]:                    and arg.s into the .DVP and launch as a seperate
102[ 0]:                    process*/
103[ 0]: void program_body (void)
104[ 0]: {
105[ 1]:   ulong winhan, prchan;
106[ 1]:   char buffer [132], directory [132], command [132], params [132];
```

```
107[ 1]:
108[ 1]:    winhan = win_me ();
109[ 1]:    win_title (winhan, "Master", 6);
110[ 1]:    win_frame (winhan, 1);
111[ 1]:    win_resize (winhan, 5, 30);
112[ 1]:    win_move (winhan, 1, 48);
113[ 1]:    win_redraw (winhan);
114[ 1]:
115[ 1]:    /*read the initial .DVP file*/
116[ 1]:    if (readpif ("prctst3.dvp"))
117[ 1]:
118[ 1]:        /*ask user for name of process to start until NULL entered*/
119[ 1]:        for (;;) {
120[ 2]:            win_printf (winhan, "Enter next program:\n");
121[ 2]:            gets (buffer);
122[ 2]:            buffer [131] = '\0';
123[ 2]:            if (*buffer == '\0')
124[ 2]:                break;
125[ 2]:
126[ 2]:            /*parse the single command into its three parts
127[ 2]:              which are then copied into the .DVP file*/
128[ 2]:            parse (buffer, &dvpbuff.drive, directory,
129[ 2]:                        command, params);
130[ 2]:            strncpy (dvpbuff.command, command, 63);
131[ 2]:            strncpy (dvpbuff.directory, directory, 63);
132[ 2]:            strncpy (dvpbuff.params, params, 63);
133[ 2]:
134[ 2]:            /*may also set fields in the .DVP file directly
135[ 2]:              (can initialize the entire file this way, in fact,
136[ 2]:              in which case, it does not need to be read from disk*/
137[ 2]:            dvpbuff.autopause  = 3;
138[ 2]:            dvpbuff.closeonexit = 1;
139[ 2]:
140[ 2]:            /*use the resulting .DVP file to start the app*/
141[ 2]:            prchan = app_start (&dvpbuff, sizeof dvpbuff);
142[ 2]:
143[ 2]:            /*acknowledge process started*/
144[ 2]:            if (prchan)
145[ 2]:                win_printf (winhan, "Program started\n\n");
146[ 2]:            else
147[ 2]:                win_printf (winhan, "Error on start\n\n");
148[ 1]:        }
149[ 1]:    else
150[ 1]:        win_printf (winhan, "Could not open .DVP file\n");
151[ 0]: }
152[ 0]:
153[ 0]: /*readpif - read a .DVP file off of disk into a buffer*/
154[ 0]: int readpif (fname)
155[ 0]:  char *fname;
156[ 0]: {
157[ 1]:    FILE *handle;
158[ 1]:
159[ 1]:    if (!(handle = fopen (fname, "rb")))
160[ 1]:      return 0;
161[ 1]:
162[ 1]:    if (fread (&dvpbuff, sizeof dvpbuff, 1, handle) != 1)
```

```
163[ 1]:    return 0;
164[ 1]:
165[ 1]:    fclose (handle);
166[ 1]:    return 1;
167[ 0]: }
168[ 0]:
169[ 0]: /*Parse - parse a path/program/params into its three constituent
170[ 0]:            parts*/
171[ 0]: void parse (buffer, drive, directory, command, params)
172[ 0]:    char *buffer, *drive, *directory, *command, *params;
173[ 0]: {
174[ 1]:    char *s, *t, *lastslash, *firstspace;
175[ 1]:
176[ 1]:    /*drive is easy*/
177[ 1]:    if (buffer[1] == ':') {
178[ 2]:        *drive = buffer[0];
179[ 2]:        buffer+= 2;
180[ 1]:    }
181[ 1]:
182[ 1]:    /*now find the last backslash and the first space in
183[ 1]:      the input string*/
184[ 1]:    firstspace = lastslash = 0;
185[ 1]:    for (s = buffer; *s; s++) {
186[ 2]:        if (*s == '\\')
187[ 2]:            lastslash = s;
188[ 2]:        if (*s == ' ') {
189[ 3]:            firstspace = s;
190[ 3]:            break;
191[ 2]:        }
192[ 1]:    }
193[ 1]:
194[ 1]:    /*now use this to break the three parts apart*/
195[ 1]:    s = buffer;              /*first the directory path*/
196[ 1]:    t = directory;
197[ 1]:    if (lastslash) {
198[ 2]:        if (s == lastslash)
199[ 2]:            *t++ = '\\';
200[ 2]:        else
201[ 2]:            for (;s != lastslash;)
202[ 2]:                *t++ = *s++;
203[ 2]:        s++;
204[ 1]:    }
205[ 1]:    *t = '\0';
206[ 1]:
207[ 1]:    t = command;            /*then the command part*/
208[ 1]:    for (;s != firstspace && *s;)
209[ 1]:        *t++ = *s++;
210[ 1]:    s++;
211[ 1]:    *t = '\0';
212[ 1]:
213[ 1]:    t = params;             /*finally the params*/
214[ 1]:    if (firstspace)
215[ 1]:        for (;*s;)
216[ 1]:            *t++ = *s++;
217[ 1]:    *t = '\0';
218[ 0]: }
```

Notice that the *.DVP* structure is not word bounded; that is, fields of longer than one byte within the structure often begin on odd byte boundaries. Although this is legal, accessing multibyte values on an 8086 processor (or better) takes longer if its address is not even. Some compilers attempt to optimize programs by forcing all multibyte fields onto even boundaries. This must be disabled before any C program that attempts to define the *.DVP* structure (including *PRCTST3*) may be compiled successfully. In Borland's Turbo C, select byte alignment under Options/Compiler/Code Generation. In Microsoft C use the */Zp1* compilation switch. In other compilers select the option that forces "byte alignment" of structures.

Shared Memory

Processes do have some drawbacks. Since processes do not share memory, each must be loaded independently into memory. Programs written in a high-level language, such as C, often share a large amount of code with all other programs written with the same development tools. The initialization code, the C library functions, and the common user functions must all be duplicated in each process. Each time a process is loaded, space must be found in memory to share this duplicated code. Many multitasking operating systems address this problem through a technique known as shared memory or dynamic linking.

With shared memory, a process may place common functions in a separate file. When the process is first loaded, the operating system looks to see if the shared file is already memory resident. If not, the shared file is loaded into memory and its use count is set to one. If it is already loaded, its use count is simply incremented.

When the process finishes and it is removed from memory, the use count of the shared memory is decremented. If the result is zero, the shared memory file is also removed from memory. If it is not zero, implying that some other process is still using it, then the shared memory file is left in place.

A program can save a lot of space if functions shared among many processes are stored in shared memory files. In the extreme, the code for virtually an entire process could be placed in a shared file, reducing the overhead for each subsequent process to barely more than that of a task.

Using shared memory under DESQview will be discussed along with other Memory Management issues in Chapter 6.

Conclusion

The next few chapters of this book deal with the problems and the advantages of dividing problems into multiple tasks and processes. Let us examine our terminology one last time. Under DESQview a task is an execution thread underneath an application. Tasks may have their own windows but they may not be independently controlled by the user from DESQview. Tasks also share code and data segments.

An application, by comparison, is the basic execution unit. Applications may be selected by the user from the DESQview window and are independently controllable. Applications may be in the same source program, in which they share common code and data segments, or in different programs, in which case they have independent code and data segments.

DESQview calls a source program a process. Thus the DESQview manual speaks of "opening an application within a separate process," meaning executing an application from an independent program. Although we often call an independent application a process to accentuate its differences from the more task-like common application, applications are treated the same under DESQview whether they are executed as independent processes or not.

Interprocess Communication

Intertask communication is a critically important aspect to any multitasking operating system. An operating system may offer a very fine task-switching algorithm coupled with an efficient switcher, but if it does not offer a convenient means of interprocess communication, it will ultimately fail.

While it is true that such a multitasker may be able to make better use of a computer's CPU time or a user's time by allowing new tasks to be started even as old tasks are being worked, the full potential of multitasking cannot be realized. If tasks cannot communicate with each other, then they are doomed to execute as small islands, oblivious to what might be taking place about them.

Global Variables

Globally accessible variables have historically been the most used communication path between parts of programs, whether they be multitasked or not. One function simply stores data into memory so that another function may use it. With tasks, it works more or less the same way. Once a task has stored data into a global variable, other tasks may then read it out. If global variables are to be used as a communication path between tasks, however, special precautions must be taken.

Whenever a memory location is accessed by two or more tasks, the potential exists for a data collision. A data collision occurs whenever one task writes data to a memory location, overwriting data written earlier to the same location by another task. As discussed in Chapter 3, data collisions can occur in a variety of ways, but generally involve a sequence such as the following:

Figure 4.1—Data Collision (Task A's Data Loss)

Task A	Task B
1) reads memory location	
2)	reads memory location
3) calculates a new value	calculates a new value
4) writes the location back	
5)	writes the location back

There are three ways that data collisions over a global variable and the ensuing loss of data may be avoided. There is no data collision if only one task is allowed to write the variable. As many tasks as desired may read the location, but if only one task is allowed to perform writes then there can be no loss of data. When possible, this is generally the solution of preference. Not only is it "iron-clad" in the sense that no mistakes are possible, it is generally the most efficient. No special system calls must be made and tasks need never suspend their execution.

Operations which do not obviously fall into this category may be bent to fit. For example, take the case of a program designed to accumulate water volume entering a tank. In this program, there are a fixed number of input pipes, each of which may contribute to the volume of the tank at any time. The contributions of each of these pipes are monitored by separate asynchronous tasks.

The obvious approach in this case would be for each task to simply add its contribution periodically to the total tank volume, which is held in some globally accessible variable. Such a plan would run the risk of data collision as two of the tasks might attempt to update the volume simultaneously.

A better solution would be to maintain a separate variable for each pipe corresponding to the accumulated contribution from that pipe. Each task updates its global variable alone. A new task, independent of the pipe monitoring tasks, is then required to periodically read the individual contributions and update the single tank volume. In this way, no variable is written by more than one task. Each of the pipe accumulations is written by the corresponding pipe monitoring task, while the total accumulation is tallied and written by the totaler.

Even when it is not possible to restrict access to a global variable to a single task, it is usually possible to prevent data collisions programmatically. That is, the natural program logic suggests a protocol for accessing certain public information, which ensures that two or more tasks do not meddle with it simultaneously. This is very often the case with initialization variables. The parent task sets a value into a global variable before starting the child task. Once started, the child task then writes information back into the global to be read by the parent task. Since the child task cannot possibly write the variable before being started, and since the parent task no longer writes to the variable once the child is active, data collisions are avoided.

If neither of these approaches is possible, then tasks that want to write to these shared memory locations must resort to operating system support. Either the writing task must disable multitasking entirely during the period that the variable is being manipulated, or a resource known as a system lock must be assigned to the variable. The name *key* might have been better than *lock*, since a task must request and be granted a system lock before it may access the variable. Tasks that request the lock while it is checked out are suspended until it is returned. Once finished, the task that holds the lock gives it back to the system for other tasks to use. The subject of locking along with the broader subject of system semaphores will be discussed in Chapter 7.

While the problem of simultaneous access may be solvable, global variables are still not the best means of intertask communication. Programs that make heavy use of them tend to be error prone. A task may forget to return the system lock. Other tasks that request the lock become permanently suspended while waiting for a now lost lock and the system deadlocks.

Worse yet, tasks may forget to request a system lock or in some other way fail to follow the protocol preventing a data collision—these protocols are, after all, strictly voluntary. Often programmers don't realize that a potential data collision exists since they may not be aware of what other tasks access their variables and in what ways. Even in single-tasked systems, global variables may not be initialized properly or may be accessed by functions in nonreentrant ways.

Problems associated with global variables are usually very difficult to track down. Such problems are often timing critical, occurring only very infrequently, and leaving little or no tracks that the experienced software detective might use to isolate the problem.

In addition, this entire discussion concentrates solely on communication between tasks that share data segments and that are linked together. Separate processes, which are not linked together, do not know the location of each others global variables. Even if they did, it is questionable whether they could both access such memory locations since they do not share data segments. Thus, communication between programs via global variables is not a possibility.

We have seen in Chapter 3 three different global communications mechanisms in use in the TSKTST1.C program. This program used the DESQview system call *api_beginc()* and *api_endc()* to enable and disable rescheduling, respectively, while the global variable TASKCOUNT is updated by any one of the children or parent tasks.

Notice that these multitasking programs are reasonably easy to read, even for the single-tasking diehard, although they may be a bit unstructured. No new techniques are required to understand or even to write such a program, except for calls to disable scheduling or to attain a system lock. As mentioned earlier, this is both the appeal and danger of global variable communication paths. Easily overlooked data collisions are exceedingly difficult to find in the completed but unstable system.

Whether or not we find global variables an acceptable communications path for tasks and applications that share code and data segments, it is not acceptable for independent processes. Even in the simple example PRCTEST.C program, I had to resort to great heroics just get a few bytes of data from the parent process to the children processes and, even at that, the result was not completely acceptable. Communication between processes via standard global variables is not really possible.

Keyboard and Files

Communicating with tasks of your own invention is one thing, but sending information to programs that don't expect to communicate with other software is another problem. Only two communications paths exist with such programs: the keyboard and the file system.

An *aware* program may communicate with an *unaware* conventional program by pushing characters into the keyboard buffer. (The terms *aware* and *unaware* reflect the fact that one program is aware of the other and one is not.) The aware program simply uses the unaware program as a slave, sending it requests to perform through the keyboard. To the unaware program, the aware program appears to be a human operator.

This communication path is not one way. Having sent the request to the unaware program, the aware program can wait for a response to appear on the screen. This is more easily done with some programs than with others. For example, Lotus 1-2-3 always displays a READY in the upper right-hand corner of the screen when it has completed a command and is prepared to accept another. An aware program can send 1-2-3 a command to execute and then wait for the READY to first disappear (indicating receipt of the command) and then reappear (indicating completion). Of course, finding the answer on the display is a bit more difficult.

This communication path exists with single-tasking operating systems as well. A program under DOS may feed characters into the keyboard buffer and then spawn a subordinate program to "discover" them. Here again, getting the results is a bit more difficult.

Feeding characters through the keyboard buffer is also a common trick among Terminate-and-Stay Resident (TSR) programs. Here communication can become slightly more sophisticated. The TSR may borrow both the keyboard and display interrupts so that all requests for key strokes as well as requests to display go through the TSR. The TSR may then simply feed characters in through the key request interrupt and collect the results at the display interrupt. A common example of these are the key macro programs, such as DESQview itself, which allow the user to define a single key to stand for an entire string. When the TSR sees a key for which it has a definition, it begins sending a string of characters.

The keyboard buffer and the screen are not generally used as a communication path between specially written aware programs.

Under DESQview, keys may be pushed into the keyboard buffer by the API function *api_pushkey()*. Since keys are pushed into the buffer like a push-down stack, they must be pushed in reverse order. That is, in a multikey command the last key should be pushed first, followed by the next to last, etc., until the first key is pushed. In order to make sure that no keys are read until all have been pushed, the calling function should disable rescheduling by calling *api_beginc()* before pushing the keys. Reenable scheduling by calling *api_endc()* only after all keys have been pushed.

Figure 4.2—Prototype Declaration for *api_pushkey()*, *key_of()*, and *key_write()*

```
                          /*push a key into keyboard buffer*/
void pushkey              /*returns nothing*/
        (unsigned key);   /*key/scan code to push*/

                          /*return the key handle of a task*/
ulong key_of              /*returns a key handle*/
        (ulong tskhan);   /*takes an task handle*/

                          /*write to a task's key handle*/
void key_write            /*returns nothing*/
        (ulong keyhan,    /*keyboard handle*/
         char  *buffer,   /*characters to write*/
         int   buflng,    /*no. of characters in buffer*/
         int   status);   /*status to assoc. with data*/
```

Keys that have no ASCII equivalent may be pushed by pushing a zero ASCII character and a non-zero scan code. (A listing of the scan codes is available in the Technical Reference Manuals for the PC, PC-XT, and PC-AT).

Of course, *api_pushkey()* is somewhat imprecise. It is difficult to guarantee that the intended program will read the keys as planned. The current application should receive the keystrokes, but in the DESQview environment users are free to pull up applications as they desire, and one of those applications might end up reading the keyboard instead.

A more deterministic approach is to *key_write()* keys directly to the application in question. When the aware parent program starts the unaware slave program, it is returned a task handle. This task handle may be used to find out the child application's keyboard handle by calling *key_of()*. It may then send the unaware process an entire message with the *key_write()* API call.

The advantage here is clear. First, the calling program does not need to worry about pushing keys in reverse order and making sure that keys are not read out of order. More importantly, the parent program can indicate to DESQview exactly which application is to receive the keyboard input, no matter what other applications the user may decide to activate in the meantime. (If this makes no sense to you, don't worry. Key handles will be examined in detail in Chapter 5.)

The second communication path with unaware programs that we mentioned is the file system. In principle, this communication path is very simple. The sending program simply opens a file, writes data into the file, and then closes it. The receiving program may then open the file and read the data out. This is also a communication method with unaware programs since many operating systems, including DOS, allow input and output to be redirected to files.

An aware program might reasonably create an input file INPUT and then execute a batch file containing something like the following:

```
UNAWARE  <INPUT  >OUTPUT
```

The unaware program UNAWARE unknowingly reads its keyboard input out of the file INPUT while writing its output to the file OUTPUT. Once the program UNAWARE has completed, the aware program may then examine the file OUTPUT to collect the results. Here again, this same technique may be used in single-tasking operating systems due to its essentially serial nature.

The file system may also be used between aware programs. In this scenario, the sending program opens a file and writes the data to be sent into it. Once all data is written, the file is then closed. The receiving program watches for the appearance of the file. Once it appears, the receiving program attempts to open it. As long as the sending program has the file open, the operating system will not allow the receiver to open it. Once the sender has closed the file, the receiver may open it and read out the contents.

The file communication path has some advantages. First, it does not require any special features. All operating systems support files. In addition, since file transactions over LANs are generally transparent to the application program, programs may communicate in a LANed environment without worrying about directly accessing the LAN.

Unfortunately, file transmission is generally slow since each transmission requires several disk accesses: a file open, one write per block and a file close, followed by similar accesses on the reader side. On the other hand, the amount of data that may be transmitted per transaction is only limited by the available disk space and not by the available RAM space. In addition, the receiving task can waste large amounts of time attempting to open files that are already opened by another task.

Performance can be enhance greatly if the communicating file is resident on a RAM disk. Not only are the data reads and writes quicker, but the opens and closes are considerably sped up. With this in mind, some operating systems support a concept called *named pipes* in which programs are tied together with what appear as files to the application, but are actually RAM resident communication paths. Named pipes have all the advantages of file transmission with considerably less overhead.

Since DESQview does not interfere with DOS's file system, DESQview supports file transmission. DESQview does not implement named pipes, however.

(Incidentally, the input file need not be created separately each time. Many programs, especially compilers, maintain what is generally known as a configuration file. The program searches for this file each time it is executed. If found, the program reads its initial configuration from this file.)

Messages

Probably the best interprocess communication method between applications is the intertask message. In this method, the sending task bundles whatever information desired into a RAM resident buffer known as a message, which it then sends to the receiving task via an operating system call. The receiving task picks up the message also via a system call.

A good example of this is the teller/bank program, also known by the more general term client/server. Assume the existence of two programs. The first, known as the teller program, serves a particular human teller or Automatic Teller Machine (ATM). The other, known as the bank, is responsible for making the actual money transactions within the bank (you can imagine that this is a very carefully written program!).

Every time the teller requests a transaction, say a balance request, the teller program bundles up a message and sends it to the bank program for processing along with the program's return address. The bank program then picks up the transaction request and services it. Seeing that it is a balance request, it looks up the balance in its records and sends it back in a separate message to the teller program from which the request originated (the teller program was careful to put his own address in the enquiry message). Once the teller program receives the response message containing the balance, it puts the value up on the display.

Let us examine the mechanism in a little more detail. What does the operating system do with a message if the receiving task is already busy or not expecting a message? Every message must be stored somewhere. The operating system could block the sender (i.e., place the sending task into state Blocked so that it does not get scheduled) until the receiving task gets around to picking up the message, or it could interrupt the receiving task and force it to take the message immediately.

Instead, most operating systems implement some type of queue mechanism, often known as a mailbox. Any task may send a message to a given mailbox. Messages are allowed to stack up in a mailbox in a First-In-First-Out basis as fast as they can be sent. The receiving task reads messages out of the mailbox. Each time the receiving task requests another message, it is given the next one off top of the stack.

The mailbox queue allows a certain *springiness* to the system. Sending tasks can generate messages faster than the receiving task can work them off (for a limited period of time) without any problems arising. They simply queue up at the mailbox until they can be worked off. But let's turn the problem around. What happens when the receiving task requests a message from the mailbox and there are none left? Generally, the receiving task is blocked until another message arrives. As soon as some other task sends a message to that queue, the receiving task is unblocked (i.e., put into state Ready) and given the message when it next executes.

Occasionally, blocking on an empty queue is not desirable, so most operating systems allow tasks to peek into the queue to see if there are any messages present. If there are messages there, then the task knows that it may request a message from the queue without being blocked. If the queue is empty, the task knows that it can safely go do something else.

Intertask messages offer some distinct advantages over the communication schemes that we have seen up until now. For example, multiple requests for service are handled by the system and are kept in order.

Returning to our teller/bank example for a moment, suppose, as is generally the case, that there are dozens of teller programs and only one bank program. Tellers sitting behind their terminals and customers at their ATM machines are all devising bank transactions simultaneously. The bank program must be able to queue up rapidly arriving transactions until it can work them off. In the interest of fairness, it would also be desirable if the requests were worked off in the order that they were made. Otherwise, a particularly active bank teller might keep other tellers from getting any transactions completed at all.

Communicating transactions back and forth via, say, global variables in this type of environment would be quite difficult since this method provides neither queuing nor First-In-First-Out capability. The user program would have to handle the problem of simultaneous request for service itself.

In addition, applications that pass messages do not have to worry about problems such as data collisions over common memory locations. A program constructs a message entirely within its own memory space. No other program is able to interfere. Once built, the request is then transmitted to the receiving program. The receiving program is free to do what it wants with the message without concern that some other task might attempt to access it at the same time. The operating system worries with the details of transmission. If there are possible data collisions involved while getting the message over to the receiving task, it is left to the operating system to worry about it and not the application code. The exact same message passing mechanism may be used with independent processes as between tightly bound tasks.

Message passing also allows the receiving task to maintain multiple queues. There are occasions when a task wants to service only certain types of requests. Operating systems often make special provisions to allow the receiving task to pull out only certain message types. In any case, a receiving task can maintain multiple message queues: one for *normal* requests and a separate queue for *special* requests. By checking the special queue first, these messages receive preferential treatment.

Finally, message passing allows tasks to be more loosely coupled than they would be with other communication techniques, such as global variables. Modular programming attempts to define the interface between functions within a system by limiting the interface to just those data that are passed to it. If the interface can be completely defined, then the module may be understood by itself without resorting to examining the program around it. This leads to lower development costs and a higher degree of reliability in the final software.

Intertask messages bring modularity to the task level, allowing the task's interfaces with the remainder of the system to be described completely in terms of the input messages that it understands and the output messages that it generates. This message coupling allows the developer great freedom in assigning and developing the tasks that make up a program. Each programmer need only mimic the input messages and examine the output messages of an assigned task. If these agree with the agreed format as contained in interface specifications, then the task works.

As we have seen, this also allows the developer freedom of another type. Tasks receive and respond to messages without knowing where these messages come from.   Returning a final time to our teller/bank program, we see that the bank program responds to transaction requests identically, whether they come from tellers or ATMs. A bank teller's terminal and an ATM machine are very different and one might imagine that the software that drives them is also very different. Since the messages they create to the bank program are the same, however, the bank program does not have to concern itself with these differences.

But the real test comes when something new comes along, say a new connection with the branch bank in the suburbs. The teller and ATM programs could have been taken into special consideration when the bank program was written, but the branch bank hookup is a new concept. As long as the branch program uses the same transaction message formats, the bank program will continue to discharge its responsibilities completely without modification!

This ability to mix and match functional units by limiting interprogram contact to a set of strictly defined messages is a great advantage, and is the real advantage of multitasking operating systems to the software developer.

Simple Messages in DESQview

DESQview supports message passing with a rich set of API calls, the majority of which begin with the prefix *mal_*. Just as tasks are known by their task handles and windows by their window handles, mailboxes are known by their mailbox handle. Like other handles, a mailbox handle is a 32-bit unsigned entity that is assigned by DESQview.   When DESQview creates a task, it automatically assigns it a default mailbox, just as it assigns default task and window descriptors. As we will see later, a task may create further mailboxes as it desires, but this is not normally necessary.

Building a message to send is straightforward. The contents of messages are not important to DESQview. It is important, however, that the sending and receiving tasks agree on the exact format of the message. In C, the easiest approach is to define a structure defining the message format. For example, the following structure definition:

```
struct message {              /*format of message to child task*/
            int xloc;         /*column of window*/
            int yloc;         /*row of window*/
            int count;        /*task count*/
        };
```

This message obviously contains three integer fields.

This message structure definition should be available to both the sending and receiving task. If both tasks are resident in the same source module, it is sufficient to merely define the structure at the beginning of the module. If the two tasks are in different source modules or in entirely different programs, as is the case with processes, the best approach is to include all message definitions in a .H include file that both the sending and receiving modules include.

The message must then be assigned space in the sender's local memory. The statement

```
        struct message msgbuff;
```

assigns space for one message.

To send a message, the sender must first assign values to each of the fields in the message. It may then use the API call *mal_write()*. This function requires that the sender know the handle of the default mailbox of the receiving task. This is a problem since mailbox handles are assigned by DESQview when the mailbox is created. We will revisit this problem several times; however, the solution is straightforward for parent tasks attempting to send messages to children tasks.

A parent task receives the child's task handle when it creates the child task.

The parent task may use this task handle to find the child's default mailbox handle by using the *mal_of()* API call. Essentially the sequence is:

```
#include "mesgdefs.h"
ulong taskhandle, mailhandle;
structure message msgbuff;

/*create the child task - save the task handle*/
taskhandle = tsk_new (childtask, stack, stacksize,
                 title, titlesize, rows, cols);

/*now use the taskhandle to find its mailbox handle*/
mailhandle = mal_of (taskhandle);

/*send it the message*/
mal_write (mailhandle, &msgbuff, sizeof(msgbuff));
```

In the call to *mal_write()*, MAILHANDLE is the handle of the destination mailbox, &MSGBUFF is the address of the message buffer, and SIZEOF(MSGBUFF) is its length. Here it is assumed that MSGDEFS.H includes the definition of the structure MESSAGE. It is also assumed that data required in the message is filled in before it is sent to the child task.

DESQview copies the message out of the message buffer when the call to *mal_write()* is made and stores the message in memory accessible to both the sending and receiving tasks. The sending task is free to reuse the message buffer as soon as the *mal_write()* call is complete.

Figure 4.3—Prototype Declarations for *mal_of()*, *mal_sizeof()*, *mal_read()*, and *mal_write()*

```
                           /*default mailbox of calling task*/
ulong  mal_me              /*returns mailbox handle*/
          ();              /*takes no arguments*/

                           /*get default mailbox for a task*/
ulong  mal_of              /*returns mailbox handle*/
          (ulong tskhandle);/*requires the task handle*/

                           /*read a message from a mailbox*/
int    mal_read            /*returns the message status*/
          (ulong  malhandle,/*handle of mailbox to read*/
```

```
            char **msgptr,   /*pointer to message buffer*/
            int   *msglngth);/*message length*/

                             /*check no. of messages in a mailbox*/
int   mal_sizeof             /*return no. of messages*/
          (ulong malhandle);/*handle of mailbox to check*/

                             /*write a message to a mailbox*/
void   mal_write             /*returns nothing*/
          (ulong malhandle, /*destination mailbox handle*/
          char *msgbuff,    /*address of message buffer*/
          int   bufflngth); /*length of message*/
```

Figure 4.4 shows an excerpt of an actual send sequence.

Figure 4.4—Send Message Excerpt from MSGTST1.C

```
struct message {             /*format of message to child task*/
            int xloc;        /*column of window*/
            int yloc;        /*row of window*/
            int count;       /*task count*/
          };
            .
            .
            .

/*start the subtask*/
titlesize = sprintf (titlebuf, "Task #%d", taskcount);
tskhan = tsk_new (subtask, stacks[taskcount], STACKSIZE,
                titlebuf, titlesize, NUMROWS, NUMCOLS);

/*now send it a message containing its location information*/
msg.xloc = x;
msg.yloc = y;
msg.count = taskcount;
mal_write (mal_of (tskhan), &msg, sizeof(msg));
```

Receiving the message in the child task is just as straightforward. The child task reads from its default mailbox (especially since this is the mailbox to which the parent task sends its message). The child task gets its own default mailbox handle by simply calling *mal_me()*. It may then check for a message using the *mal_sizeof()* API call or simply read the mailbox, suspending itself if no messages are present by calling *mal_read()*. Figure 4.5 contains the reading excerpt from MSGTST1.C.

Figure 4.5—Receive Message Excerpt from MSGTST1.C

```
struct message *msgptr;
int msglngth;

/*wait for an initiation message with location information*/
mal_read (mal_me(), &msgptr, &msglngth);
```

Notice in Figure 4.3 that the second argument to *mal_read()* is of type CHAR **, which is "a pointer to a pointer to a character." We see why in Figure 4.5. The sending task simply declares a MSGBUF of type MESSAGE structure. This buffer is locally resident and its elements are accessed as MSGBUF.X, MSGBUF.Y, and so on. In the call to *mal_write()*, DESQview copies MSGPTR into a buffer that it takes from its own space.

DESQview does not copy the message again into the reader task's memory space. Instead, the reading task provides DESQview the address of a pointer to MESSAGE structure. Thus, MSGPTR is declared to be of type STRUCT MESSAGE *. Once it returns from the call to *mal_read()*, it will point to the message buffer stored within DESQview. In order for DESQview to change it, the reading task must pass the address of MSGPTR and not the contents of MSGPTR and hence the &MSGPTR in the call to *mal_read()*.

The fact that messages sent using *mal_write()* are actually stored in DESQview's memory has some important implications. First, the receiving task should be very careful about writing into them. Exceeding the limits of a message buffer causes the user task to overwrite DESQview's space, which is likely to be fatal. Second, if the message contains any information that the receiving task needs saved, it must copy the message into another buffer before executing another *mal_read()*. DESQview will reuse the buffer, causing the message to go away as soon as the receiving task attempts to read another message.

If we combine the read and write operations into one task, we end up with MSGTST1.C. In this version, the parent task starts the child *subtask()* just as before. It then immediately creates a message containing the child task window's X and Y location—information previously communicated via global variables—and sends it to the default mailbox for the new task.

The parent task must also send the task its number in the message. A global variable would not even be possible in this case as the parent task does not know when the child task will read the message. Depending on the order in which operations are performed, all five tasks may be started before the first task reads its message.

Notice that *fork()* refers to the elements of the MESSAGE structure as MSGBUF.X and MSGBUF.Y, while *subtask()* refers to them as MSG-PTR->X and MSGPTR->Y. This difference in structure operators stems from the fact that the message is defined within the sending task, but *msg_read()* only returns a pointer to the message.

Notice also that we have not completely done away with global variables. The child tasks continue to decrement TCOUNT to indicate their demise to the parent task. Since these tasks only decrement the count after the user has acknowledged the *win_disperor()* call, we are assured that a data collision is impossible, so we can dispense with the locking precautions of Chapter 3.

```
 1[ 0]: /*************************************************************
 2[ 0]:    Message Test #1 - create several visible tasks.  Have the
 3[ 0]:                      parent task direct each subtask via an
 4[ 0]:                      intertask message.
 5[ 0]: *************************************************************/
 6[ 0]:
 7[ 0]: #include <stdio.h>
 8[ 0]: #include "dvapi.h"
 9[ 0]:
10[ 0]: /*locally declared programs*/
11[ 0]: void main (void);
12[ 0]: void program_body (void);
13[ 0]: ulong fork (int, int, int, char *, int);
14[ 0]: int subtask (void);
15[ 0]:
16[ 0]: /*minimum API version required is DESQview 2.00*/
17[ 0]: #define required 0x200
18[ 0]:
19[ 0]: /*main - standard pattern for DESQview programs*/
20[ 0]: void main (void)
21[ 0]: {
22[ 1]:    int  version;
23[ 1]:
24[ 1]:    version = api_init();
```

```
25[ 1]:   if (version < required)
26[ 1]:        printf ("This program requires DESQview %d.%02d or later.\n",
27[ 1]:                   required >> 8, required & 0xff);
28[ 1]:   else {
29[ 2]:        /*tell DESQview what extensions to enable
30[ 2]:          and start application*/
31[ 2]:        api_level (required);
32[ 2]:        program_body();
33[ 1]:   }
34[ 1]:   /*if DESQview present (even if wrong version), shut it down*/
35[ 1]:   if (version)
36[ 1]:        api_exit();
37[ 0]: }
38[ 0]:
39[ 0]: /*program body - start up 5 tasks and wait for them to quit*/
40[ 0]:
41[ 0]: #define NUMTASKS     5          /*start up 5 subtasks*/
42[ 0]: #define NUMROWS     10
43[ 0]: #define NUMCOLS     25
44[ 0]:
45[ 0]: int X[NUMTASKS] = {60, 40, 20,  1, 30},
46[ 0]:     Y[NUMTASKS] = { 1,  5, 10, 15, 20};
47[ 0]:
48[ 0]: int tcount;                     /*number of tasks active*/
49[ 0]:
50[ 0]: struct message {                /*format of message to child task*/
51[ 1]:                 int xloc;       /*column of window*/
52[ 1]:                 int yloc;       /*row of window*/
53[ 1]:                 int count;      /*task count*/
54[ 0]:              };
55[ 0]:
56[ 0]: void program_body (void)
57[ 0]: {
58[ 1]:   int i;
59[ 1]:   ulong winhan;
60[ 1]:   #define STACKSIZE 1000        /*allocate some stack for each*/
61[ 1]:   char stacks [NUMTASKS][STACKSIZE];
62[ 1]:
63[ 1]:   winhan = win_new ("Main Program", 12, 10, 38);
64[ 1]:   win_move (winhan, 1, 1);
65[ 1]:   win_logattr (winhan, 1);
66[ 1]:   win_attr (winhan, 1);
67[ 1]:   win_unhide (winhan);
68[ 1]:   win_top (winhan);
69[ 1]:
70[ 1]:   /*now start subtask NUMTASKS number of times*/
71[ 1]:   for (tcount = 0; tcount < NUMTASKS; tcount++)
72[ 1]:        fork (X[tcount], Y[tcount], tcount, stacks [tcount], STACKSIZE)
73[ 1]:
74[ 1]:   /*wait for them all to quit - show we are still alive in mean time*/
75[ 1]:   i = 0;
76[ 1]:   while (tcount) {
77[ 2]:        win_printf (winhan, "Waiting; taskcount = %d, count = %d\n",
78[ 2]:                                tcount, i++);
79[ 2]:        api_pause ();
80[ 1]:   }
```

```
 81[ 1]:
 82[ 1]:    /*now put the window away*/
 83[ 1]:    win_free (winhan);
 84[ 0]: }
 85[ 0]:
 86[ 0]: /*fork - fork a new task*/
 87[ 0]: ulong fork (x, y, taskcount, stack, stacksize)
 88[ 0]:    int x, y, taskcount;
 89[ 0]:    char *stack;
 90[ 0]:    int stacksize;
 91[ 0]: {
 92[ 1]:    char titlebuf [80], titlesize;
 93[ 1]:    ulong tskhan;
 94[ 1]:    struct message msg;
 95[ 1]:
 96[ 1]:    /*start the subtask*/
 97[ 1]:    titlesize = sprintf (titlebuf, "Task #%d", taskcount);
 98[ 1]:    tskhan = tsk_new (subtask, stack, stacksize, titlebuf, titlesize,
 99[ 1]:                   NUMROWS, NUMCOLS);
100[ 1]:
101[ 1]:    /*now send it a message containing its location information*/
102[ 1]:    msg.xloc = x;
103[ 1]:    msg.yloc = y;
104[ 1]:    msg.count = taskcount;
105[ 1]:    mal_write (mal_of (tskhan), &msg, sizeof(msg));
106[ 1]:
107[ 1]:    /*finally return the task handle*/
108[ 1]:    return tskhan;
109[ 0]: }
110[ 0]:
111[ 0]: /*subtask - an example subtask which opens a window, counts down
112[ 0]:                and then removes itself*/
113[ 0]: int subtask (void)
114[ 0]: {
115[ 1]:    int i;
116[ 1]:    ulong winhan;
117[ 1]:    struct message *msgptr;
118[ 1]:    int msglngth;
119[ 1]:
120[ 1]:    /*wait for an initiation message with location information*/
121[ 1]:    mal_read (mal_me(), &msgptr, &msglngth);
122[ 1]:
123[ 1]:    /*set up window*/
124[ 1]:    winhan = win_me();
125[ 1]:    win_move (winhan, msgptr->yloc, msgptr->xloc);
126[ 1]:    win_logattr (winhan,1);
127[ 1]:    win_attr (winhan, msgptr->count+2);
128[ 1]:    win_unhide (winhan);
129[ 1]:    win_top (winhan);
130[ 1]:
131[ 1]:
132[ 1]:    /*now print out, politely giving up control after each round*/
133[ 1]:    for (i = 200; i; i--) {
134[ 2]:      win_printf (winhan, "I'm counting down %d\n", i);
135[ 2]:      api_pause ();
136[ 1]:
```

```
137[ 1]:
138[ 1]:    /*acknowlege task over*/
139[ 1]:    win_disperor (winhan, "Finished", 8, 1, 10, 1, 0);
140[ 1]:
141[ 1]:    /*decrement the task count*/
142[ 1]:    tcount--;
143[ 0]: }
```

It may seem curious that the prototype definitions in Figure 4.3 for *mal_read()* and *mal_write()* do not exactly match the way we have used them. Specifically, *mal_read()* and *mal_write()* refer to pointers to a character buffer while we pass them pointers to a structure of type MES-SAGE. In the days prior to the ANSI draft standard for C, it was common place to show a function accepting or returning a pointer to a character when the function accepts a pointer to any variable type.

In this case, however, we could have passed a simple character (or integer) array to *mal_write()*. Our send sequence might have looked like the following:

```
int msg [3];

msg[0] = x;
msg[1] = y;
msg[2] = taskcount;
mal_write (mal_of (tskhan), msg, 3);
```

This practice has several problems and is strongly discouraged. First, the resulting program is more difficult to read. It may be perfectly clear to the programmer that MSG[0] is the X location for the task to place its window and that MSG[2] is its task count, but it certainly won't be clear to anyone else. Worse yet, this approach is rife with potential for error. If another program assumes that the task count is MSG[1], there is nothing to correct the errant assignment. As a result, the program will not work, for what is a very subtle reason.

Further, this technique ignores the reality of programming. The only thing that is certain about a program when it is written is that it is going to change. Adding another integer field in between Y and TASKCOUNT is very difficult using the array model. The program can never be sure that he has found and corrected all of the proper occurrences of MSG[2] to MSG[3] and not corrected the MSG[2]'s, which really refer to the new field. Structure definitions, by comparison, are changed in one place and then in all affected modules recompiled.

Structures are a very powerful part of the C language and should be used. Their absence is one of the major limitations in older languages such as Fortran (indeed, it is generally the ex-Fortran programmer who uses array constructs such as the one shown). Structure definitions allow programmers to combine variables of different type into a composite whose structure is clear to both the reader and the programmer.

Replying to Messages

Having received a message, it is often the case that a task would like to reply to the message sender. Even in our teller/bank example, the bank was required to respond to the teller. In order to respond, the receiving task need only know the mailbox in which the sender will be looking for the answer. A message sent to this mailbox is picked up by the sending task as its response. The most straightforward approach is for the sender to include the return address in the message itself.

In DESQview, the sending task may send a mailbox handle within the message. If it uses the default mailbox to receive responses, it may send its task handle instead. The reading task can always use *mal_of()* to convert this task handle to a mailbox handle, and the task handle is a lot more useful for other functions.

Although very clean in appearance, our first message program was made aesthetically less pleasing by the continued use of the global variable TCOUNT as a return communication path. This approach only works for tasks and applications that share code and data segments. Just as before, separate processes would have to resort to special tricks in order to get this to work properly. The tasks shown in MSGTST2 communicate with each other using only messages.

```
 1[ 0]: /*****************************************************************
 2[ 0]:   Message Test #2 - create several visible tasks.  Have the main
 3[ 0]:                     task direct the subtasks via messages and
 4[ 0]:                     have the subtasks respond via messages as
 5[ 0]:                     well.
 6[ 0]: *****************************************************************/
 7[ 0]:
 8[ 0]: #include <stdio.h>
 9[ 0]: #include "dvapi.h"
10[ 0]:
11[ 0]: /*locally declared programs*/
12[ 0]: void main (void);
13[ 0]: void program_body (void);
14[ 0]: ulong fork (int, int, int, char *, int);
15[ 0]: int subtask (void);
16[ 0]:
17[ 0]: /*minimum API version required is DESQview 2.00*/
18[ 0]: #define required 0x200
19[ 0]:
20[ 0]: /*main - standard pattern for DESQview programs*/
21[ 0]: void main (void)
22[ 0]: {
23[ 1]:    int  version;
24[ 1]:
25[ 1]:    version = api_init();
26[ 1]:    if (version < required)
27[ 1]:        printf ("This program requires DESQview %d.%02d or later.\n",
28[ 1]:                 required >> 8, required & 0xff);
29[ 1]:    else {
30[ 2]:        /*tell DESQview what extensions to enable
31[ 2]:          and start application*/
32[ 2]:        api_level (required);
33[ 2]:        program_body();
34[ 1]:    }
35[ 1]:    /*if DESQview present (even if wrong version), shut it down*/
36[ 1]:    if (version)
37[ 1]:        api_exit();
38[ 0]: }
39[ 0]:
40[ 0]: /*program body - start up 5 tasks and wait for them to quit*/
41[ 0]:
42[ 0]: #define NUMTASKS    5              /*start up 5 subtasks*/
43[ 0]: #define NUMROWS    10
44[ 0]: #define NUMCOLS    25
45[ 0]:
46[ 0]: int X[NUMTASKS] = {60, 40, 20,  1, 30},
47[ 0]:     Y[NUMTASKS] = { 1,  5, 10, 15, 20};
48[ 0]:
49[ 0]: struct message {                   /*format of message to child task*/
50[ 1]:                  int xloc;         /*column of window*/
51[ 1]:                  int yloc;         /*row of window*/
52[ 1]:                  int count;        /*task count*/
53[ 1]:                  ulong parent;     /*handle of parent task*/
54[ 0]:                 };
55[ 0]:
56[ 0]: struct response {                  /*format of response message*/
```

```
57[ 1]:                      ulong child;  /*return the child handle*/
58[ 1]:                      int   count;  /*and its count*/
59[ 0]:                      };
60[ 0]:
61[ 0]: void program_body (void)
62[ 0]: {
63[ 1]:    int i;
64[ 1]:    int tcount;
65[ 1]:    ulong winhan;
66[ 1]:    struct response *msgptr;
67[ 1]:    int       msglngth;
68[ 1]:    #define STACKSIZE 1000        /*allocate some stack for each*/
69[ 1]:    char stacks [NUMTASKS][STACKSIZE];
70[ 1]:
71[ 1]:    winhan = win_new ("Main Program", 12, 10, 38);
72[ 1]:    win_move (winhan, 1, 1);
73[ 1]:    win_logattr (winhan, 1);
74[ 1]:    win_attr (winhan, 1);
75[ 1]:    win_unhide (winhan);
76[ 1]:    win_top (winhan);
77[ 1]:
78[ 1]:    /*now start subtask NUMTASKS number of times*/
79[ 1]:    for (tcount = 0; tcount < NUMTASKS; tcount++)
80[ 1]:        fork (X[tcount], Y[tcount], tcount, stacks [tcount], STACKSIZE)
81[ 1]:
82[ 1]:    /*wait for them all to quit - show we are still alive in mean time*/
83[ 1]:    i = 0;
84[ 1]:    while (tcount) {
85[ 2]:        /*if a message appears, read it and decrement the task count*/
86[ 2]:        if (mal_sizeof (mal_me())) {
87[ 3]:            mal_read (mal_me(), &msgptr, &msglngth);
88[ 3]:            win_printf (winhan, "\nReceived a quit from %d\n\n",
89[ 3]:                        msgptr->count);
90[ 3]:            tcount--;
91[ 2]:        }
92[ 2]:
93[ 2]:        win_printf (winhan, "Waiting; taskcount = %d, count = %d\n",
94[ 2]:                            tcount, i++);
95[ 2]:        api_pause ();
96[ 1]:    }
97[ 1]:
98[ 1]:    /*now put the window away*/
99[ 1]:    win_free (winhan);
100[ 0]: }
101[ 0]:
102[ 0]: /*fork - fork a new task*/
103[ 0]: ulong fork (x, y, taskcount, stack, stacksize)
104[ 0]:    int x, y, taskcount;
105[ 0]:    char *stack;
106[ 0]:    int stacksize;
107[ 0]: {
108[ 1]:    char titlebuf [80], titlesize;
109[ 1]:    ulong tskhan;
110[ 1]:    struct message msg;
111[ 1]:
112[ 1]:    /*start the subtask*/
```

```
113[ 1]:    titlesize = sprintf (titlebuf, "Task #%d", taskcount);
114[ 1]:    tskhan = tsk_new (subtask, stack, stacksize, titlebuf, titlesize,
115[ 1]:                    NUMROWS, NUMCOLS);
116[ 1]:
117[ 1]:    /*now send it a message containing its location information*/
118[ 1]:    msg.xloc = x;
119[ 1]:    msg.yloc = y;
120[ 1]:    msg.count = taskcount;
121[ 1]:    msg.parent = tsk_me();
122[ 1]:    mal_write (mal_of (tskhan), &msg, sizeof(msg));
123[ 1]:
124[ 1]:    /*finally return the task handle*/
125[ 1]:    return tskhan;
126[ 0]: }
127[ 0]:
128[ 0]: /*subtask - an example subtask which opens a window, counts down
129[ 0]:             and then removes itself*/
130[ 0]: int subtask (void)
131[ 0]: {
132[ 1]:    int i;
133[ 1]:    ulong winhan;
134[ 1]:    struct message *msgptr;
135[ 1]:    struct response msg;
136[ 1]:    int   msglngth;
137[ 1]:
138[ 1]:    /*wait for an initiation message with location information*/
139[ 1]:    mal_read (mal_me(), &msgptr, &msglngth);
140[ 1]:
141[ 1]:    /*set up window*/
142[ 1]:    winhan = win_me();
143[ 1]:    win_move (winhan, msgptr->yloc, msgptr->xloc);
144[ 1]:    win_logattr (winhan,1);
145[ 1]:    win_attr (winhan, msgptr->count+2);
146[ 1]:    win_unhide (winhan);
147[ 1]:    win_top (winhan);
148[ 1]:
149[ 1]:
150[ 1]:    /*now print out, politely giving up control after each round*/
151[ 1]:    for (i = 200; i; i--) {
152[ 2]:      win_printf (winhan, "I'm counting down %d\n", i);
153[ 2]:      api_pause ();
154[ 1]:    }
155[ 1]:
156[ 1]:    /*acknowlege task over*/
157[ 1]:    win_disperor (winhan, "Finished", 8, 1, 10, 1, 0);
158[ 1]:
159[ 1]:    /*now send a message back of our demise*/
160[ 1]:    msg.child = tsk_me();
161[ 1]:    msg.count = msgptr->count;
162[ 1]:    win_write (mal_of (msgptr->parent), &msg, sizeof(msg));
163[ 0]: }
```

Just as before, the main task starts each *subtask()* and then sends it a message, indicating its task number and where it should place itself on the screen, only this time the main task also includes its own task handle, which it gets by calling *tsk_me()*. Just as before, each of the children tasks enters a count down loop. Once the loop is exhausted, it outputs a message and then terminates; but before it terminates, it sends a message back to the main program, indicating the fact that it has completed. Each child task addresses its terminate message to *mal_of(msgptr->parent)*, MSG-PTR->PARENT being the task handle of the parent task.

Once all the children tasks have been started, the parent task must then prepare to read its mailbox to pick up its responses. It cannot simply post a read on the mailbox, however, as it will not get control back until a message arrives. Instead, we want the parent task to continue sending a waiting message to the screen, indicating the current outstanding task count. Therefore, within the waiting loop, the parent task uses the API call *mal_sizeof()* to determine the number of messages waiting there. If *mal_sizeof()* returns a zero, then there are no messages, and the task proceeds on. If the number of messages is not zero, then the parent can call *mal_read()* without being suspended. For every response message read, the parent task simply decrements TCOUNT, which is now a local variable.

Although the most straightforward approach, it is not necessary for the sending task to send its task handle along in the message. The receiving task can get the task handle of the sender of the last message read by calling the API function *mal_addr()*. The same program, now using this function call, appears in MSGTST3.

```
 1[ 0]: /****************************************************************
 2[ 0]:    Message Test #3 - have the subtasks communicate back by
 3[ 0]:                      noting the default mailbox of the sending
 4[ 0]:                      tasks.
 5[ 0]: ****************************************************************/
 6[ 0]:
 7[ 0]: #include <stdio.h>
 8[ 0]: #include "dvapi.h"
 9[ 0]:
10[ 0]: /*locally declared programs*/
11[ 0]: void main (void);
12[ 0]: void program_body (void);
13[ 0]: ulong fork (int, int, int, char *, int);
14[ 0]: int subtask (void);
```

```
15[ 0]:
16[ 0]: /*minimum API version required is DESQview 2.00*/
17[ 0]: #define required 0x200
18[ 0]:
19[ 0]: /*main - standard pattern for DESQview programs*/
20[ 0]: void main (void)
21[ 0]: {
22[ 1]:   int  version;
23[ 1]:
24[ 1]:   version = api_init();
25[ 1]:   if (version < required)
26[ 1]:       printf ("This program requires DESQview %d.%02d or later.\n",
27[ 1]:                   required >> 8, required & 0xff);
28[ 1]:   else {
29[ 2]:       /*tell DESQview what extensions to enable
30[ 2]:        and start application*/
31[ 2]:       api_level (required);
32[ 2]:       program_body();
33[ 1]:   }
34[ 1]:   /*if DESQview present (even if wrong version), shut it down*/
35[ 1]:   if (version)
36[ 1]:       api_exit();
37[ 0]: }
38[ 0]:
39[ 0]: /*program body - start up 5 tasks and wait for them to quit*/
40[ 0]:
41[ 0]: #define NUMTASKS     5              /*start up 5 subtasks*/
42[ 0]: #define NUMROWS     10
43[ 0]: #define NUMCOLS     25
44[ 0]:
45[ 0]: int X[NUMTASKS] = {60, 40, 20,  1, 30},
46[ 0]:     Y[NUMTASKS] = { 1,  5, 10, 15, 20};
47[ 0]:
48[ 0]: struct message {                   /*format of message to child task*/
49[ 1]:                   int xloc;        /*column of window*/
50[ 1]:                   int yloc;        /*row of window*/
51[ 1]:                   int count;       /*task count*/
52[ 0]:                };
53[ 0]:
54[ 0]: struct response {
55[ 1]:                   int   count;  /*and its count*/
56[ 0]:                };
57[ 0]:
58[ 0]: void program_body (void)
59[ 0]: {
60[ 1]:   int i;
61[ 1]:   int tcount;
62[ 1]:   ulong winhan;
63[ 1]:   struct response *msgptr;
64[ 1]:   int           msglngth;
65[ 1]:   #define STACKSIZE 1000          /*allocate some stack for each*/
66[ 1]:   char stacks [NUMTASKS][STACKSIZE];
67[ 1]:
68[ 1]:   winhan = win_new ("Main Program", 12, 10, 38);
69[ 1]:   win_move (winhan, 1, 1);
70[ 1]:   win_logattr (winhan, 1);
```

```
71[ 1]:    win_attr (winhan, 1);
72[ 1]:    win_unhide (winhan);
73[ 1]:    win_top (winhan);
74[ 1]:
75[ 1]:    /*now start subtask NUMTASKS number of times*/
76[ 1]:    for (tcount = 0; tcount < NUMTASKS; tcount++)
77[ 1]:        fork (X[tcount], Y[tcount], tcount, stacks [tcount], STACKSIZE)
78[ 1]:
79[ 1]:    /*wait for them all to quit - show we are alive in mean time*/
80[ 1]:    i = 0;
81[ 1]:    while (tcount) {
82[ 2]:        /*if a message appears, read it and dec the task count*/
83[ 2]:        if (mal_sizeof (mal_me())) {
84[ 3]:            mal_read (mal_me(), &msgptr, &msglngth);
85[ 3]:            win_printf (winhan, "\nReceived a quit from %d\n\n",
86[ 3]:                        msgptr->count);
87[ 3]:            tcount--;
88[ 2]:        }
89[ 2]:
90[ 2]:        win_printf (winhan, "Waiting; taskcount = %d, count = %d\n",
91[ 2]:                        tcount, i++);
92[ 2]:        api_pause ();
93[ 1]:    }
94[ 1]:
95[ 1]:    /*now put the window away*/
96[ 1]:    win_free (winhan);
97[ 0]: }
98[ 0]:
99[ 0]: /*fork - fork a new task*/
100[ 0]: ulong fork (x, y, taskcount, stack, stacksize)
101[ 0]:    int x, y, taskcount;
102[ 0]:    char *stack;
103[ 0]:    int stacksize;
104[ 0]: {
105[ 1]:    char titlebuf [80], titlesize;
106[ 1]:    ulong tskhan;
107[ 1]:    struct message msg;
108[ 1]:
109[ 1]:    /*start the subtask*/
110[ 1]:    titlesize = sprintf (titlebuf, "Task #%d", taskcount);
111[ 1]:    tskhan = tsk_new (subtask, stack, stacksize, titlebuf, titlesize,
112[ 1]:                NUMROWS, NUMCOLS);
113[ 1]:
114[ 1]:    /*now send it a message containing its location information*/
115[ 1]:    msg.xloc = x;
116[ 1]:    msg.yloc = y;
117[ 1]:    msg.count = taskcount;
118[ 1]:    mal_write (mal_of (tskhan), &msg, sizeof(msg));
119[ 1]:
120[ 1]:    /*finally return the task handle*/
121[ 1]:    return tskhan;
122[ 0]: }
123[ 0]:
124[ 0]: /*subtask - an example subtask which opens a window, counts down
125[ 0]:            and then removes itself*/
126[ 0]: int subtask (void)
```

```
127[ 0]: {
128[ 1]:    int i;
129[ 1]:    ulong winhan;
130[ 1]:    ulong taskhan, mailhan;
131[ 1]:    struct message *msgptr;
132[ 1]:    struct response msg;
133[ 1]:    int   msglngth;
134[ 1]:
135[ 1]:    /*wait for an initiation message with location information*/
136[ 1]:    mal_read (mal_me(), &msgptr, &msglngth);
137[ 1]:
138[ 1]:    /*set up window*/
139[ 1]:    winhan = win_me();
140[ 1]:    win_move (winhan, msgptr->yloc, msgptr->xloc);
141[ 1]:    win_logattr (winhan,1);
142[ 1]:    win_attr (winhan, msgptr->count+2);
143[ 1]:    win_unhide (winhan);
144[ 1]:    win_top (winhan);
145[ 1]:
146[ 1]:
147[ 1]:    /*now print out, politely giving up control after each round*/
148[ 1]:    for (i = 200; i; i--) {
149[ 2]:       win_printf (winhan, "I'm counting down %d\n", i);
150[ 2]:       api_pause ();
151[ 1]:    }
152[ 1]:
153[ 1]:    /*acknowlege task over*/
154[ 1]:    win_disperor (winhan, "Finished", 8, 1, 10, 1, 0);
155[ 1]:
156[ 1]:    /*now send a message back of our demise*/
157[ 1]:    msg.count = msgptr->count;
158[ 1]:    mailhan = mal_me();              /*get my own mail handle*/
159[ 1]:    taskhan = mal_addr (mailhan);  /*use that to get the sender's
160[ 1]:                                     task handle*/
161[ 1]:
162[ 1]:    /*send message to the original sender's default mailbox*/
163[ 1]:    win_write (mal_of (taskhan), &msg, sizeof(msg));
164[ 0]: }
```

This further simplifies the job of responding to a tasking message.

Message Status

It is often the case that a particular task may receive several different type of messages. Returning to our teller/bank example, the bank program might reasonably receive requests to look up a balance or to make a withdrawal, a deposit, or a transfer of funds. It is also reasonable to assume that these different message types have different formats since they require different data. If all of these message types were defined at the same time, the transaction type may be merely included within the message itself. For example, the bank and teller program developers may agree that the first byte of the message should indicate the message type and, hence, the format of the remainder of the message.

Suppose, however, that some of the message formats are fixed. For example, assume that the formats of teller request messages are fixed using the first byte to indicate the message type, while ATM messages are fixed using the second byte for this purpose. The bank program has a dilemma. As soon as the bank program knows what type of message it is dealing with, it knows its format, but it must know the message format before it can known the message type. For teller requests it should look in one place, and for ATMs it should look somewhere else. For any given message, the bank program cannot know where in the message to look.

The bank program could look at the sending task to see if it is a teller or ATM program, but this is very inflexible. For one thing, the names of the programs may change. For another, the messages may have been rerouted in some fashion to which the bank program is not privy. In any case, the bank program should not need to worry itself with how the message requests arrived.

DESQview offers a concept known as *message status*. When a message is sent, the sender indicates the message type along with the call. The receiver can then receive this status at the same time as it receives the message itself. This receiver uses this message status to determine the message type and, therefore, its format. Some operating systems also allow the receiving task to preferentially receive messages of a particular type, effectively granting them higher priority.

A further use for status is to indicate the original source of the message. For example, even though they are of the same format, local teller messages and remote teller messages may be assigned different status. Of course, if the format of the messages is truly the same, this information could have been placed within the message itself; however, it might be more convenient to place it in the status field.

When we used the API call *mal_write()* before, the status was set to zero. A task which wants to specifically set the message status must use the API call *mal_addto()*. This API call is identical to the *mal_write()* call except that it allows the sending task to specify a message status. Although we did not use it before, the *mal_read()* API call returns the message status when it receives a message. It is also possible to get the status of the last message read from a specified mailbox via the *mal_status()* API call. Notice that the message status is limited to one byte and so cannot exceed the range 0 to 255.

Figure 4.6—Prototype Declarations for *mal_addto()*, *mal_status()*, and *mal_subfrom()*

```
                          /*send a message by value with status*/
void  mal_addto           /*returns nothing*/
         (ulong malhandle, /*handle of target mailbox*/
          char *msgbuf,   /*message buffer to send*/
          int  msglngth,  /*length of message*/
          int  status);   /*message status to send*/

                          /*get status of last message received*/
int   mal_status          /*return status*/
         (ulong malhandle);/*handle of mailbox to check*/

                          /*send a message by reference*/
void  mal_subfrom         /*returns nothing*/
         (ulong malhandle, /*handle of target mailbox*/
          char *msgbuf,   /*message buffer to send*/
          int  msglngth,  /*length of message*/
          int  status);   /*message status to send*/
```

The API call *mal_status()* also offers the possibility for a small trick. Generally, tasks should not attempt to track messages once they have been sent. However, if a different message status is assigned to each different source for a particular message, then *mal_status()* may be used to tell a task when its message has been read. If a task calls *mal_status()* on the mailbox handle to which it has sent a message, it will receive the type of the last message read from that mailbox. If the status equals its own status number, then the task knows that its message was the last one read. Of course, this is not a very good technique. Due to the vagaries of multitasking timing, the receiving task might read two messages before the sending task can call *mal_status()* again and the information would be lost.

Passing Messages by Reference

Normally when messages are sent from one task to another, they are copied into a safe buffer area accessible by both the sending and receiving tasks. This is in keeping with our concept of minimizing the interaction between the sending and receiving tasks to just the message itself. The sending task may do what it likes with the message buffer once it has been sent, as it is a copy of the buffer which the receiving task gets and not the original.

Of course, there is a certain amount of overhead incurred by all this copying about. The amount of overhead is a function of the size of the message. For messages of reasonable size, the overhead is not noticeable. In this case, the benefits far outweigh the price in CPU time. When messages start to become quite large, the price in terms of CPU time can become noticeable. With extremely large messages, an even worse problem can arise. The operating system may not have sufficient buffer space to hold the message or the host computer may not even have sufficient room to hold two copies of the message at once!

In this case, it becomes necessary to pass messages by reference. When passing by reference, the operating system merely passes along the address of the sender's buffer and not the contents. The address that the receiving task receives from *mal_read()* is that of the sender's original message.

Although potentially faster, there are some severe restrictions on this technique. First, the sending and receiving tasks must both have access to the memory contained by the buffer. Normally this can only be assured if both tasks are within the same process or if the message is contained in shared common memory.

Second, the sending task is not free to reuse the message buffer until the receiving task has completed using it. Thus, the sending task must send the buffer and forget about it or the sending and receiving tasks must agree upon some type of protocol. Either the receiving task can send a small message indicating it has finished with the message, or it may set a flag within the message itself. The cleanest approach is for the receiving task to actually send the buffer back. The cost of sending the large buffer back is very small and independent of the size of the buffer.

Notice that passing messages by reference is not a new capability. A program can always create a large buffer of information and then store its address into a message that is passed by value. The actual message is a scant four bytes long (the length of a long address), irrespective of the size of the buffer pointed at. This is probably preferable as it is more clear to the reader that what is actually being passed is the address of a large buffer.

DESQview supports passing messages by reference with the *mal_subfrom()* API call. This call resembles the *mal_addto()* call in that both a message and its status are required. Our message passing example program rewritten to use *mal_subfrom()* is shown in MSGTST4.

In MSGTST4, the parent program starts each child process like before and then sends it its marching papers via an interprocess message. Since the message has been passed by reference, however, it must wait this time until the child task sends the message back before it can continue and reuse it for the next task.

The children tasks must copy from the message any information of interest before sending the message back. Data must be copied into local space since the subtask does not know when the parent task will change its contents again. Alternatively, the parent task must wait for the subtask to finish before it may receive its message back and continue on with the next subtask.

```
 1[ 0]: /*************************************************************
 2[ 0]:     Message Test #4 - communicate between tasks using "pass by
 3[ 0]:                     reference" messages.
 4[ 0]: *************************************************************/
 5[ 0]:
 6[ 0]: #include <stdio.h>
 7[ 0]: #include "dvapi.h"
 8[ 0]:
 9[ 0]: /*locally declared programs*/
10[ 0]: void main (void);
11[ 0]: void program_body (void);
12[ 0]: ulong fork (int, int, int, char *, int);
13[ 0]: int subtask (void);
14[ 0]:
15[ 0]: /*minimum API version required is DESQview 2.00*/
16[ 0]: #define required 0x200
17[ 0]:
18[ 0]: /*main - standard pattern for DESQview programs*/
19[ 0]: void main (void)
20[ 0]: {
21[ 1]:    int  version;
22[ 1]:
23[ 1]:    version = api_init();
24[ 1]:    if (version < required)
25[ 1]:        printf ("This program requires DESQview %d.%02d or later.\n",
26[ 1]:                required >> 8, required & 0xff);
27[ 1]:    else {
28[ 2]:        /*tell DESQview what extensions to enable
29[ 2]:          and start application*/
30[ 2]:        api_level (required);
31[ 2]:        program_body();
32[ 1]:    }
33[ 1]:    /*if DESQview present (even if wrong version), shut it down*/
34[ 1]:    if (version)
35[ 1]:        api_exit();
36[ 0]: }
37[ 0]:
38[ 0]: /*program body - start up 5 tasks and wait for them to quit*/
39[ 0]:
40[ 0]: #define NUMTASKS    5            /*start up 5 subtasks*/
41[ 0]: #define NUMROWS    10
42[ 0]: #define NUMCOLS    25
43[ 0]:
44[ 0]: int X[NUMTASKS] = {60, 40, 20,  1, 30},
45[ 0]:     Y[NUMTASKS] = { 1,  5, 10, 15, 20};
46[ 0]:
47[ 0]: struct message {                    /*format of message to child task*/
48[ 1]:                 int xloc;           /*column of window*/
49[ 1]:                 int yloc;           /*row of window*/
50[ 1]:                 int count;          /*task count*/
51[ 1]:                 ulong parent;       /*handle of parent task*/
52[ 0]:                 };
53[ 0]:
54[ 0]: struct response {                   /*format of response message*/
55[ 1]:                 ulong child;   /*return the child handle*/
56[ 1]:                 int   count;   /*and its count*/
```

```
57[ 0]:                          };
58[ 0]:
59[ 0]: void program_body (void)
60[ 0]: {
61[ 1]:    int i;
62[ 1]:    int tcount;
63[ 1]:    ulong winhan;
64[ 1]:    struct response *msgptr;
65[ 1]:    int          msglngth;
66[ 1]:    #define STACKSIZE 1000        /*allocate some stack for each*/
67[ 1]:    char stacks [NUMTASKS][STACKSIZE];
68[ 1]:
69[ 1]:    winhan = win_new ("Main Program", 12, 10, 38);
70[ 1]:    win_move (winhan, 1, 1);
71[ 1]:    win_logattr (winhan, 1);
72[ 1]:    win_attr (winhan, 1);
73[ 1]:    win_unhide (winhan);
74[ 1]:    win_top (winhan);
75[ 1]:
76[ 1]:    /*now start subtask NUMTASKS number of times*/
77[ 1]:    for (tcount = 0; tcount < NUMTASKS; tcount++)
78[ 1]:        fork (X[tcount], Y[tcount], tcount, stacks [tcount], STACKSIZE)
79[ 1]:
80[ 1]:    /*wait for them all to quit - show we are alive in mean time*/
81[ 1]:    i = 0;
82[ 1]:    while (tcount) {
83[ 2]:        /*if a message appears, read it and dec the task count*/
84[ 2]:        if (mal_sizeof (mal_me())) {
85[ 3]:            mal_read (mal_me(), &msgptr, &msglngth);
86[ 3]:            win_printf (winhan, "\nReceived a quit from %d\n\n",
87[ 3]:                        msgptr->count);
88[ 3]:            tcount--;
89[ 2]:        }
90[ 2]:
91[ 2]:        win_printf (winhan, "Waiting; taskcount = %d, count = %d\n",
92[ 2]:                        tcount, i++);
93[ 2]:        api_pause ();
94[ 1]:    }
95[ 1]:
96[ 1]:    /*now put the window away*/
97[ 1]:    win_free (winhan);
98[ 0]: }
99[ 0]:
100[ 0]: /*fork - fork a new task*/
101[ 0]: ulong fork (x, y, taskcount, stack, stacksize)
102[ 0]:    int x, y, taskcount;
103[ 0]:    char *stack;
104[ 0]:    int stacksize;
105[ 0]: {
106[ 1]:    char titlebuf [80], titlesize;
107[ 1]:    ulong tskhan;
108[ 1]:    struct message  msg;
109[ 1]:    struct message *msgptr;
110[ 1]:    int     msglngth;
111[ 1]:
112[ 1]:    /*start the subtask*/
```

```
113[ 1]:   titlesize = sprintf (titlebuf, "Task #%d", taskcount);
114[ 1]:   tskhan = tsk_new (subtask, stack, stacksize, titlebuf, titlesize,
115[ 1]:                    NUMROWS, NUMCOLS);
116[ 1]:
117[ 1]:   /*now send it a message by reference containing its
118[ 1]:     location information*/
119[ 1]:   msg.xloc = x;
120[ 1]:   msg.yloc = y;
121[ 1]:   msg.count = taskcount;
122[ 1]:   msg.parent = tsk_me();
123[ 1]:   mal_subfrom (mal_of (tskhan), &msg, sizeof(msg), taskcount);
124[ 1]:
125[ 1]:   /*now wait for the message to be sent back*/
126[ 1]:   mal_read (mal_me(), &msgptr, &msglngth);
127[ 1]:   if (msgptr != &msg)
128[ 1]:       win_disperor (win_me(), "Received msg did not match", 26,
129[ 1]:                    1, 28, 1, 0);
130[ 1]:
131[ 1]:   /*finally return the task handle*/
132[ 1]:   return tskhan;
133[ 0]: }
134[ 0]:
135[ 0]: /*subtask - an example subtask which opens a window, counts down
136[ 0]:               and then removes itself*/
137[ 0]: int subtask (void)
138[ 0]: {
139[ 1]:   int i;
140[ 1]:   ulong winhan;
141[ 1]:   struct message *msgptr;
142[ 1]:   struct response msg;
143[ 1]:   int   msglngth;
144[ 1]:   int   localx, localy, localcount;
145[ 1]:   ulong localparent;
146[ 1]:
147[ 1]:   /*wait for an initiation message with location information -
148[ 1]:     as message is being passed by reference, get the data from it
149[ 1]:     and send it back as soon as possible*/
150[ 1]:   mal_read (mal_me(), &msgptr, &msglngth);
151[ 1]:   localx    =    msgptr->xloc;
152[ 1]:   localy    =    msgptr->yloc;
153[ 1]:   localcount  = msgptr->count;
154[ 1]:   localparent = msgptr->parent;
155[ 1]:   mal_subfrom (mal_of (localparent), msgptr, msglngth, 0);
156[ 1]:
157[ 1]:   /*set up window*/
158[ 1]:   winhan = win_me();
159[ 1]:   win_move (winhan, localy, localx);
160[ 1]:   win_logattr (winhan,1);
161[ 1]:   win_attr (winhan, localcount + 2);
162[ 1]:   win_unhide (winhan);
163[ 1]:   win_top (winhan);
164[ 1]:
165[ 1]:
166[ 1]:   /*now print out, politely giving up control after each round*/
167[ 1]:   for (i = 200; i; i--) {
168[ 2]:     win_printf (winhan, "I'm counting down %d\n", i);
```

```
169[ 2]:     api_pause ();
170[ 1]:   }
171[ 1]:
172[ 1]:   /*acknowlege task over*/
173[ 1]:   win_disperor (winhan, "Finished", 8, 1, 10, 1, 0);
174[ 1]:
175[ 1]:   /*now send a message back of our demise*/
176[ 1]:   msg.child = tsk_me();
177[ 1]:   msg.count = localcount;
178[ 1]:   win_write (mal_of (localparent), &msg, sizeof(msg));
179[ 0]: }
```

Notice that the final message from each of the children tasks advising the parent task of its demise cannot reasonably be sent by reference since the task is preparing to exit. A task that is about to abort can only safely send messages by reference if the address space that the message occupies does not originate within the task as a task must return its memory to the system when it quits. Tasks, especially when they are in their own process, should always send messages by value if there is any chance of the task quitting before the receiving task has a chance to copy the data out of the message. (In this particular case, there is no problem since the stack space used by the children tasks originally belonged to the parent task anyway, but it still isn't a good idea.)

Despite the problems presented with passing messages by reference, I do not want to imply that passing addresses is a bad idea in all cases. Passing addresses of large memory blocks is very often a useful and necessary technique. In any case, it is better to store the address of the memory block to be passed within a message that is passed by value. We will revisit the entire subject of large memory blocks in our discussion of Memory Management in Chapter 6.

Multiple Mailboxes

So far we have only discussed tasks with a single mailbox. It is sometimes desirable to allow a single task to sport more than one mailbox address. This most often arises when a task must communicate with other tasks to fulfill a request. Returning to our teller/bank example, suppose that the teller task sends a withdrawal request to the bank program as before. This time, however, when the bank program looks up the account, it notices that this account was opened in a branch office in the suburbs. Due to the way the bank is organized, this account's records are out in the suburban bank.

No problem, the bank program simply forwards the withdrawal request to the bank program on the suburban computer. As soon as the response returns, it can be forwarded back to the local teller program. There are only a few snags with this approach. First, the local bank program will want to forward the response from the suburban bank as soon as it arrives, so as to liven response time. (Remember that the teller has been waiting while the message was forwarded and processed at the suburban location. Besides, the main bank has no extra processing left to do anyway.) Further, the local bank program will not want to send any more requests to the suburban bank until it answers the one it has, otherwise the local bank program will have quite a job sorting out which response goes with which request.

If there is only one input queue, however, the following problem arises. Suppose that another request that requires action by the suburban program is queued ahead of the suburban bank program's response. (This is shown graphically in Figure 4.7.) The program cannot respond to the suburban bank's response since it is buried in the queue, and it cannot work off the queue since there is another request requiring the suburban bank waiting.

This dilemma is avoided by having two mailboxes: one devoted to bank requests and the other for responses from the suburban bank programs. In this way, the bank program can work off the response mailbox preferentially, resulting in better response time for tellers and avoidance of the deadlock described above.

DESQview creates and opens the default mailbox when it creates the task; however, further mailboxes may be created with the *mal_new ()* API call. A new mailbox must be opened with the *mal_open ()* call before messages may be sent to it. Reading a mailbox that has not already been opened automatically opens it. Only one task may have a mailbox open.

Figure 4.7—Bank program deadlocked awaiting Response from Suburban Bank, which it cannot reach because an "unworkable" Suburban Bank Request is in the queue

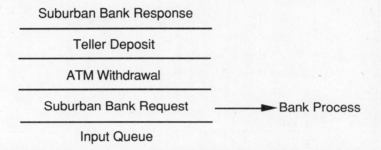

Suburban Bank Response

Teller Deposit

ATM Withdrawal

Suburban Bank Request ————▶ Bank Process

Input Queue

Once a mailbox is no longer necessary, its space may be recovered by freeing it with the *mal_free()* call. This frees the mailbox plus any messages that may be queued to it.

If a task maintains multiple mailboxes, it must check them all from time to time for messages. Simply reading the mailboxes in circular fashion will not work. The task will suspend on a single empty mailbox even if the other mailboxes are full of unanswered messages. There are several ways to address this problem. A task may simply poll each of the mailboxes in round-robin fashion using the *mal_sizeof()* call. As soon as the task finds a mailbox with a length greater than zero, it knows it can safely *mal_read()* the message out without being suspended.

Figure 4.8—Prototypes of *mal_find()*, *mal_free()*, *mal_name()*, *mal_new()*, and *mal_open()*

```
                              /*find a mailbox by name*/
ulong mal_find                /*returns a mailbox handle*/
          (char *name,        /*mailbox name*/
           int  length);      /*name length*/

                              /*free a mailbox*/
void  mal_free                /*returns nothing*/
          (ulong malhandle);/*handle of mailbox to free*/
```

```
                          /*name a mailbox*/
void  mal_name            /*returns nothing*/
        (ulong malhandle, /*mailbox to receive name*/
         char *name,      /*mailbox name*/
         int   length);   /*name length*/

                          /*create a new mailbox*/
ulong mal_new             /*returns a mailbox handle*/
        ();               /*takes no arguments*/

                          /*open a mailbox for use*/
void  mal_open            /*returns nothing*/
        (ulong malhandle);/*handle of mailbox*/
```

Named Mailboxes

In our previous programming examples, the parent task always knew how to get in touch with its children tasks by converting the task handle that it received during creation into a default mailbox handle. The children only knew their parent's address because they were told, either explicitly within the message itself or implicitly via the *mal_addr()* call. But what if a task has multiple mailboxes? How does a task find the handle of the proper mailbox to which its message should be sent? Or what it the two tasks do not know each other's task handle. In the teller/bank program example we have been using up until now, it is not obvious that a child-parent relationship exists at all.

The answer lies in named mailboxes. A task may create a new mailbox, open it, and then assign it a previously agreed upon name. Other tasks may then look for the mailbox of this name. Returning to our teller/bank example once again, the bank program might reasonably create a mailbox and assign it the name BANK. Having done so, as each teller program is executed, it need only look for the mailbox named BANK.

Notice that the tellers may not reasonably create mailboxes named TELLER. For one thing, there is more than one teller program, so confusion is bound to arise. Besides, in our simple model, it is not necessary. Tellers originate requests. These requests contain the return address. The bank does not know (or care) whether it is responding to tellers, ATMs, or other banks. If the bank program needs to know the identity and type of each of the teller programs, it simply requires each teller program to identify itself with a registration message to the BANK before it will respond to any transaction requests. The registration message could contain both the return mailbox address and any passwords required for security.

Under DESQview, a mailbox is assigned a name with the *mal_name()* API call. Once named, other tasks may find the mailbox's handle with the *mal_find()* call. If *mal_find()* cannot find a mailbox with the given name, it returns a zero.

The example programs REQUEST.C and SERVER.C included with the API C Library use the concept of named queues in the same way that our example bank program does. Our MSGTEST program rewritten to used named mailboxes appears as MSGTST5. Notice how the parent task no longer places its own mailbox or task handle in the message being sent to the subtasks. Instead, it creates a new mailbox, which it names PARENT. The children tasks merely respond to PARENT when they are finished.

Named mailboxes provide the key link that gives intertask messages their true power. Our teller programs can send queries without knowing anything about the bank program other than the name of the mailbox it uses and the format of the messages to send. The teller programs don't know, for example, how the bank program works, whether it is one program or many, or even whether the bank program is in the same computer as they are. For example, at a remote site the BANK mailbox may be monitored by a program that merely picks up messages and relays them to the central office.

**Figure 4.9—Bank process with its named input mailbox
servicing several teller processes, each with an
unnamed mailbox for receiving responses**

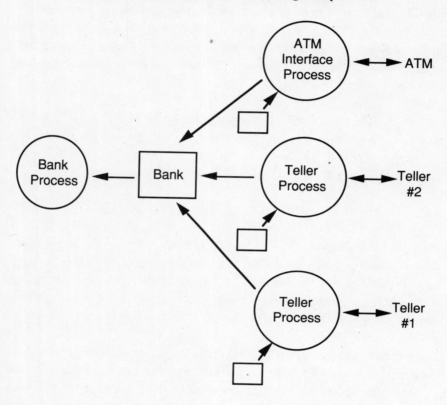

```
 1[ 0]: /*****************************************************************
 2[ 0]:    Message Test #5 - create subtasks again, but this time have
 3[ 0]:                      subtasks respond to a named queue PARENT.  A
 4[ 0]:                      more detailed example of named queues appears
 5[ 0]:                      on the API C Library as REQUEST/SERVER.
 6[ 0]: *****************************************************************/
 7[ 0]:
 8[ 0]: #include <stdio.h>
 9[ 0]: #include "dvapi.h"
10[ 0]:
11[ 0]: /*locally declared programs*/
12[ 0]: void main (void);
13[ 0]: void program_body (void);
14[ 0]: ulong fork (int, int, int, char *, int);
15[ 0]: int subtask (void);
```

```
16[ 0]:
17[ 0]: /*minimum API version required is DESQview 2.00*/
18[ 0]: #define required 0x200
19[ 0]:
20[ 0]: /*main - standard pattern for DESQview programs*/
21[ 0]: void main (void)
22[ 0]: {
23[ 1]:   int  version;
24[ 1]:
25[ 1]:   version = api_init();
26[ 1]:   if (version < required)
27[ 1]:       printf ("This program requires DESQview %d.%02d or later.\n",
28[ 1]:               required >> 8, required & 0xff);
29[ 1]:   else {
30[ 2]:       /*tell DESQview what extensions to enable
31[ 2]:         and start application*/
32[ 2]:       api_level (required);
33[ 2]:       program_body();
34[ 1]:   }
35[ 1]:   /*if DESQview present (even if wrong version), shut it down*/
36[ 1]:   if (version)
37[ 1]:       api_exit();
38[ 0]: }
39[ 0]:
40[ 0]: /*program body - start up 5 tasks and wait for them to quit*/
41[ 0]:
42[ 0]: #define NUMTASKS    5           /*start up 5 subtasks*/
43[ 0]: #define NUMROWS     10
44[ 0]: #define NUMCOLS     25
45[ 0]:
46[ 0]: int X[NUMTASKS] = {60, 40, 20,  1, 30},
47[ 0]:     Y[NUMTASKS] = { 1,  5, 10, 15, 20};
48[ 0]:
49[ 0]: struct message {                /*format of message to child task*/
50[ 1]:                 int xloc;       /*column of window*/
51[ 1]:                 int yloc;       /*row of window*/
52[ 1]:                 int count;      /*task count*/
53[ 0]:               };
54[ 0]:
55[ 0]: struct response {               /*format of response message*/
56[ 1]:                 int   count;    /*and its count*/
57[ 0]:               };
58[ 0]:
59[ 0]: void program_body (void)
60[ 0]: {
61[ 1]:   int i;
62[ 1]:   int tcount;
63[ 1]:   ulong winhan, malhan;
64[ 1]:   struct response *msgptr;
65[ 1]:   int,        msglngth;
66[ 1]:   #define STACKSIZE 1000         /*allocate some stack for each*/
67[ 1]:   char stacks [NUMTASKS][STACKSIZE];
68[ 1]:
69[ 1]:   winhan = win_new ("Main Program", 12, 10, 38);
70[ 1]:   win_move (winhan, 1, 1);
71[ 1]:   win_logattr (winhan, 1);
```

```
 72[ 1]:   win_attr (winhan, 1);
 73[ 1]:   win_unhide (winhan);
 74[ 1]:   win_top (winhan);
 75[ 1]:
 76[ 1]:   /*create a response queue and name it PARENT (must be opened
 77[ 1]:     before it can be named)*/
 78[ 1]:   malhan = mal_new ();
 79[ 1]:   mal_open (malhan);
 80[ 1]:   mal_name (malhan, "PARENT", 6);
 81[ 1]:
 82[ 1]:   /*now start subtask NUMTASKS number of times*/
 83[ 1]:   for (tcount = 0; tcount < NUMTASKS; tcount++)
 84[ 1]:       fork (X[tcount], Y[tcount], tcount, stacks [tcount], STACKSIZE)
 85[ 1]:
 86[ 1]:   /*wait for them all to quit - show we are alive in mean time*/
 87[ 1]:   i = 0;
 88[ 1]:   while (tcount) {
 89[ 2]:       /*if a message appears, read it and dec the task count*/
 90[ 2]:       if (mal_sizeof (malhan)) {
 91[ 3]:           mal_read (malhan, &msgptr, &msglngth);
 92[ 3]:           win_printf (winhan, "\nReceived a quit from %d\n\n",
 93[ 3]:                       msgptr->count);
 94[ 3]:           tcount--;
 95[ 2]:       }
 96[ 2]:
 97[ 2]:       win_printf (winhan, "Waiting; taskcount = %d, count = %d\n",
 98[ 2]:                            tcount, i++);
 99[ 2]:       api_pause ();
100[ 1]:   }
101[ 1]:
102[ 1]:   /*now put the mailbox and window away*/
103[ 1]:   mal_free (malhan);
104[ 1]:   win_free (winhan);
105[ 0]: }
106[ 0]:
107[ 0]: /*fork - fork a new task*/
108[ 0]: ulong fork (x, y, taskcount, stack, stacksize)
109[ 0]:   int x, y, taskcount;
110[ 0]:   char *stack;
111[ 0]:   int stacksize;
112[ 0]: {
113[ 1]:   char titlebuf [80], titlesize;
114[ 1]:   ulong tskhan;
115[ 1]:   struct message msg;
116[ 1]:
117[ 1]:   /*start the subtask*/
118[ 1]:   titlesize = sprintf (titlebuf, "Task #%d", taskcount);
119[ 1]:   tskhan = tsk_new (subtask, stack, stacksize, titlebuf, titlesize,
120[ 1]:                     NUMROWS, NUMCOLS);
121[ 1]:
122[ 1]:   /*now send it a message containing its location information*/
123[ 1]:   msg.xloc = x;
124[ 1]:   msg.yloc = y;
125[ 1]:   msg.count = taskcount;
126[ 1]:   mal_write (mal_of (tskhan), &msg, sizeof(msg));
127[ 1]:
```

```
128[ 1]:    /*finally return the task handle*/
129[ 1]:    return tskhan;
130[ 0]: }
131[ 0]:
132[ 0]: /*subtask - an example subtask which opens a window, counts down
133[ 0]:              and then removes itself*/
134[ 0]: int subtask (void)
135[ 0]: {
136[ 1]:    int i;
137[ 1]:    ulong winhan, malhan;
138[ 1]:    struct message *msgptr;
139[ 1]:    struct response msg;
140[ 1]:    int   msglngth;
141[ 1]:
142[ 1]:    /*wait for an initiation message with location information*/
143[ 1]:    mal_read (mal_me(), &msgptr, &msglngth);
144[ 1]:
145[ 1]:    /*set up window*/
146[ 1]:    winhan = win_me();
147[ 1]:    win_move (winhan, msgptr->yloc, msgptr->xloc);
148[ 1]:    win_logattr (winhan,1);
149[ 1]:    win_attr (winhan, msgptr->count+2);
150[ 1]:    win_unhide (winhan);
151[ 1]:    win_top (winhan);
152[ 1]:
153[ 1]:
154[ 1]:    /*now print out, politely giving up control after each round*/
155[ 1]:    for (i = 200; i; i--) {
156[ 2]:       win_printf (winhan, "I'm counting down %d\n", i);
157[ 2]:       api_pause ();
158[ 1]:    }
159[ 1]:
160[ 1]:    /*acknowlege task over*/
161[ 1]:    win_disperor (winhan, "Finished", 8, 1, 10, 1, 0);
162[ 1]:
163[ 1]:    /*now send a message back to PARENT of our demise*/
164[ 1]:    msg.count = msgptr->count;
165[ 1]:    malhan = mal_find ("PARENT", 6);
166[ 1]:    win_write (malhan, &msg, sizeof(msg));
167[ 0]: }
```

Conclusion

As soon as a problem is divided into more than one task, the need arises to communicate information between those tasks. Without this communication, single-user multitasking becomes little more than a switcher, which a sophisticated user might use to "compile in the background."

Communicating with programs not designed to execute in a multitasking environment is problematic. Generally such programs only expect input to arrive through the keyboard or a file and output to leave through the screen, the printer, or a file. The aware task must make itself look to the unaware task as much like one or more of these devices as possible. DESQview has included some hooks to aide in this effort.

Of course, communication between two aware tasks is much easier. The most obvious approach is to use the same tools available to the single-tasking programmer, namely those of variables that, being globally defined, are known to both tasks. Although this technique has some advantages, we rapidly saw how its many problems can make programs difficult to debug. Due to the random nature of data collisions, programs that are thought to be error free may randomly crash during use at unpredictable (but perhaps widely separated) intervals and in unpredictable ways.

Communicating between tasks via messages passed between mailboxes offers the advantage of loosely coupled tasks communicating via well-defined and monitorable messages. Such systems display less of the unpredictable nature of the more data collision prone approaches.

As we will see, the interprocess message paradigm has not stopped. What began as a simple way of getting information from one task to another will grow in importance in the next few chapters, becoming the real importance behind multitasking under DESQview.

c h a p t e r 5

Generalized
Message Input

Chapter 4 introduced interprocess messages as a way of getting information from here to there. Although we discussed several ways of communicating information between independent tasks, messages sent through mailboxes between tasks were the most versatile and least error prone.

The same intertask communication problem exists, however, when communicating between a task and the operating system. The operating system has information to send to the user application. Key strokes, mouse clicks, and expiring timers may all be communicated to simultaneously executing programs. But these events occur asynchronously, i.e., at random time intervals. A program cannot predict when external events are likely to occur. In any case, a program that is suspended awaiting keyboard input will not be executing when the key is finally entered.

The problem is simply that the operating system is not a part of the user program with which it must communicate. In single-tasking operating systems, the operating system generally executes as part of the caller's task. A program that makes a system call does not receive control until the operating system is completed. When not replying to a user program request, the operating system does not execute except to process interrupts.

In a multitasking operating system such as DESQview, this is not the case. A key stroke, for example, must be transmitted from the operating system's interrupt handler to the suspended task awaiting it, without completely disrupting the other tasks that might be executing as well.

It may seem surprising that the DESQview operating system reverts to the same technique for transmitting information to application tasks as these tasks use to communicate with each other. After all, operating systems lie at the lowest level. They have access to facilities of which user programs can only dream. Nevertheless, messages are about the best way to send information from one task to another.

As we will see, there are several different types of mailboxes capable of receiving different types of messages from the operating system. Semantically, it is advantageous to distinguish between the different types of mailboxes. In DESQview, the term *object* is used as the generic name given to the different types. We will see that there are keyboard objects (mailboxes to receive keyboard messages), pointer objects (mailboxes for mouse messages), etc. A mailbox designed to receive messages from other user tasks, such as we have seen up until now, is then a mailbox object under this nomenclature, even though this might seem slightly redundant.

Keyboard Input

Let us consider for a minute how single-tasking software reads the keyboard of the PC using the BIOS (Basic Input/Output System) calls.

When a key is depressed at the PC's keyboard, a small microprocessor in the keyboard itself detects and decodes that key. This information is then sent to the host PC where it generates an interrupt. The interrupt temporarily stops execution of the current program and forces the processor to execute the special interrupt program. This software reads the key from the keyboard and stores it into a queue that looks much like a mailbox. Once the key has been stored, the interrupted user program is allowed to continue processing.

There are three BIOS functions stored in the PC's Read-Only Memory that user programs may use to read keys stored in this queue. The user software may perform a read request. This is a blocking read; i.e., if no key strokes are present, the program is suspended until the user strikes a key. Therefore, a *size of*-like function call is also provided so the user program may determine whether a key is available in the queue or not. A program may perform multiple *size of* requests until a key is known to be present in the input queue, at which point it may read the character without fear of waiting. Finally, the third BIOS request is provided to read the status of the keyboard.

Even though no true multitasking is taking place, the DOS operating system has the same problem as DESQview: storing up asynchronously occurring key strokes until the application program gets around to asking for them. If we view the keyboard interrupt handler as a separate task from the user program, then DOS must bridge the communications gap between two asynchronously executing tasks. It is not surprising, then, that the solution employed is so similar to the way in which messages are sent to and read from DESQview objects.

Of course, in a multitasking operating environment like DESQview, there is more than one program that might request keyboard input. To keep the requests straight, DESQview assigns each task its own keyboard object. As they arrive from the keyboard, key strokes are stuffed into messages and sent to the currently active keyboard object, also known as the *Keyboard Owner*. There is a set of rules to decide what is the current *Keyboard Owner*. In practice, the effect is that the program uppermost on the display will receive any characters entered.

The rules for deciding which keyboard object is currently active are as follows: keyboard objects must be associated with windows before they may be active, as it is the position of the window that the system uses to determine what is active. (Remember, roughly the same rule applies to tasks and applications. Tasks must also have windows associated with them. Whenever a task is selected, its windows are brought to the top and given a double border.)

A search is made of all windows starting with the top window and working downward. The first window that:

a) has a keyboard object;

b) has the same parent as the topmost window *or* is above the topmost task window; and

c) is opened in keystroke mode, has the hardware cursor, *or* has keystroke-selectable fields

is the Keyboard Owner.

Rule C will apply when we discuss panels. For now, we are limiting ourselves to the keystroke mode. The other two rules basically say that a window with a keyboard object and who's task has the topmost window is the *Keyboard Owner*. Characters entered from the keyboard are sent to that keyboard object.

Reading a keyboard object is the same as reading a mailbox object. The keyboard-BIOS interrupt is redirected so that programs attempting to read the keyboard using the BIOS call actually read the keyboard object as well.

A default keyboard object is opened for every new task, the handle of which is returned from the *key_me()* API call. The *key_read()* API call works the same as it does with mailbox objects, returning the top message and suspending the caller if there are none left. The message consists of nothing more than the ASCII character read and is normally only one byte long.

Figure 5.1—Prototype Declarations for *key_getc()*, *key_me()*, *key_read()*, and *key_status()*

```
                                /*get a single char from keyboard*/
unsigned key_getc               /*returns extended code + 0x100
                                  or ASCII code*/
          (ulong keyhan);       /*keyboard object to read*/

                                /*return default keyboard object*/
ulong    key_me                 /*returns keyboard handle*/
          (void);               /*takes no arguments*/

                                /*read a keyboard object*/
void     key_read               /*returns nothing*/
          (ulong keyhan,        /*keyboard object to read*/
           char **msgptr,       /*address of pointer to message*/
           int   *msglngth);    /*address of message length*/

                                /*read the key status of last read -
                                  normally contains extended char
code*/
int      key_status             /*returns the key status*/
          (ulong keyhan);       /*keyboard object*/
```

Not all keys on the PC's keyboard have an ASCII equivalent associated with them. For normal keys, this integer is the ASCII character code. For extended keys, it is the extended character code + 256. The extended-character code is zero for the standard keys. It is returned from a *key_status()* call made immediately after the *key_read()*.

The sequence reads a single character and, if zero, its extended-character code resembles the following:

```
char *charptr;
    int extchar, length;

    key_read (key_me (), &charptr, &length);
    if (*charptr == 0)
        extchar = key_status (key_me ());
```

After this call, **charptr* will point to the character read and *length* will contain a one. The same effect as the *key_read()* can be achieved with the *key_getc()* API call, which returns a single character entered from the keyboard:

```
unsigned character;

character = key_getc (key_me ());
```

Here the ASCII and extended-character code are combined into a single unsigned integer. The ASCII character is found in the lower byte of the integer and the extended character in the upper byte. Thus, normal keys have values below 0x100 while special keys such as function keys have values above.

Both of these code segments have a very large problem, however. Both assume that the message received from the keyboard object only contains a single character. While this is certainly true of characters from the keyboard, remember that another task may send a message to our keyboard object (as discussed in Chapter 4). To our task, such a message appears to have originated from the keyboard. These messages, however, are not limited to a single character in length.

Either of the approaches above will read the first character of a multi-character message and discard the remainder. It is preferable to allow for the possibility that the message may be of any length; for example, the code segment below that reads characters from the keyboard and prints them to the default window. While this code segment certainly works for normal messages containing a single character, it works equally well for messages of any length.

```
char *msgptr;
int   msglngth;

key_read (key_me (), &msgptr, &msglngth);
while (msglngth--)
    win_printf (win_me (), "%c", *msgptr++);
```

The other object-related functions work in a similar fashion with key objects. The *key_sizeof()* API call returns the number of messages in the keyboard object. The *key_of()* call allows a task to find the default keyboard object for any task for which it has a handle. This allows a task to send a message through the keyboard with the *key_write()* API call.

As mentioned, *key_write()* is an excellent way to communicate with tasks that are DESQview unaware. It can also be used to great effect with DESQview-specific programs. Take, for example, program-user shells designed to add a friendlier human interface to a powerful program with a deficient interface. Shells that add a menu-driven interface to DOS have been available for years. Shells written to use DESQview's capabilities have abilities beyond those of conventional shells.

Normally a shell program must insert hooks into the base program in order to regain control once the base program begins executing. This is not necessary in a multitasking environment, as the shell program can launch the base program as a background process. As *Keyboard Owner,* the shell program continues to receive user input from the keyboard once the base program is executed. The base application receives its keyboard input from the user shell via *key_write().*

This allows the user shell to execute initialization sequences and to act as a user-friendly filter for the application. For example, the shell might open a menu of options above the base program's display. Click one of these options and the shell program formulates the corresponding command and ships it to the base program in the background using *key_write().* As long as the shell remains *Keyboard Owner*, user input must first pass through it where it can be filtered before it is forwarded on to the application program.

If at anytime the shell became clumsy or hinders access to a powerful feature within the base program, the user need only select the background program by using the mouse or the *Switch* command in the DESQview window. Making the base program the foreground application makes it the *Keyboard Owner*, effectively moving the shell program out of the way. The user can now converse directly with the application program as if the shell program did not exist. The user can restore the shell program at any time by selecting it, thereby returning it to status of *Keyboard Owner.*

Separate keyboard objects are automatically associated with task windows.
It is occasionally desirable to associate keyboard objects with windows that
are not separate tasks, such as drop-down menus. This can be done by
creating a new keyboard object and attaching it to the window.

A new keyboard object is created using the *key_new()* API call. Once created, the keyboard must be opened via the *key_open()* call before it may be
used. It is the *key_open()* call that associates the keyboard object with a
window. This keyboard object will become *Keyboard Owner* when the
associated window is uppermost in the system. The keyboard object is returned to the system with the *key_free()* API call. Notice that it is also
possible to close a keyboard object, including the default keyboard, and
reopen it with a different window.

Figure 5.2—Prototype Declaration for Remaining Keystroke-Mode Keyboard API Calls

```
                            /*set a keyboard property*/
void key_addto              /*returns nothing*/
         (ulong keyhan,     /*keyboard handle*/
          unsigned flags);  /*properties to assign:
                                KBF_FIELD put into field mode
                                KBF_CURSOR enable hardware cursor
                                KBF_INSERT insert mode
                                KBF_ASYNC  asynch menu mode
                                KBF_ALLESC all keys go to
                                           key_setesc function*/

                            /*detach a keyboard from a window*/
void key_close              /*returns nothing*/
         (void);            /*accepts no arguments*/

                            /*free a keyboard object*/
void key_free               /*returns nothing*/
         (void);            /*accepts no arguments*/


                            /*create a new keyboard object*/
ulong key_new               /*returns a keyboard object*/
         (void);            /*accepts no arguments*/

                            /*find the default keyboard object
                              of a task*/
ulong key_of                /*returns a keyboard object*/
```

```
              (ulong taskhan);   /*accepts a task handle*/

                                 /*attach a keyboard to a window*/
void   key_open                  /*returns nothing*/
              (ulong winhan);    /*window handle to attach*/

                                 /*return number of messages queued
                                   to keyboard object*/
int    key_sizeof                /*returns number of messages*/
              (ulong keyhan);    /*keyboard object*/

                                 /*remove a keyboard property*/
void   key_subfrom               /*returns nothing*/
              (ulong   keyhan,   /*keyboard object*/
               usigned flags);   /*property to remove*/

                                 /*send a message to a keyboard object*/
void   key_write                 /*returns nothing*/
              (ulong   keyhan,   /*target keyboard object*/
               char    *string,  /*character string to send*/
               int     length,   /*length of string*/
               int     status);  /*status to send with it*/
```

Finally, just as with other objects, a keyboard object has properties that the
user software can control. The most important property is the mode. Up
until now, we have been assuming that a separate message is built for
each character read from the keyboard because this mode most resembles
standard DOS and because it is the easiest to use for programs with
modest input requirements. This is known as *keystroke mode*.

DESQview supports another mode known as *field mode*. In this mode,
the user program puts up an entire screen of fields, known as a *panel*. The
user may move about among fields within the panel, filling in fields
and making selections while under the control of DESQview. The format of the keyboard input messages in field mode are a function of the
panel.

Panels are a very powerful tool, but as they can be quite difficult to build
properly, Quarterdeck offers a utility known as the *Panel-Design Tool*.
Panels and the Panel-Design Tool are discussed in Chapter 8.

Properties that users may control in keystroke mode are *hardware-cursor enable* and *insert mode*. Selecting hardware cursor enable means that the window associated with this keyboard object will contain the hardware cursor. This is an important consideration as there is only one hardware cursor.

Keyboard object properties are set using the *key_addto()* call and cleared with the *key_subfrom()* call. The available properties are listed above with the *key_addto()* prototype. Defines exist within DVAPI.H to make setting and clearing these properties easier. Notice that the *win_hcur()* API call must be used to update the hardware cursor location after output calls, as DESQview does not normally update the hardware cursor.

A simple example of opening a keyboard object, reading from it, and then closing it upon request is presented in KEYTST1.

```
 1[ 0]: /****************************************************
 2[ 0]:    Keyboard Test - Read and display keyboard messages.
 3[ 0]: ****************************************************/
 4[ 0]:
 5[ 0]: #include <stdio.h>
 6[ 0]: #include "dvapi.h"
 7[ 0]:
 8[ 0]: /*locally declared programs*/
 9[ 0]: void main (void);
10[ 0]: void program_body (void);
11[ 0]:
12[ 0]: /*minimum API version required is DESQview 2.00*/
13[ 0]: #define required 0x200
14[ 0]:
15[ 0]: /*main - standard pattern for DESQview programs*/
16[ 0]: void main (void)
17[ 0]: {
18[ 1]:   int  version;
19[ 1]:
20[ 1]:   version = api_init();
21[ 1]:   if (version < required)
22[ 1]:       printf ("This program requires DESQview %d.%02d or later.\n",
23[ 1]:               required >> 8, required & 0xff);
24[ 1]:   else {
25[ 2]:       /*tell DESQview what extensions to enable
26[ 2]:         and start application*/
27[ 2]:       api_level (required);
28[ 2]:       program_body();
29[ 1]:   }
30[ 1]:   /*if DESQview present (even if wrong version), shut it down*/
31[ 1]:   if (version)
32[ 1]:       api_exit();
```

```
33[ 0]: }
34[ 0]:
35[ 0]: /*program body - open a window, attach a keyboard object and
36[ 0]:                    read key messages from it*/
37[ 0]:
38[ 0]: void program_body (void)
39[ 0]: {
40[ 1]:    int i;
41[ 1]:    ulong winhan, keyhan;
42[ 1]:    char *msgptr;
43[ 1]:    int  msglngth;
44[ 1]:
45[ 1]:    /*open our standby window*/
46[ 1]:    winhan = win_new ("Main Program", 12, 10, 38);
47[ 1]:    win_move (winhan, 1, 1);
48[ 1]:    win_logattr (winhan, 1);
49[ 1]:    win_attr (winhan, 1);
50[ 1]:    win_unhide (winhan);
51[ 1]:    win_top (winhan);
52[ 1]:
53[ 1]:    /*open a keyboard object and attach it to the window*/
54[ 1]:    keyhan = key_new();
55[ 1]:    key_open (keyhan, winhan);
56[ 1]:    key_addto (keyhan, KBF_CURSOR);
57[ 1]:
58[ 1]:    /*read character messages in a loop until 'X' entered*/
59[ 1]:    win_printf (winhan, "Enter characters (X to stop):\n");
60[ 1]:    for (i = 0; ; i++) {
61[ 2]:        /*read another message from keyboard*/
62[ 2]:        key_read (keyhan, &msgptr, &msglngth);
63[ 2]:
64[ 2]:        /*exit when capital X entered*/
65[ 2]:        if (*msgptr == 'X')
66[ 2]:            break;
67[ 2]:
68[ 2]:        /*print characters read (include message status)*/
69[ 2]:        win_printf (winhan, "%d - Read ", i);
70[ 2]:        while (msglngth--)
71[ 2]:            win_printf (winhan, "%c", *msgptr++);
72[ 2]:        win_printf(winhan, " (status = %x)\n",
73[ 2]:                            key_status (keyhan));
74[ 2]:        win_hcur (winhan);
75[ 2]:
76[ 2]:        /*on the 10th key send a message to our own keyboard
77[ 2]:           as an example of messages to the keyboard*/
78[ 2]:        if (i == 10)
79[ 2]:            key_write (keyhan, "At line 10", 10, 0xff);
80[ 1]:    }
81[ 1]:
82[ 1]:    /*free the keyboard object and the window*/
83[ 1]:    key_free (keyhan);
84[ 1]:    win_free (winhan);
85[ 0]: }
```

Pointer Input

Input from a mouse is handled like input from the keyboard in many ways. Messages are built and sent to the task signaling its new state whenever the mouse is moved or a button is depressed.

Like the keyboard, there is only one mouse. Unlike the keyboard, however, the mouse is a pointing device. When two tasks attempt to read the keyboard at one time, DESQview establishes a protocol based upon which window is uppermost on the display. No such rules are necessary for the mouse, however, as the user can simply point at the intended task.

If a task is to access the mouse, it must open a pointer object explicitly using the *ptr_new()*. A pointer object is not automatically opened up when a task is created. Since there is no default pointer object, there is no *ptr_me()* or *ptr_of()* API calls. Before a pointer object may be used, it must be attached to a window, just as with a keyboard object, via the *ptr_open()* API call. A pointer object may be closed and the space recovered with the *ptr_free()*.

The presence of messages in the pointer object may be determined with the *ptr_sizeof()* API call. Messages are read from the pointer object using the *ptr_read()* API call. Messages are normally generated whenever the pointer is moved or a single button is depressed (chording the mouse, i.e.. depressing both buttons simultaneously brings up the DESQview menu). These messages are sent to the pointer object attached to the window the pointer currently occupies.

Since there is more information to communicate, the format of the messages sent from the pointer is more complicated than that sent from the keyboard. The structure of pointer messages is as follows:

```
struct pointer_message {      /*format of pointer message*/
            unsigned row;     /*row of pointer*/
            unsigned col;     /*column of pointer*/
            char  status;     /*pointer status -
                        drnnnnbb
                            bb - 0, 1 or 2 -> button
```

```
                              r - 1 -> released (  "      ")
                              n - number of times pressed-1*/
        char  field;   /*number of field mouse is in*/
   };
```

The row and column are 16-bit values indicating the screen row and column currently occupied by the pointer. The status indicates whether a button has just been depressed and how many times. (The button indication is only valid for the message immediately after the button is depressed. If the button is depressed and held down as the mouse is moved, only the message generated immediately after the mouse is depressed will have the button indication set. The subsequent messages indicating the pointer location will not have the button set.) The status field of the last pointer message read may be retrieved again from the pointer object by issuing the *ptr_status()* API call, if necessary.

Figure 5.3—Prototype Declarations of the Pointer Functions

```
                         /*set pointer control flags*/
void  ptr_addto          /*returns nothing*/
        (ulong ptrhan,   /*pointer handle*/
      unsigned flags); /*flags to set:
                            PTF_CLICKS - clicks only
                            PTF_UPDOWN - both up and down
                            PTF_RELSCR - screen relative
                            PTF_MULTI  - multiclick
                            PTF_BACK   - background also
                            PTF_NOTTOP - also if not top
                            PTF_HIDE   - hide pointer*/

                         /*free a pointer object*/
void  ptr_free           /*returns nothing*/
        (ulong ptrhan);  /*pointer handle to free*/

                         /*get current scaling factor*/
void  ptr_getscale       /*returns nothing directly*/
        (ulong ptrhan,   /*handle to check*/
         int  *rows,      /*returned vert units per window*/
         int  *cols);     /*returned hor  units per window*/

                         /*create a new pointer object*/
ulong ptr_new            /*returns pointer handle*/
        (void);          /*accepts no arguments*/

                         /*assoc pointer with a window*/
void  ptr_open           /*returns nothing*/
        (ulong ptrhan,   /*pointer object to open*/
         ulong winhan);   /*window to which to attach*/
```

```
                          /*read a message from pointer object*/
void  ptr_read            /*returns nothing directly*/
          (ulong  ptrhan,  /*pointer object to read*/
           char **buffer,   /*address of message*/
           int   *length);  /*length of message*/

                          /*set scaling factor*/
void  ptr_setscale        /*returns nothing*/
          (ulong ptrhan,   /*handle to set*/
           int  *rows,     /*vert units per window*/
           int  *cols);    /*hor  units per window*/

                          /*return no. messages in queue*/
int   ptr_sizeof          /*returns no. messages...*/
          (ulong ptrhan);  /*...in this pointer object*/

                          /*get button status of last read*/
int   ptr_status          /*read button status...*/
          (ulong ptrhan);  /*...from this pointer object*/

                          /*clear pointer control flags*/
void  ptr_subfrom         /*returns nothing*/
          (ulong ptrhan,   /*pointer handle*/
           unsigned flags); /*flags to clear (see ptr_addto)*/
```

Just as with the keyboard, a mouse object has different modes of operation that are setable by the user software. Normally, the pointer device sends a message whenever the pointer is moved. It may be more desirable for the pointer to only send messages when a mouse button is depressed. Or the user program may prefer to be informed of both when the key is depressed, as well as when it is released.

The pointer modes are set using the *ptr_addto()* and cleared with the *ptr_subfrom()* API calls. Constants have been defined in DVAPI.H to make controlling the pointer modes easier. Pointer modes are on an object-by-object basis. Thus, setting a particular mode for one pointer object has no effect on other pointer objects. Setting *PTF_CLICKS* causes DESQview to only send messages when a mouse button is depressed. Adding *PTF_UPDOWN* mode generates a message both when the a button is depressed and released. In *PTF_MULTI* mode, DESQview accumulates mouse clicks one third of a second or less apart, reporting them along with a count of the number only once. This facilitates detection of double clicks.

Normally, the row and column pointer positions are reported relative to the upper left corner of the window to which the pointer object is attached. In rare occasions, it may be useful to know the location of the pointer relative to the display screen rather than the window. This can be arranged by setting the *PTF_RELSCR* flag.

The *PTF_HIDE* flag is particularly useful for menu type applications. Normally, the pointer position is noted by DESQview using a white diamond. This may be distracting for menu applications where the color of the menu option is used to indicate the currently selected state or for drawing applications using other types of markers to indicate the pointer position. By setting the *PTF_HIDE* flag, such applications can remove the white diamond marker. Of course, this applies only when the pointer is within that window. When moved outside of the window, DESQview's white diamond magically reappears (only to disappear once again when reentering the *PTF_HIDE* window).

Finally, the *PTF_BACK* and *PTF_NOTTOP* flags determine the relationship of the pointer to windows. Since windows do not necessarily completely cover each other, the user may see background windows and attempt to point at them. Whether or not the program wants to acknowledge the pointer when it strays outside of the topmost window depends upon the program. Normally, DESQview only sends messages to the topmost window of the foreground application. Setting either *PTF_NOTTOP* or *PTF_BACK* allows windows other than the topmost to receive pointer messages, but they are not the same.

If a pointer has *PTF_NOTTOP* mode set, pointer messages are sent to it if it is attached to the foreground application, even if it is not the topmost window within the application. For example, assume that selecting an option on a drop menu opens a submenu of possibilities. This is contained within a new window, but this new window does not obscure the original menu of choices. If the old menu does not have *PTF_NOTTOP* mode, then the user can only select the options presented by the submenu. On the other hand, if this mode is selected, then the user can still select choices from the original menu even if the submenu is still present.

Setting *PTF_BACK*, by comparison, causes a pointer object to receive pointer messages even if it belongs to a window attached to an application that is not currently the foreground application. Take the example of a communications package. This package might want to allow communications to go on in the background. Thus, it is entirely possible that when the program needs user input it will be in the background. Using *win_topsys()* to open a menu above the current application can be used to make a menu visible, but that window must have *PTF_BACK* mode set to allow the user to select from it without bringing the communications program to the front. Of course, both *PTF_BACK* and *PTF_NOTTOP* may be set, in which case a window receives pointer messages as long as it is visible, no matter what its relationship to other windows might be.

The following program listing is an adaption of our task program, modified now to demonstrate the use of pointer objects. The main task starts three subtasks and then waits for their demise before continuing. Each task opens a window and then attaches a pointer object to it. Each of these objects is made slightly different by the call to *ptr_addto()*. In one of the windows the pointer is invisible, while in another window DESQview only reports button clicks. Each task continues until the pointer is placed in the upper left-hand corner (and clicked, if necessary). When the subtask sees both the row and column equal to zero, the task terminates with a message back to the main program.

```
 1[ 0]: /********************************************************
 2[ 0]:    Pointer Test - read pointer messages in multiple tasks.
 3[ 0]: ********************************************************/
 4[ 0]:
 5[ 0]: #include <stdio.h>
 6[ 0]: #include "dvapi.h"
 7[ 0]:
 8[ 0]: /*locally declared programs*/
 9[ 0]: void main (void);
10[ 0]: void program_body (void);
11[ 0]: void subtask (void);
12[ 0]:
13[ 0]: /*minimum API version required is DESQview 2.00*/
14[ 0]: #define required 0x200
15[ 0]:
16[ 0]: /*main - standard pattern for DESQview programs*/
17[ 0]: void main (void)
18[ 0]: {
19[ 1]:   int  version;
```

```
20[ 1]:
21[ 1]:    version = api_init();
22[ 1]:    if (version < required)
23[ 1]:        printf ("This program requires DESQview %d.%02d or later.\n",
24[ 1]:                    required >> 8, required & 0xff);
25[ 1]:    else {
26[ 2]:        /*tell DESQview what extensions to enable
27[ 2]:          and start application*/
28[ 2]:        api_level (required);
29[ 2]:        program_body();
30[ 1]:    }
31[ 1]:    /*if DESQview present (even if wrong version), shut it down*/
32[ 1]:    if (version)
33[ 1]:        api_exit();
34[ 0]: }
35[ 0]:
36[ 0]: /*program body - open a window, attach a pointer object and
37[ 0]:                    read pointer messages.  Display a message
38[ 0]:                    for each message read.*/
39[ 0]:
40[ 0]: struct pointer_message {        /*format of pointer message*/
41[ 1]:                unsigned row;   /*row of pointer*/
42[ 1]:                unsigned col;   /*column of pointer*/
43[ 1]:                char    status; /*pointer status -
44[ 1]:                                    nrnnnnbb
45[ 1]:                                    bb - 0, 1 or 2 -> button
46[ 1]:                                    r - 1 -> released
47[ 1]:                                    n - number of times
48[ 1]:                                    pressed - 1*/
49[ 1]:                char  field;    /*number of field mouse is in*/
50[ 0]:                };
51[ 0]:
52[ 0]: struct position_message {        /*format of a position message*/
53[ 1]:                unsigned row;   /*row position of window*/
54[ 1]:                unsigned col;   /*column position of window*/
55[ 1]:                ulong response;/*response handle*/
56[ 0]:                };
57[ 0]:
58[ 0]: void program_body (void)
59[ 0]: {
60[ 1]:    int i;
61[ 1]:    ulong tskhan;
62[ 1]:    struct position_message msg;
63[ 1]:    char            **msgptr;
64[ 1]:    int             length;
65[ 1]:    #define STACKSIZE 1000
66[ 1]:    #define NOTASKS     3
67[ 1]:    char stacks [NOTASKS][STACKSIZE];
68[ 1]:
69[ 1]:    win_printf (win_me (),
70[ 1]:                "Place cursor in upper left corner of window\n"
71[ 1]:                "to close that task (you may need to click mouse)\n");
72[ 1]:    for (i = NOTASKS; i; i--) {
73[ 2]:        tskhan = tsk_new (subtask, stacks [i], STACKSIZE,
74[ 2]:                            "Subtask", 7, 10, 40);
75[ 2]:        msg.row = i * 5;
```

```
76[ 2]:        msg.col = i * 15;
77[ 2]:        msg.response = mal_me ();
78[ 2]:        mal_write (mal_of (tskhan), &msg, sizeof(msg));
79[ 1]:   }
80[ 1]:
81[ 1]:   /*receive as many messages as tasks*/
82[ 1]:   for (i = NOTASKS; i; i--)
83[ 1]:        mal_read (mal_me (), &msgptr, &length);
84[ 0]: }
85[ 0]:
86[ 0]: void subtask (void) {
87[ 1]:   ulong winhan, ptrhan;
88[ 1]:   struct pointer_message *msgptr;
89[ 1]:   int               msglngth;
90[ 1]:   struct position_message *mailptr;
91[ 1]:   int                  maillngth;
92[ 1]:
93[ 1]:   /*open a subtask window and position it where we are told*/
94[ 1]:   winhan = win_me ();
95[ 1]:   mal_read (mal_me (), &mailptr, &maillngth);
96[ 1]:   win_move (winhan, mailptr->row, mailptr->col);
97[ 1]:   win_logattr (winhan, 1);
98[ 1]:   win_attr (winhan, 1);
99[ 1]:   win_unhide (winhan);
100[ 1]:   win_top (winhan);
101[ 1]:
102[ 1]:   /*open a pointer object and attach it to the window*/
103[ 1]:   ptrhan = ptr_new();
104[ 1]:   ptr_open (ptrhan, winhan);
105[ 1]:
106[ 1]:   /*set: 1) all windows so they work in background
107[ 1]:         2) middle window so it only responds to clicks
108[ 1]:         3) top window so it hides pointer*/
109[ 1]:   ptr_addto (ptrhan, PTF_BACK|
110[ 1]:                  (PTF_CLICKS * (mailptr->row == 10))|
111[ 1]:                  (PTF_HIDE   * (mailptr->row == 5))
112[ 1]:                  );
113[ 1]:
114[ 1]:   /*read messages in a loop until pointer placed in upper left
115[ 1]:     hand corner*/
116[ 1]:   do {
117[ 2]:        ptr_read (ptrhan, &msgptr, &msglngth);
118[ 2]:        win_printf (winhan, "row = %d, col = %d, status = %x\n",
119[ 2]:                              msgptr->row,
120[ 2]:                              msgptr->col,
121[ 2]:                              msgptr->status);
122[ 1]:   } while (msgptr->row || msgptr->col);
123[ 1]:
124[ 1]:   /*now free our pointer object and respond to parent task with a
125[ 1]:     NULL message*/
126[ 1]:   ptr_free (ptrhan);
127[ 1]:   mal_write (mailptr->response, "", 1);
128[ 1]:
129[ 0]: }
```

Unlike a keyboard, the mouse has one other property: *scale*. Scale determines how many rows or columns exist from one end of the screen to another. For example, with the proper scale, row and column values reported may vary from 0 to 99, even though the screen is in 25x80 mode. This serves two purposes. For one, it might be more rational to consider a screen that has the same number of units in one dimension as in the other.

Secondly, and perhaps more importantly, a scale factor might be suggested by the application itself. In a spreadsheet application, for example, the program may not care about the position of the pointer except when it moves from one cell to another. Such a program would want to set the scale to correspond with the spreadsheet cell size so that the row and column reported in the pointer messages would correspond directly to the cell pointed at.

As a by-product, setting the scale also affects how often pointer messages are sent to the application. Pointer messages are only sent when the scaled location changes. However, messages are never sent more often than the number of display rows and columns would suggest, no matter what scale factor is selected.

Scale factor is set using the *ptr_setscale()* function call. This function accepts the pointer handle, and the vertical and horizontal-scale factor to apply. The scale factor is compared with the logical size of the attached window. The row and column are always reported as zero when the pointer is in the upper left-hand corner. A multiplication factor is determined such that the row and column are reported as the scale factor minus 1 when the pointer is in the lower right-hand corner. The *ptr_getscale()* API call can be used to query the scale factor of a given pointer object.

Timer Objects

Measuring time, or, more exactly, the passage of same, is a problem in a multitasking environment. In the singletasking world, there are several techniques for delaying a specified amount of time. A program can merely sit in a tight loop executing meaningless instructions to delay a specified amount of time. Since each passage through the loop can be made almost as short as desired, time can be measured quite accurately with this technique.

Often no-operation, or simply no-op loops (so named because the contents of the loops consist of *NOP do nothing* type instructions), are a very bad technique. The actual amount of time a loop requires to execute is very dependent upon performance details specific to the machine. The CPU type, the clock speed, the bus size, and the number of memory-wait states all have a pronounced effect on the time required to execute such a loop. A loop designed to work just right for an 8-MHz AT will take an inexorably long time on a conventional PC and will fly by on a modern 25-MHz 80386 machine.

In a multitasking system, no-op timing loops are even worse. First, the program doing the waiting can never be sure how many times it is being interrupted by other programs. Every interruption adds to the time required to execute the delay loop. In addition, no-op loops appear to be performing useful work to the operating system. Thus, a task with such a loop robs time from other tasks, and slows the entire system without accomplishing any real work.

A better approach to timing in a single-tasking system is to watch the system clock. The system clock is a count-down timer that periodically generates an interrupt. This interrupt is fielded by the PC's BIOS and is used to increment a global variable that any task can read, either directly or via a BIOS call. On the down side, the system ticks much less often than a timing loop requires to execute, resulting in rougher time approximations. At 18.2 clicks per second for the PC, however, the system clock is accurate enough for human time frames.

In a multitasking system, this technique is hardly better than the no-op loop. Waiting in a tight loop for the clock to tick off time is just as wasteful of computer time has a no-op loop. In addition, if control is not passed to the task at least once per timer tick, ticks may be lost, therefore resulting in lost time.

Rather than count the individual clocks ticks, the timing program could read the time initially and then calculate the clock value when the desired time as been reached. This has the advantage of not being sensitive to missed clock ticks. This could be combined with a system call to give up control (such as *api_pause()*) so that every time the task gained control it checked and, if the appointed time had not been reached, it would immediately surrender it again.

Such a solution would be acceptable from a multitasking standpoint, if not particularly elegant. Prompt scheduling of the timing task would not be critical, since it would be insensitive to missed timer ticks. In addition, the timing task would not waste CPU time in meaningless loops, preferring instead to surrender valuable computing time to background tasks.

Of course, time is lost scheduling a task that will do nothing more than turn around and give control back. A much cleaner solution is to suspend the task until the requisite amount of time has transpired before ever giving control back. All that is needed is a mechanism for suspending and then unsuspending a task.

The message system already provides a mechanism for suspending a task. Reading an object that is empty results in suspension of the calling task. This would fit our timing needs exactly if it could be arranged to automatically place a message in the queue, thus unsuspending the task when the proper time is reached. This is exactly how timer objects work.

Figure 5.4—Prototype Declarations for the Timer Functions

```
                           /*start a timer for an interval*/
void  tim_addto            /*returns nothing*/
         (ulong timhan,    /*timer handle*/
          ulong interval); /*interval to wait [1/100 sec]*/

                           /*stop the current timer*/
void  tim_erase            /*returns nothing*/
         (ulong timhan);   /*timer handle*/

                           /*free a timer object*/
void  tim_free             /*returns nothing*/
         (ulong timhan);   /*timer handle*/

                           /*read time remaining before timer
                              queue expires*/
ulong tim_len              /*returns time left [1/100 sec]*/
         (ulong timhan);   /*timer handle*/

                           /*create a new timer object*/
ulong tim_new              /*returns object handle*/
         (void);           /*takes no arguments*/

                           /*wait for timer to expire*/
ulong tim_read             /*returns time since midnight [1/100 sec]*/
         (ulong timhan);   /*timer object handle*/

                           /*determine time since timer started*/
ulong tim_sizeof           /*return time [1/100 sec]*/
         (ulong timhan);   /*timer object handle*/

                           /*set timer for a time of day*/
void  tim_write            /*returns nothing*/
         (ulong timhan,    /*timer object handle*/
          ulong time);     /*time since midnight*/
```

A timer object is created via the *tim_new()* API call. Since a timer object is not automatically created when a task is started, there is no default timer object retrievable with a *tim_me()* function. As with other objects, *tim_free()* frees an object, returning its memory to the system. Reading a timer object via the *tim_read()* suspends the calling task until a message appears. DESQview automatically sends a message to a timer object when its preset time expires. There are two ways to set the time, either of which automatically opens the timer object. The *tim_addto()* API call sets the timer to expire after a given amount of time has expired, irrespective of what the current time might be. The complementary function, *tim_write()*, sets the timer object to expire when a given time of day is

reached. The *tim_len()* API call may be made to read the amount of time
left before a timer expires.

All time units are in terms of 1/100ths of a second. Even so, the clock is
only accurate to 1/18.2 second. Thus, specifying a time out of 1/100th of a
second actually results in a delay of up to 1/18.2 second (or more, due to
multitasking vagueness).

```
 1[ 0]: /****************************************************************
 2[ 0]:   Timer Test - read timer objects for various lengths of time
 3[ 0]:                 (uses the initial row position of the task window
 4[ 0]:                 as the time to wait).
 5[ 0]: ****************************************************************/
 6[ 0]:
 7[ 0]: #include <stdio.h>
 8[ 0]: #include "dvapi.h"
 9[ 0]:
10[ 0]: /*locally declared programs*/
11[ 0]: void main (void);
12[ 0]: void program_body (void);
13[ 0]: void subtask (void);
14[ 0]:
15[ 0]: /*minimum API version required is DESQview 2.00*/
16[ 0]: #define required 0x200
17[ 0]:
18[ 0]: /*main - standard pattern for DESQview programs*/
19[ 0]: void main (void)
20[ 0]: {
21[ 1]:    int  version;
22[ 1]:
23[ 1]:    version = api_init();
24[ 1]:    if (version < required)
25[ 1]:        printf ("This program requires DESQview %d.%02d or later.\n",
26[ 1]:                  required >> 8, required & 0xff);
27[ 1]:    else {
28[ 2]:        /*tell DESQview what extensions to enable
29[ 2]:          and start application*/
30[ 2]:        api_level (required);
31[ 2]:        program_body();
32[ 1]:    }
33[ 1]:    /*if DESQview present (even if wrong version), shut it down*/
34[ 1]:    if (version)
35[ 1]:        api_exit();
36[ 0]: }
37[ 0]:
38[ 0]: /*program body - open a window, attach a pointer object and
39[ 0]:                  set and watch timer events.*/
40[ 0]:
41[ 0]: struct position_message {        /*format of a position message*/
42[ 1]:                unsigned row;  /*row position of window*/
43[ 1]:                unsigned col;  /*column position of window*/
44[ 1]:                ulong response;/*response handle*/
```

```
45[ 0]:                        };
46[ 0]:
47[ 0]: void program_body (void)
48[ 0]: {
49[ 1]:    int i;
50[ 1]:    ulong tskhan;
51[ 1]:    struct position_message msg;
52[ 1]:    char                   **msgptr;
53[ 1]:    int                      length;
54[ 1]:    #define STACKSIZE 1000
55[ 1]:    #define NOTASKS        3
56[ 1]:    char stacks [NOTASKS][STACKSIZE];
57[ 1]:
58[ 1]:    for (i = NOTASKS; i; i--) {
59[ 2]:         tskhan = tsk_new (subtask, stacks [i], STACKSIZE,
60[ 2]:                             "Subtask", 7, 10, 30);
61[ 2]:         msg.row = i * 5;
62[ 2]:         msg.col = i * 20;
63[ 2]:         msg.response = mal_me ();
64[ 2]:         mal_write (mal_of (tskhan), &msg, sizeof(msg));
65[ 1]:    }
66[ 1]:
67[ 1]:    /*receive as many messages as tasks*/
68[ 1]:    for (i = NOTASKS; i; i--)
69[ 1]:         mal_read (mal_me (), &msgptr, &length);
70[ 0]: }
71[ 0]:
72[ 0]: void subtask (void)
73[ 0]: {
74[ 1]:    ulong winhan, timhan;
75[ 1]:    struct position_message *mailptr;
76[ 1]:    int                      maillngth;
77[ 1]:    int i;
78[ 1]:
79[ 1]:    /*open a subtask window and position it where we are told*/
80[ 1]:    winhan = win_me ();
81[ 1]:    mal_read (mal_me (), &mailptr, &maillngth);
82[ 1]:    win_move (winhan, mailptr->row, mailptr->col);
83[ 1]:    win_logattr (winhan, 1);
84[ 1]:    win_attr (winhan, 1);
85[ 1]:    win_unhide (winhan);
86[ 1]:    win_top (winhan);
87[ 1]:
88[ 1]:    /*create a timer object*/
89[ 1]:    timhan = tim_new();
90[ 1]:
91[ 1]:    /*use the window row position as the initial number of seconds
92[ 1]:       to wait - quit when time expires*/
93[ 1]:    i = mailptr->row;
94[ 1]:    while (i--) {
95[ 2]:         tim_addto (timhan, 100);  /*delay one second*/
96[ 2]:         tim_read (timhan);        /*now wait for timer to expire*/
97[ 2]:         win_printf (winhan, "%d seconds remain\n", i);
98[ 1]:    }
99[ 1]:
100[ 1]:    /*now free our timer object and respond to parent task with a
```

```
101[ 1]:    NULL message*/
102[ 1]:    tim_free (timhan);
103[ 1]:    mal_write (mailptr->response, "", 1);
104[ 0]: }
```

Signals

As we have seen, messages can originate from DESQview as well as from
other user programs. It is not so surprising that DESQview might
generate messages in response to physical stimuli, such as the keyboard,
mouse, and timers. Somewhat less obvious is the fact that DESQview can
also alert user programs about changes in its environment, especially
since DESQview manages these alterations without the help of the user
program.

Most environments present programs that run under them with an essentially synchronous environment. The program might present a
question it expects answered or a menu from the user may make a choice.
Besides answering the question, however, there is little that the user can
do (apart from aborting the application).

DESQview presents an asynchronous environment to application programs. At almost any time, the user is free to perform such operations as
moving or resizing windows, starting a new application, freezing the
current one, etc. DESQview calls these window operations events. (In
computer jargon, an event is any external happening the computer must
handle. Keystrokes, timer ticks, and mouse clicks are all events. We will
use the term *window events* to refer to messages resulting from window
movements.)

Normally, a user program is not concerned with window events that are
occurring about it. If the user decides to move a window to a new place on
the screen, DESQview continues to handle output to the screen just as it
handles the clipping of windows behind it. Programs may execute in a
window or in the background under DESQview in exactly the same

manner as they do in the foreground (as long as they do not attempt to write directly to screen memory on a non-80386 system).

If a program does become concerned with windowing events, it has several recourses. First, it may disallow the event. For example, it may be critical to their proper appearance that the windows placed on the screen by an application remain in their original positions. In such a case, the event may be disallowed by the application program. The user is simply precluded from the operation. In our example, the user might be prevented from either moving or resizing the key windows.

Sometimes an event is acceptable as long as the program is made aware. Once the user completes the operation, DESQview sends a message to the application that owns the window, informing it of the new location, size, etc. The exact format and contents of the message depend upon the event.

When a window is created, the default is to allow all events and to not notify the user software. Events are disabled using the *win_disallow()* API call. The list of events that may be disallowed appear with the function in Figure 5.5. A disallowed event may be reenabled with the *win_allow()* API call.

A user program alerts DESQview that it wants to be notified of events via the *win_notify()* API call. A list of these events appears with the description of *win_notify()* in Figure 5.5. Having established notification of a particular event, the program may deselect notification via the *win_cancel()* function call.

Figure 5.5—Prototype Definitions for Event Message API Functions

```
                              /*set notification of window events*/
void  win_notify              /*returns nothing*/
         (ulong winhan,       /*window in which to set notification*/
          int   event);       /*event to notify is one of:
                                    NTF_HMOVE   - horizontal move
                                    NTF_VMOVE   - vertical move
                                    NTF_HSIZE   - horizontal size
```

```
                                 NTF_VSIZE   - vertical size
                                 NTF_HSCROLL - horizontal scroll
                                 NTF_VSCROLL - vertical scroll
                                 NTF_CLOSE   -+closing
                                 NTF_HIDE    -+hidden
                                 NTF_HELP    - help is requested
                                 NTF_POINTER - pointer msg sent
                                 NTF_FORE    -+app moved to foreground
                                 NTF_BACK    -+app moved to background
                                 NTF_VIDEO   -+video mode changed
                                 NTF_CUT     - Cut request made
                                 NTF_COPY    - Copy request made
                                 NTF_PASTE   - Paste request made
                                 NTF_DVKEY   - DESQview menu requested
                                 NTF_DVDONE  - DESQview menu dropped*/


                             /*cancel notification of an event*/
        void   win_cancel    /*returns nothing*/
                (ulong winhan,  /*window in which to cancel notification*/
                 int   event);   /*event to cancel*/


                             /*name a new notification window*/
        void   win_dflt      /*returns nothing*/
                (ulong winhan);  /*window handle*/


                             /*disallow an event*/
        void  win_disallow   /*returns nothing*/
                (ulong winhan,  /*window in which to disallow event*/
                 int   event);   /*event to disallow:
                                 ALW_HMOVE   - horizontal move
                                 ALW_VMOVE   - vertical move
                                 ALW_HSIZE   - horizontal size
                                 ALW_VSIZE   - vertical size
                                 ALW_HSCROLL - horizontal scroll
                                 ALW_VSCROLL - vertical scroll
                                 ALW_CLOSE   -+closing app
                                 ALW_HIDE    -+hiding app
                                 ALW_FREEZE  -+freezing app
                                 ALW_COPY    - Copy request made
                                 ALW_DVMENU  -*access to DESQview menu
                                 ALW_SWITCH  -*access to Switch menu
                                 ALW_OPEN    -*access to Open menu
                                 ALW_QUIT    -*quitting DESQview*/


                             /*(re)allow an event*/
        void  win_allow      /*returns nothing*/
                (ulong winhan,  /*window handle*/
                 int   event);   /*event to re-enable*/
```

Events fall into three categories: those specific to a particular window
(such as moving or resizing), those specific to a particular application
(such as Closing an application from the DESQview menu), and those

applying to the entire environment (such as bringing up the DESQview menu).

Events local to a window are easily understood. In this case, disabling the event or establishing notification of the event does not have any effect on other windows. The notification message is sent to the default mailbox of the task owning the window.

One of the more interesting local-window events that may be notified is the *Help* event. Normally selecting the *?* command from the DESQview menu results in DESQview help being displayed. If the mouse is pointed at a window with *Help* notification enabled, however, selecting *Help* results in a notification message to the task. Such a task may respond by opening its own *Help* window and providing information. This represents a great way to integrate the program's help into the existing DESQview help mechanism in a manner completely seamless to the user.

Window events may be specific to the application. (These have been marked with a + in Figure 5.5.) Application-specific events are somewhat more complicated than window-specific ones. Disable and notification must be set on the application program's initial window to have any effect. The user program may disable the *Close, Hide,* or *Freeze* commands. The *Close* command is used to terminate a program from the DESQview menu. The *Hide* and *Freeze* options allow the user to remove an application entirely from the screen or remove the application from memory without actually terminating it. Disabling these capabilities reduces the ability of the user to stop the current program to whatever commands it offers. In the event of notification, the notification message is sent to the application's initial window.

Notification allows programs to work effortlessly with DESQview. For example, a word processor might request *Close* notification. Normally, closing an application from the DESQview menu results in the immediate termination of the program. In the case of the word processor, this might result in the user losing any edits made. When *Close* notification is enabled, selecting *Close* from the DESQview menu results in a *Close*-notification message being sent to the application. The word processor might ask the operator whether it should save any edits and then exit upon receipt of such message. When *Close* notification is enabled, DESQview takes no other action beyond sending notification.

Finally, some window events are system wide. (These have been marked with a * in Figure 5.5) Disallowing the system-wide commands, such as *Opening*, *Switching*, or even bringing up the DESQview menu, preclude the operator from interacting directly with DESQview. This allows the program to control all operator interaction in a more conventional, *single-tasked* fashion.

An example notification program appears in NOTTST1.C. While it is executing, move or resize the displayed window either with the mouse or via the *Rearrange* command from the DESQview menu. Each time the window is changed, a message appears indicating the notification message the program received. Moving the window to the upper left-hand corner of the screen terminates the program.

Notice that each notification has a slightly different format, although the general form is given by the structure:

```
                /*format of a notification message*/
struct not_message {
                char        action;
                ulong       window;
                signed char row;
                signed char col;
                signed char field;
                signed char displacement;
                };
```

The action indicates the event causing the notification. The value of this variable is the same as the events noted with *win_notify()*. This value is always present. The window field contains the handle of the window to which the event applies for window-specific events. The next two values are very event specific, but predictable. They represent the new row and column of the upper left corner of the window for the horizontal and vertical window move, the vertical and horizontal size of the window for the window resize, etc. The field number indicates the field that is being pointed at (fields are explained in more detail in our discussion of Panels). Finally, the displacement field is used to indicate the number of columns scrolled in the horizontal and vertical scroll operations.

```
 1[ 0]: /*******************************************************************
 2[ 0]:     Window Notification Test - open a window and set notification
 3[ 0]:                               messages.  Display messages received.
 4[ 0]: *******************************************************************/
 5[ 0]:
 6[ 0]: #include <stdio.h>
 7[ 0]: #include "dvapi.h"
 8[ 0]:
 9[ 0]: /* prototype declarations of user functions*/
10[ 0]: void main (void);
11[ 0]: void program_body (void);
12[ 0]:
13[ 0]: /*minimum API version required is DESQview 2.00*/
14[ 0]: #define required 0x200
15[ 0]:
16[ 0]: /*main - standard pattern for DESQview programs*/
17[ 0]: void main (void)
18[ 0]: {
19[ 1]:   int  version;
20[ 1]:
21[ 1]:   version = api_init();
22[ 1]:   if (version < required)
23[ 1]:       printf ("This program requires DESQview %d.%02d or later.\n",
24[ 1]:               required >> 8, required & 0xff);
25[ 1]:   else {
26[ 2]:       /*tell DESQview what extensions to enable
27[ 2]:         and start application*/
28[ 2]:       api_level (required);
29[ 2]:       program_body();
30[ 1]:   }
31[ 1]:   /*if DESQview present (even if wrong version), shut it down*/
32[ 1]:   if (version)
33[ 1]:       api_exit();
34[ 0]: }
35[ 0]:
36[ 0]: /*program_body - open a window and set its attributes
37[ 0]:                   to notify when the operator accesses them,
38[ 0]:                   then wait for messages indicating they have
39[ 0]:                   been accessed.  Quit the program when the user
40[ 0]:                   brings the window to the upper left-hand corner
41[ 0]:                   or shrinks the window to 1 column square*/
42[ 0]:
43[ 0]: int notification [] = {NTF_HMOVE, NTF_VMOVE, NTF_HSIZE, NTF_VSIZE,
44[ 0]:                   NTF_HELP,  0};
45[ 0]:
46[ 0]:                   /*format of a notification message*/
47[ 0]: struct not_message {
```

```
48[ 1]:                    char        action;
49[ 1]:                    ulong       window;
50[ 1]:                    signed char row;
51[ 1]:                    signed char col;
52[ 1]:                    signed char field;
53[ 1]:                    signed char displacement;
54[ 0]:                 };
55[ 0]:
56[ 0]: void program_body (void)
57[ 0]: {
58[ 1]:   ulong winhan;
59[ 1]:   int *ptr;
60[ 1]:   char *text;
61[ 1]:   struct not_message *msg;
62[ 1]:   int              msglngth;
63[ 1]:
64[ 1]:   /* create a window and set it to use logical attributes */
65[ 1]:   winhan = win_new ("User Window", 11, 15, 50);
66[ 1]:   win_move (winhan, 5, 10);
67[ 1]:   win_logattr (winhan, 1);
68[ 1]:   win_attr (winhan, 1);
69[ 1]:   win_unhide (winhan);
70[ 1]:   win_top (winhan);
71[ 1]:
72[ 1]:   /*set its notification properties*/
73[ 1]:   for (ptr = notification; *ptr; ptr++)
74[ 1]:       win_notify (winhan, *ptr);
75[ 1]:
76[ 1]:   /*Now receive notification messages.  Print them out
77[ 1]:     in the window.  Exit loop when row and col both equal
78[ 1]:     1 (corresponding to window in upper left corner or
79[ 1]:     window shrunk to 1 col square)*/
80[ 1]:   win_printf (winhan, "Move and resize window and notice messages.\n"
81[ 1]:                       "Program quits when window placed in upper\n"
82[ 1]:                       "hand corner of screen\n\n");
83[ 1]:   do {
84[ 2]:       mal_read (mal_me (), &msg, &msglngth);
85[ 2]:       switch (msg->action) {
86[ 3]:           case NTF_HMOVE:  text = "horizontally moved";
87[ 3]:                            break;
88[ 3]:           case NTF_VMOVE:  text = "vertically moved";
89[ 3]:                            break;
90[ 3]:           case NTF_HSIZE:  text = "horizontally sized";
91[ 3]:                            break;
92[ 3]:           case NTF_VSIZE:  text = "vertically sized";
93[ 3]:                            break;
94[ 3]:           case NTF_HELP:   text = "requested help from";
95[ 2]:       }
96[ 2]:       win_printf (winhan, "\nHey, you %s me (%d,%d)",
97[ 2]:                           text, msg->row, msg->col);
98[ 1]:   } while ((msg->row != 1) || (msg->col != 1));
99[ 1]:
100[ 1]:   /*finally release the window and git*/
101[ 1]:   win_free (winhan);
102[ 0]: }
```

The above structure is not aligned on whole-word boundaries. Most compilers provide the option to align variables on word boundaries to increase access speed on 16 and 32-bit processors. Often word alignment is the default. With this message, as with most messages in DESQview, compiler alignment must be on byte boundaries for the structure definition to accurately reflect the message received.

By their very nature, event messages are the most unpredictable of all message types, arriving at almost any time. It is therefore entirely possible that the user task is not looking for a message when the event notification is made. In such a case, it may be some time before the user program notices the message and takes action on it.

It is possible to request that DESQview interrupt the user program using an automated version of the signal mechanism seen earlier. The signal function must then read the notification message from the task's default mailbox to determine what the event was before it can take action on the event. Even if the user program is executing a section of code it is not expecting (and, therefore, not looking for message input), interrupting with a signal function allows quick response to the event notification. Once the event has been handled, the signal function simply returns, returning control to the point of interruption.

As mentioned before, a signal is not a true interrupt. Rather, DESQview modifies the task's saved control information so that the interrupt routine is executed the next time the task gains control.

A signal function is established with the *win_async()* API call. This call accepts the window handle and the address of the function. The signal function receives no arguments from DESQview. The signal function may be removed by calling *win_async()* again and specifying a *NULL* function address.

When an event occurs that has had notification enabled with the *win_notify()* API call, DESQview first sends a notification message and then signals the task. This causes the signal function to be executed the next time the task is scheduled. The signal function should read the task's default mailbox object using the *mal_read()* call. It may then examine the first byte of the message to determine the event. Once the event has been processed, the signal function may execute a return that returns control to normal task processing. The signal function should be careful to read all notify messages queued up to it before it exits. Events which occur in rapid succession may generate several messages before the signal function can start. Notice that if the task mailbox is also used for normal message traffic, the signal function must be careful. Normal intertask messages may lie ahead of the event message in the queue. The program NOTTST2.C shows a signal version of the notification program above. It is executed exactly like the previous version. In this version, the main program is in a tight loop, outputting to the window to simulate message unrelated activity. Before beginning the loop, however, the program declares the function *notify()* to be the signal function for handling window events.

When the window is moved or sized, *notify()* is scheduled to run on an interrupt basis. The function reads the input message to determine what type of notification is being made. The global variables *MOVES* and *SIZINGS* are used to keep track of the number of messages of each type received. Just as before, placing the window in the upper left corner of the screen or shrinking it to one square column terminates the program. The signal function should be careful to read all notify messages queued up to it before it exits. Events which occur in rapid succession may generate several messages before the signal function can start. Notice that the signal function *notify()* is simpler than its predecessor. The signal function must dispense with the signal before another signal arrives.

```
 1[ 0]: /****************************************************************
 2[ 0]:      Window Notification Test - use an asynchronous notification
 3[ 0]:                                  function rather than intertask
 4[ 0]:                                  messages.
 5[ 0]: ****************************************************************/
 6[ 0]:
 7[ 0]: #include <stdio.h>
 8[ 0]: #include "dvapi.h"
 9[ 0]:
10[ 0]: /* prototype declarations of user functions*/
11[ 0]: void main (void);
```

```
12[ 0]: void program_body (void);
13[ 0]: void notify (void);
14[ 0]:
15[ 0]: /*minimum API version required is DESQview 2.00*/
16[ 0]: #define required 0x200
17[ 0]:
18[ 0]: /*main - standard pattern for DESQview programs*/
19[ 0]: void main (void)
20[ 0]: {
21[ 1]:   int  version;
22[ 1]:
23[ 1]:   version = api_init();
24[ 1]:   if (version < required)
25[ 1]:       printf ("This program requires DESQview %d.%02d or later.\n",
26[ 1]:                   required >> 8, required & 0xff);
27[ 1]:   else {
28[ 2]:       /*tell DESQview what extensions to enable
29[ 2]:         and start application*/
30[ 2]:       api_level (required);
31[ 2]:       program_body();
32[ 1]:   }
33[ 1]:   /*if DESQview present (even if wrong version), shut it down*/
34[ 1]:   if (version)
35[ 1]:       api_exit();
36[ 0]: }
37[ 0]:
38[ 0]: /*program_body - open a window and set its attributes
39[ 0]:                    to notify when the operator accesses them.
40[ 0]:                    All set an asynchronous notification function
41[ 0]:                    to be called when a movement occurs.  Quit the
42[ 0]:                    program when the user brings the window to the
43[ 0]:                    upper left-hand corner or shrinks the window
44[ 0]:                    to 1 column square*/
45[ 0]:
46[ 0]: int notification [] = {NTF_HMOVE, NTF_VMOVE, NTF_HSIZE, NTF_VSIZE,
47[ 0]:                     0};
48[ 0]:
49[ 0]:                    /*format of a notification message*/
50[ 0]: struct not_message {
51[ 1]:                    char        action;
52[ 1]:                    ulong       window;
53[ 1]:                    signed char row;
54[ 1]:                    signed char col;
55[ 1]:                    signed char field;
56[ 1]:                    signed char displacement;
57[ 0]:                    };
58[ 0]: int run;        /*execute as long as run == 1*/
59[ 0]: ulong winhan;   /*notification window*/
60[ 0]: ulong malhan;   /*notification mailbox*/
61[ 0]: int moves, sizings; /*number of move and sizing notifications*/
62[ 0]: void program_body (void)
63[ 0]: {
64[ 1]:   int *ptr;
65[ 1]:
66[ 1]:   /* create a window and set it to use logical attributes */
67[ 1]:   winhan = win_new ("User Window", 11, 15, 50);
```

```
68[ 1]:   win_move (winhan, 5, 10);
69[ 1]:   win_logattr (winhan, 1);
70[ 1]:   win_attr (winhan, 1);
71[ 1]:   win_unhide (winhan);
72[ 1]:   win_top (winhan);
73[ 1]:
74[ 1]:   /*set its notification properties*/
75[ 1]:   malhan = mal_me ();
76[ 1]:   for (ptr = notification; *ptr; ptr++)
77[ 1]:       win_notify (winhan, *ptr);
78[ 1]:
79[ 1]:   /*now set a signal function for asynchronous notification of
80[ 1]:     events*/
81[ 1]:   win_async (winhan, notify);
82[ 1]:
83[ 1]:   /*just sit in a loop outputting to the screen until the
84[ 1]:     notify window asks us to quit*/
85[ 1]:   win_printf (win_me (),
86[ 1]:               "Move and resize window\n"
87[ 1]:               "Program terminates when window placed in upper"
88[ 1]:               "left corner\n");
89[ 1]:   run = 1;
90[ 1]:   moves = sizings = 0;
91[ 1]:   while (run)
92[ 1]:       win_printf (winhan, "\nMoves = %d, sizings = %d",
93[ 1]:                           moves, sizings);
94[ 1]:   win_printf (winhan, "\n\nMain prog terminating!\n");
95[ 1]:
96[ 1]:   /*finally release the window and git*/
97[ 1]:   win_free (winhan);
98[ 0]: }
99[ 0]:
100[ 0]: /*Notify - handle signals from DESQview indicating the occurrence
101[ 0]:             of window events*/
102[ 0]: void notify (void)
103[ 0]: {
104[ 1]:   char *text;
105[ 1]:   struct not_message *msg;
106[ 1]:   int              msglngth;
107[ 1]:
108[ 1]:    while (mal_sizeof (malhan)) {
109[ 2]:        mal_read (malhan, &msg, &msglngth);
110[ 2]:        switch (msg->action) {
111[ 3]:            case NTF_HMOVE:  moves++;
112[ 3]:                             break;
113[ 3]:            case NTF_VMOVE:  moves++;
114[ 3]:                             break;
115[ 3]:            case NTF_HSIZE:  sizings++;
116[ 3]:                             break;
117[ 3]:            case NTF_VSIZE:  sizings++;
118[ 2]:        }
119[ 2]:        /*tell main program when it's time to quit*/
120[ 2]:        run = (msg->row != 1) || (msg->col != 1);
121[ 1]:    }
122[ 0]: }
```

Object Queues

Different types of objects present a problem. A program may reasonably expect input to any one of several different objects at any given time. Take, for instance, the problem of a menu. Users might be requested to either select the first letter of the desired menu option or click on it with the mouse, and they might also select *Help* from the DESQview menu if they are confused by the choices. Finally, if no input is received within 20 seconds or so, the program should assume that the user is confused and provide some type of help anyway.

This reasonable scenario involves four different objects, any one of which could provide input. Entering the first letter of the option generates a message to the keyboard object. Pointing and clicking on a menu option results in a message to the window's pointer object. Selecting *Help* results in a notification message to the task's mailbox object. Finally, the expiration of the timer generates a message to the task's timer object.

Monitoring these four different objects simultaneously can be a problem. The window event can be tied to a signal function, but the other three cannot. Reading one of these queues without knowing if a message is present is out of the question. Read the keyboard object, for example, and the task is suspended until a key is depressed, no matter what happens to the mouse, timer, or mailbox object.

One workable approach is to poll each of the four queues using the *_sizeof()* API calls, pausing in the loop to give up control if no messages are found before trying them all again. This solution works reasonably well.

The program OBJTST1.C shown below represents just such a program. This program opens a window on the screen and it attaches a timer, a pointer, and a keyboard object to it. The pointer is set to *report key clicks only mode* while the keyboard object is left in key mode. The timer is programmed to expire in two seconds and is reprogrammed to expire every two seconds thereafter. The program then enables window-event notification to report whenever the user moves or resizes the window.

Each pass through the loop, the program calls *api_pause()*. This returns control to DESQview to allow it to schedule other tasks that might be waiting for execution time. The program then checks each of the possible objects for messages. (The timer object must be checked specially by looking at the time remaining to execute rather than the number of messages present.) When a message appears, it is read and interpreted. Keystrokes are merely written to the screen (the ASCII character only), pointer messages display pointer position, and window events display the new window location. In a real program, such as the menu described above, more sophisticated action would be taken on the different inputs.

While the program is executing, a time-out message appears in the window every two seconds. While these are ticking off, enter keys from the keyboard or click within the window. Notice that both cause immediate messages to appear. Finally, try moving or resizing the window using either the mouse or the DESQview Rearrange command to see the notification messages. Enter an *x* at the keyboard to terminate the program.

```
 1[ 0]: /*****************************************************************
 2[ 0]:   Object Test #1  - open up a keyboard, pointer, timer, and
 3[ 0]:                      notification object.  Check each in a loop.
 4[ 0]:                      Report any messages which appear.
 5[ 0]:                      Terminate when an 'X' entered.
 6[ 0]: *****************************************************************/
 7[ 0]:
 8[ 0]: #include <stdio.h>
 9[ 0]: #include "dvapi.h"
10[ 0]:
11[ 0]: /*locally declared programs*/
12[ 0]: void main (void);
13[ 0]: void program_body (void);
14[ 0]:
15[ 0]: /*minimum API version required is DESQview 2.00*/
16[ 0]: #define required 0x200
17[ 0]:
18[ 0]: /*main - standard pattern for DESQview programs*/
19[ 0]: void main (void)
20[ 0]: {
21[ 1]:   int  version;
22[ 1]:
23[ 1]:   version = api_init();
24[ 1]:   if (version < required)
```

```
25[ 1]:          printf ("This program requires DESQview %d.%02d or later.\n",
26[ 1]:                  required >> 8, required & 0xff);
27[ 1]:   else {
28[ 2]:          /*tell DESQview what extensions to enable
29[ 2]:            and start application*/
30[ 2]:          api_level (required);
31[ 2]:          program_body();
32[ 1]:   }
33[ 1]:   /*if DESQview present (even if wrong version), shut it down*/
34[ 1]:   if (version)
35[ 1]:          api_exit();
36[ 0]: }
37[ 0]:
38[ 0]: /*program body - open a window, attach a timer, and pointer object
39[ 0]:                  to it and set notification.  Then wait for a
40[ 0]:                  keystroke, a mouse click, a timer or notification
41[ 0]:                  of the window being moved or resized.*/
42[ 0]:
43[ 0]: /*Message formats*/
44[ 0]: struct pointer_message {          /*format of pointer message*/
45[ 1]:              unsigned row;
46[ 1]:              unsigned col;
47[ 1]:              char    status;
48[ 1]:              char    field;
49[ 0]:              };
50[ 0]: struct not_message {              /*format of a notification message*/
51[ 1]:              char        action;
52[ 1]:              ulong       window;
53[ 1]:              signed char row;
54[ 1]:              signed char col;
55[ 1]:              signed char field;
56[ 1]:              signed char displacement;
57[ 0]:              };
58[ 0]:
59[ 0]: /*notifications to enable*/
60[ 0]: unsigned notification [] = {NTF_HMOVE, NTF_VMOVE,
61[ 1]:                             NTF_HSIZE, NTF_VSIZE,
62[ 0]:                             0};
63[ 0]:
64[ 0]: /*define length of timer tick*/
65[ 0]: #define TIMERTICK 200L
66[ 0]:
67[ 0]: void program_body (void)
68[ 0]: {
69[ 1]:   ulong winhan, keyhan, malhan, timhan, ptrhan;
70[ 1]:   char lastchar, *text, *bufptr, buffer [80];
71[ 1]:   unsigned char i;
72[ 1]:   unsigned j, *nptr;
73[ 1]:
74[ 1]:   struct pointer_message *msgptr;
75[ 1]:   int                    msglngth;
76[ 1]:   struct not_message     *malptr;
77[ 1]:   int                    mallngth;
78[ 1]:   char                   *keyptr;
79[ 1]:   int                    keylngth;
80[ 1]:
```

```
 81[ 1]:    /* create a window and set it up*/
 82[ 1]:    winhan = win_new ("Multiple Object Window", 22, 15, 50);
 83[ 1]:    win_move (winhan, 5, 10);
 84[ 1]:    win_logattr (winhan, 1);
 85[ 1]:    win_attr (winhan, 1);
 86[ 1]:    win_unhide (winhan);
 87[ 1]:    win_top (winhan);
 88[ 1]:
 89[ 1]:    /*use the default task mailbox for event notifications*/
 90[ 1]:    malhan = mal_me();
 91[ 1]:
 92[ 1]:    /*open a keyboard object and attach it to the window*/
 93[ 1]:    keyhan = key_new();
 94[ 1]:    key_open (keyhan, winhan);
 95[ 1]:    key_addto (keyhan, KBF_CURSOR);
 96[ 1]:
 97[ 1]:    /*open a pointer object and attach it to the window*/
 98[ 1]:    ptrhan = ptr_new();
 99[ 1]:    ptr_open (ptrhan, winhan);
100[ 1]:    ptr_addto (ptrhan, PTF_BACK|PTF_CLICKS);
101[ 1]:
102[ 1]:    /*set the window's notification properties*/
103[ 1]:    for (nptr = notification; *nptr; nptr++)
104[ 1]:        win_notify (winhan, *nptr);
105[ 1]:
106[ 1]:    /*finally, create a timer object and set it to go off
107[ 1]:      in 2 secondss*/
108[ 1]:    timhan = tim_new();
109[ 1]:    tim_addto (timhan, TIMERTICK);
110[ 1]:
111[ 1]:    /*read each of the objects in turn, being constantly on
112[ 1]:      the ready for messages to arrive*/
113[ 1]:    win_printf (winhan,
114[ 1]:                "Click mouse in window, resize window or type at\n"
115[ 1]:                "keyboard and notice messages received.\n"
116[ 1]:                "Also notice the timer ticking at the same time.\n"
117[ 1]:                "Enter 'X' to terminate.\n\n");
118[ 1]:    i = j = lastchar = 0;
119[ 1]:    do {
120[ 2]:        j++;
121[ 2]:        api_pause();
122[ 2]:
123[ 2]:        /*check for pointer message*/
124[ 2]:        if (ptr_sizeof (ptrhan)) {
125[ 3]:            ptr_read (ptrhan, &msgptr, &msglngth);
126[ 3]:            win_printf (winhan,
127[ 3]:                    "%3d(%4x) - pointer (r=%2d, c=%2d)\n",
128[ 3]:                    i++, j, msgptr->row, msgptr->col);
129[ 2]:        }
130[ 2]:
131[ 2]:        if (mal_sizeof (malhan)) {
132[ 3]:            mal_read (malhan, &malptr, &mallngth);
133[ 3]:            switch (malptr->action) {
134[ 4]:                case NTF_HMOVE:  text = "horizontal move";
135[ 4]:                                 break;
136[ 4]:                case NTF_VMOVE:  text = "vertical   move";
```

```
137[ 4]:                                      break;
138[ 4]:               case NTF_HSIZE:  text = "horizontal size";
139[ 4]:                                      break;
140[ 4]:               case NTF_VSIZE:  text = "vertical   size";
141[ 3]:              }
142[ 3]:              win_printf (winhan, "%3d(%4x) - %s (%d,%d)\n",
143[ 3]:                       i++, j, text, malptr->row, malptr->col);
144[ 2]:          }
145[ 2]:
146[ 2]:          if (!tim_len (timhan)) {
147[ 3]:              tim_read (timhan);
148[ 3]:              win_printf (winhan, "%3d(%4x) - timer expired\n",
149[ 3]:                                  i, j);
150[ 3]:              tim_addto (timhan, TIMERTICK); /*reset clock*/
151[ 2]:          }
152[ 2]:
153[ 2]:          if (key_sizeof (keyhan)) {
154[ 3]:              key_read (keyhan, &keyptr, &keylngth);
155[ 3]:              lastchar = *keyptr;
156[ 3]:              for (bufptr = buffer; keylngth--; )
157[ 3]:                      *bufptr++ = *keyptr++;
158[ 3]:              *bufptr = '\0';
159[ 3]:              win_printf (winhan,
160[ 3]:                          "%3d(%4x) - keyboard message:%s\n",
161[ 3]:                          i++, j, buffer);
162[ 2]:          }
163[ 1]:      } while (lastchar != 'X');
164[ 1]:
165[ 1]:      /*now free our objects and quit*/
166[ 1]:      key_free (keyhan);
167[ 1]:      ptr_free (ptrhan);
168[ 1]:      tim_free (timhan);
169[ 1]:      win_free (winhan);
170[ 0]: }
```

This program has an inherent inefficiency. DESQview must reschedule the program repeatedly so that it can check each of its queues. (This is reflected by the rapidly increasing loop counter J.) What is needed is a single queue to which a message is sent whenever any of the other objects contain a message. A task could read such a queue and be suspended until a message arrives to any one of its objects. The task, now unsuspended, could then read the message from the appropriate object. DESQview offers just such a queue, known as the object queue. (Admittedly, the object queue is just as much an object as the mailbox, keyboard, and pointer queues, but the term *object object*, although accurate, is semantically unappealing.) Once opened, the object queue receives a message whenever any of the other objects receive a message. This message consists of a single long word; the handle of the object receiving the message. If an object contains more than one message, its handle will appear in the object queue multiple times. (However, if the application is suspended on a read to an object when a message is sent to it, an entry is not made in the object queue.)

Figure 5.6—Prototype Declarations for *obj_open()*, *obj_read()*, and *obj_sizeof()*

```
                              /*open the object queue*/
void   obj_open               /*returns nothing*/
          (void);             /*and takes no arguments*/
                              /*read the object queue*/
ulong obj_read                /*returns object handle*/
          (void);             /*takes no arguments*/
                              /*check for handles in object queue*/
void   obj_sizeof             /*returns handle count*/
          (void);             /*takes no arguments*/
```

There is only one object queue per task and it is created when the task is created. Thus, there are no *obj_new()* or *obj_free()* API functions. The object queue does differ from other objects in that it has no handle, so there is no *obj_of()* or *obj_me()* call, and a handle is not required to read the object queue. There is an *obj_open* call, but reading the object queue automatically opens it. The function *obj_sizeof()* does exist, so it is possible to check the object queue without suspending.

The following code segment suspends the calling task until a message arrives:

```
    ulong inputhandle, obj_read (void);

    inputhandle = obj_read();
```

After returning from the call, the variable *inputhandle* contains the handle of an object. This handle must be compared against all of the handles currently opened to determine which one now has the message in it. It is not possible to determine the type of the object by simply examining the handle. (It is possible under DESQview 2.2 using the new OBJTYPE direct call , however, the API C Library 1.0 does not support this.)

The multiple-object program rewritten to use the object queue appears below. Note that this program has been changed as little as possible to dramatize the differences between the object queue and the poll approach.

The most obvious factor is how little the two programs differ. The overall loop is still there, but the call to *api_pause ()* is now replaced with an *obj_read()* call. Each of the cases is checked, this time against the returned object handle instead of calls to *_sizeof()*. In execution, the two programs are quite similar except for one striking difference.

The variable *J* is used to count the number of times through the loop (displayed in hex). Rerun the first program and notice that this number rapidly becomes quite large, wrapping around in a few minutes (depending upon the speed of the base machine). In the second program, *J* only increases by one upon each event. This is indicative of the fact that the second program does not regain control until there is really something to do. No time is wasted scheduling a task that has no useful work to perform.

```
 1[ 0]: /**********************************************************************
 2[ 0]:    Object Test #2 - this is essentially the same program as OBJTST1,
 3[ 0]:                     except that instead of polling the several
 4[ 0]:                     objects this program waits on the object queue
 5[ 0]:                     for indication that one of the objects has
 6[ 0]:                     something in it.  Notice how much slower the
 7[ 0]:                     loop count increments in this program than in
 8[ 0]:                     its predecessor.
 9[ 0]: **********************************************************************/
10[ 0]:
11[ 0]: #include <stdio.h>
12[ 0]: #include "dvapi.h"
13[ 0]:
14[ 0]: /*locally declared programs*/
15[ 0]: void main (void);
16[ 0]: void program_body (void);
17[ 0]:
18[ 0]: /*minimum API version required is DESQview 2.00*/
19[ 0]: #define required 0x200
20[ 0]:
21[ 0]: /*main - standard pattern for DESQview programs*/
22[ 0]: void main (void)
23[ 0]: {
24[ 1]:    int  version;
25[ 1]:
26[ 1]:    version = api_init();
27[ 1]:    if (version < required)
```

```
28[ 1]:          printf ("This program requires DESQview %d.%02d or later.\n",
29[ 1]:                  required >> 8, required & 0xff);
30[ 1]:   else {
31[ 2]:          /*tell DESQview what extensions to enable
32[ 2]:            and start application*/
33[ 2]:          api_level (required);
34[ 2]:          program_body();
35[ 1]:   }
36[ 1]:   /*if DESQview present (even if wrong version), shut it down*/
37[ 1]:   if (version)
38[ 1]:          api_exit();
39[ 0]: }
40[ 0]:
41[ 0]: /*program body - open a window, attach a timer, and pointer object
42[ 0]:                  to it and set notification.  Then wait for a
43[ 0]:                  keystroke, a mouse click, a timer or notification
44[ 0]:                  of the window being moved or resized.*/
45[ 0]:
46[ 0]: /*Message formats*/
47[ 0]: struct pointer_message {         /*format of pointer message*/
48[ 1]:                  unsigned row;
49[ 1]:                  unsigned col;
50[ 1]:                  char  status;
51[ 1]:                  char  field;
52[ 0]:                  };
53[ 0]: struct not_message {             /*format of a notification message*/
54[ 1]:                  char        action;
55[ 1]:                  ulong       window;
56[ 1]:                  signed char row;
57[ 1]:                  signed char col;
58[ 1]:                  signed char field;
59[ 1]:                  signed char displacement;
60[ 0]:                  };
61[ 0]:
62[ 0]: /*notifications to enable*/
63[ 0]: unsigned notification [] = {NTF_HMOVE, NTF_VMOVE,
64[ 1]:                            NTF_HSIZE, NTF_VSIZE,
65[ 0]:                            0};
66[ 0]:
67[ 0]: /*time between time ticks*/
68[ 0]: #define TICKTIME 200L            /*2 seconds*/
69[ 0]:
70[ 0]: void program_body (void)
71[ 0]: { _
72[ 1]:   ulong winhan, keyhan, malhan, timhan, ptrhan, inputhan;
73[ 1]:   char lastchar, *text, *bufptr, buffer [80];
74[ 1]:   unsigned char i;
75[ 1]:   unsigned j, *nptr;
76[ 1]:
77[ 1]:   struct pointer_message *msgptr;
78[ 1]:   int                     msglngth;
79[ 1]:   struct not_message     *malptr;
80[ 1]:   int                     mallngth;
81[ 1]:   char                   *keyptr;
82[ 1]:   int                     keylngth;
83[ 1]:
```

```
 84[ 1]:   /* create a window and set it up*/
 85[ 1]:   winhan = win_new ("Multiple Object Window", 22, 15, 50);
 86[ 1]:   win_move (winhan, 5, 10);
 87[ 1]:   win_logattr (winhan, 1);
 88[ 1]:   win_attr (winhan, 1);
 89[ 1]:   win_unhide (winhan);
 90[ 1]:   win_top (winhan);
 91[ 1]:
 92[ 1]:   /*use the default task mailbox for event notifications*/
 93[ 1]:   malhan = mal_me ();
 94[ 1]:
 95[ 1]:   /*open a keyboard object and attach it to the window*/
 96[ 1]:   keyhan = key_new();
 97[ 1]:   key_open (keyhan, winhan);
 98[ 1]:   key_addto (keyhan, KBF_CURSOR);
 99[ 1]:
100[ 1]:   /*open a pointer object and attach it to the window*/
101[ 1]:   ptrhan = ptr_new();
102[ 1]:   ptr_open (ptrhan, winhan);
103[ 1]:   ptr_addto (ptrhan, PTF_BACK|PTF_CLICKS);
104[ 1]:
105[ 1]:   /*set the window's notification properties*/
106[ 1]:   for (nptr = notification; *nptr; nptr++)
107[ 1]:       win_notify (winhan, *nptr);
108[ 1]:
109[ 1]:   /*finally, create a timer object and set it to go off
110[ 1]:     in 2 seconds*/
111[ 1]:   timhan = tim_new();
112[ 1]:   tim_addto (timhan, TICKTIME);
113[ 1]:
114[ 1]:   /*use the object queue to determine when there is
115[ 1]:     input to read*/
116[ 1]:   win_printf (winhan,
117[ 1]:               "Click mouse in window, resize window or type at\n"
118[ 1]:               "keyboard and notice messages received.\n"
119[ 1]:               "Also notice the timer ticking at the same time.\n"
120[ 1]:               "Enter 'X' to terminate.\n\n");
121[ 1]:   i = j = lastchar = 0;
122[ 1]:   do {
123[ 2]:       j++;
124[ 2]:       inputhan = obq_read ();        /*wait for notification of msg*/
125[ 2]:
126[ 2]:       /*was input from the mouse*/
127[ 2]:       if (inputhan == ptrhan) {
128[ 3]:           ptr_read (ptrhan, &msgptr, &msglngth);
129[ 3]:           win_printf (winhan,
130[ 3]:                       "%3d(%4x) - pointer (r=%2d, c=%2d)\n",
131[ 3]:                       i++, j, msgptr->row, msgptr->col);
132[ 2]:
133[ 2]:
134[ 2]:       /*or window notification*/
135[ 2]:       if (inputhan == malhan) {
136[ 3]:           mal_read (malhan, &malptr, &mallngth);
137[ 3]:           switch (malptr->action) {
138[ 4]:               case NTF_HMOVE:  text = "horizontal move";
139[ 4]:                                   break;
```

```
140[ 4]:                    case NTF_VMOVE:  text = "vertical   move";
141[ 4]:                        break;
142[ 4]:                    case NTF_HSIZE:  text = "horizontal size";
143[ 4]:                        break;
144[ 4]:                    case NTF_VSIZE:  text = "vertical   size";
145[ 3]:                }
146[ 3]:                win_printf (winhan, "%3d(%4x) - %s (%d,%d)\n",
147[ 3]:                            i++, j, text, malptr->row, malptr->col);
148[ 2]:            }
149[ 2]:
150[ 2]:            /*or, perhaps, timer event*/
151[ 2]:            if (inputhan == timhan) {
152[ 3]:                tim_read (timhan);
153[ 3]:                win_printf (winhan, "%3d(%4x) - timer expired\n",
154[ 3]:                            i, j);
155[ 3]:                tim_addto (timhan, TICKTIME); /*reset clock*/
156[ 2]:            }
157[ 2]:
158[ 2]:            /*must be from the keyboard then*/
159[ 2]:            if (inputhan == keyhan) {
160[ 3]:                key_read (keyhan, &keyptr, &keylngth);
161[ 3]:                lastchar = *keyptr;
162[ 3]:                for (bufptr = buffer; keylngth--; )
163[ 3]:                    *bufptr++ = *keyptr++;
164[ 3]:                *bufptr = '\0';
165[ 3]:                win_printf (winhan,
166[ 3]:                            "%3d(%4x) - keyboard message:%s\n",
167[ 3]:                            i++, j, buffer);
168[ 2]:            }
169[ 1]:        } while (lastchar != 'X');
170[ 1]:
171[ 1]:        /*now free our objects and quit*/
172[ 1]:        key_free (keyhan);
173[ 1]:        ptr_free (ptrhan);
174[ 1]:        tim_free (timhan);
175[ 1]:        win_free (winhan);
176[ 0]: }
```

All objects may have their contents removed and discarded using one of
the _erase() API calls shown in Figure 5.7. This may be useful in several
different cases; for example, after changing modes so that messages sent
in the previous mode do not confuse software expecting only messages of
the new mode. Since there is a one-to-one relationship between entries in
the object queue and in the object itself, however, removing objects must be
handled carefully.

Suppose, for example, that a message is sent to the keyboard object. If the
object queue is opened, the keyboard handle will be sent there also. Now, if
the user executes the *key_erase()* function on the keyboard handle, the

keyboard message will be discarded, but the keyboard handle will remain in the object queue. When the program then reads the object queue for further input, it will conclude that a key message is waiting. When it then reads the keyboard object, the task will be suspended until another key is entered. (In fact, the object queue and keyboard object would continue to stay one message out of phase were it not for the fact that a message sent to an object with a task *already* waiting on it does not generate an entry in the object queue.) If no messages are expected, the program may simply erase the object queue itself. The *obj_erase()* not only erases all object handles from the queue, it also performs an erase operation upon each handle found there. This ascertains that all messages are discarded and the object queue is left in synch with all of the objects.

A somewhat more surgical alternative is presented by the *obj_subfrom()* API call. This function removes every incidence of a given handle from the object queue. This is useful whenever an object is erased or closed to make sure that no object handles remain in the object queue. Erasing an object and then removing it from the object queue is a good way to get an object back in sync with the object queue.

Figure 5.7—Prototype Declarations for the Erase Functions

```
                                /*erase messages from the keyboard object*/
void  key_erase                 /*returns nothing*/
          (ulong keyhan);       /*keyboard handle*/

                                /*erase messages from the mailbox object*/
void  mal_erase                 /*returns nothing*/
          (ulong malhan);       /*mailbox handle*/

                                /*erase objects from the object queue*/
void  obj_erase                 /*returns nothing*/
          (void);               /*takes no arguments*/

                                /*remove an object for object queue*/
void  obj_subfrom               /*returns nothing*/
          (ulong objhan);       /*handle of object to remove*/

                                /*erase messages from the pointer object*/
void  ptr_erase                 /*returns nothing*/
          (ulong ptrhan);       /*pointer handle*/
```

Note, however, that a potential timing problem exists. Tasks that erase an object and then remove it from the object queue should protect themselves from messages that might arrive in the middle by surrounding the operation with *api_beginc()* and *api_endc()* calls.

Powerful Paradigms

Message passing was first introduced as a convenient mechanism for communicating between tasks. As we have seen, however, the same problems application tasks have in getting information from here to there, operating systems have communicating with their applications. DESQview takes the basic message-passing mechanism and generalizes it to handle almost all communications with tasks.

Generalization is a powerful software tool—in fact, it's probably the most powerful. One of the biggest advances UNIX made over other operating systems of its time was the generalization of treating all devices as files. This allowed programs to read from files, keyboards, or external devices without change. With file redirection and pipes, the user was allowed to make this decision even at execution time, a fact hailed as a major advantage even today.

The *message paradigm* employed by DESQview is potentially an even more important generalization. In the message paradigm, a task is easily seen as having a specified set of inputs (the input messages) and outputs (the output messages) with some processing in between. While this is equally true in a nonmessage-based system, the multivaried forms of input and output tend to obscure the fact. In a well-constructed message-based system, this division of logic is very obvious.

Systems divided into smaller engines, each with a small set of input and output messages, have distinct advantages over the software systems we see in common commercial use today. These systems are more easily written and debugged, since each task can be developed by itself without intimate knowledge or interaction with the tasks surrounding it. Such systems are more easily supported. Adding support for a new and different piece of hardware entails nothing more than developing the single engine that interacts with the new hardware; the remainder of the system remains blissfully ignorant of the details of the new hardware.

Finally, the biggest advantage of all is that users may remain in control of these building blocks, stacking and packing them in ways that best solves their problems.

chapter 6

Memory Management

When working with relatively small tasks and passing messages of limited size (such as we have seen so far), programmers don't need to concern themselves to any great degree with memory considerations. Before addressing real-world problems requiring programs of any appreciable size, DOS programmers must understand the memory organization of the system. Under DESQview, the situation is no different, and the programmer has some options, as we shall see.

Memory Models

A memory model is the way a processor looks at memory, sort of a battle plan of attack. For example, an instruction attempts to read a location in memory. The memory model that describes exactly which steps transpire before the contents of that location are safe and sound in an internal register within the CPU, where they may be processed. The memory model is built into the processor's hardware, even though the model may have profound effects on the way in which the software is written. Few, if any, CPUs not built as clones of one another have identical memory models.

Invariably at the very mention of memory models, some programmers begin to groan. "The 68000 microprocessor from Motorola has no memory model," they say. "I can directly access any byte of physical memory at any time."

First of all, that statement is patently false. If any byte of memory can be accessed at any time, then that *is* the memory model: all of the addressable physical memory is like a single array. This is the "simple linear-addressing memory model." Second, though the 68000's memory model is simpler than most, there is more to it than the single sentence. For example, the 68000 can access memory both as bytes or as words. It cannot, however, access words on odd addresses. There are twelve addressing modes for the source operand of which nine may be used for the destination operand. Since the 68000 has memory mapped Input/Output, its I/O address space must also come out of the memory space somewhere. These factors are all a part of this chip's overall memory model.

The Intel 8086 family of microprocessors has what is called a *segmented memory model*. In this model, memory may only be accessed through one of the segment registers. The logical address specified by the software is combined with the segment offset to form a physical address, which is then used to access physical memory.

Much has been said and written about segmentation in Intel microprocessors; most of which has been disapproving. Many of the criticisms levied have originated from programmers not familiar with the benefits of different memory models. The linear-addressing model is not the only, or necessarily the best, memory model in existence. (Not one modern mini- or mainframe computer uses this model.)

CPUs that use a simple linear-addressing model lack both memory protection and memory mapping. Without memory protection, the operating system cannot protect itself from application programs. Each may access the memory of other applications or the operating system in addition to its own. A bug in any one of the applications usually crashes the entire system.

With memory mapping, each application can be written to execute in a fixed logical address range, probably starting with zero. When loaded, the operating system can pick the physical address most suitable and map the application's logical address into the chosen physical address. The operating system may even change the location of a program in physical memory without affecting the application itself. Without such mapping, each application must either be written to execute at its own predetermined, fixed address, or else it must take other precautions such as special loaders or addressing modes to be location independent. Simple linear-address spaces are normally found in processors meant to handle simple jobs rapidly, such as hardware controllers. They are also seen in older CPUs, where technology did not allow the inclusion of more involved memory models.

Memory protection and mapping are actually two separate issues; however, they are normally handled with the same mechanism. There are few processors that implement one and not the other. Both require that the logical memory be divided up into blocks. Each block is described by a type of descriptor that carries the physical address of the block in memory and flags to control access to the block.

Most often these blocks are of fixed size and are known as pages. In the paged memory model, the page descriptors are variously known as page pointers, page registers, or simply page table entries since they are invariably combined into a lookup table known as a *page table*. When a program attempts to access physical memory, the upper bits of the logical address (usually known as the selector) are used as a vector into this page table. The address contained with the page table entry is then added to the lower bits of the offset to arrive at a physical address.

Notice that the logical address need not have the same number of bits as the physical address that it generates. Although it would never have more, it may well have less. Take, for example, the following hypothetical example:

Figure 6.1—24-Bit Logical to 32-Bit Physical Memory Conversion in a Paged Memory Model with 4K Pages

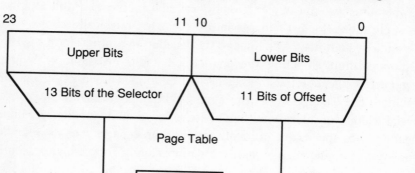

An address generated by an instruction within the CPU is known as the logical address, and consists of two parts. The selector bits select a page-table entry from the page table. The value of the page table contains the physical address of this page in memory. The offset bits from the logical address are then added to the page-table value to arrive at the final physical address.

In this example, the page size is 4K, which is equal to 0x1000 hex bytes. Address offsets must range from zero to 0x0FFF in order to cover the entire page. This requires 11 bits, which leaves the upper 13 bits of the logical address to act as a selector for the page table. This means we can select 8K pages (0x2000 hex). Each of the entries in the page table contains a 32-bit physical address. The selected 32-bit address is summed with the 11 bits of offset to generate a 32-bit physical address.

If we assume the lower two or three bits of the page offset to be zero (this forces pages on a four- or eight-byte boundary), we can also allocate protection flags in these bits for our machine. For example, the least significant bit might be a read/only flag. When set, an application may read from this page of memory but may not write to it. We might also define a user/system flag so that a page with this bit set may only be accessible when the application is performing a system call, and not when it is executing normally.

Each application has its own page table. Thus, a given application may be mapped to an entirely different range of physical memory than another, even though they might occupy the same logical address range. Also, there is no requirement for the physical pages to be consecutive. The operating system may pick up pages wherever it finds them and add them to the page table. The memory appears consecutive to the application with its logical addressing.

Page mapping allows a computer to make efficient use of more physical memory than any individual task can access. In our example machine, each application is limited to the 16MBs defined by its 24 bits of logical address. The machine may have the full 4 gigabytes of physical memory defined by the 32-bit physical address length. This extra memory is not wasted (nor doomed to the infamous *RAM disk* or *printer spooler*). In our machine, up to 256 tasks could be executing at the same time, each with a full complement of 16MBs allotted to it.

Page mapping invariably involves some time inefficiency. It takes time to perform the extra steps of looking up the page table entry and performing the extra addition. This can be minimized, however. For one thing, programs generally only execute three pages at a time. The code occupies one page, the stack a second, and data the third. If our processor is built to cache these page table entries in internal registers, the time required to look up the page table entries in memory would be avoided. The CPU only has to access the page table in memory when the code or stack wanders across a page boundary onto the next page or when the occasional access is made to far-off addresses. Some caching of page table entries must be performed to keep time overhead to a minimum. Nevertheless, some overhead is inevitable.

There is also a small amount of memory inefficiency. Suppose, for example, that an application on our sample processor requires 13K of memory. Since our page size is 4K, we must allocate to the application 16K of memory (the largest multiple greater than or equal to the required amount). Therefore, it is in the CPU designer's interest to make the page size small to reduce the amount of waisted page space. The smaller the page size, however, the more entries in the page table, which itself takes up memory (up to 32K in our theoretical processor). Smaller page sizes also means that more page table entries must be cached to avoid excessive time overhead. Typically, memory pages range between 2K and 8K in size.

Segments in the 80286 microprocessor differ from pages in three significant ways. First, they are not of fixed length. The segment descriptor not only contains the physical address of the segment, but the length of the segment as well. Secondly, segments allow a higher degree of protection. Not only do segments define several levels of priority instead of simply User and System, but different types of segments are defined to describe different types of memory blocks. Finally, segment descriptor caching is not automatic as with pages. Instead, the CPU has several special registers known as segment registers. To access a segment, the software must first load the segment address into one of the segment registers. This allows the software to control the caching of the segment descriptors for greater efficiency on the one hand, but on the other hand places the burden to do so on the software.

Intel intended for each application to have its own set of segment descriptors that it could load. Only the operating system could parcel these out, so only it had control of access to physical memory. Unfortunately, Intel made two design decisions in implementing their segmentation scheme which, in retrospect, seem very unwise.

First, since segment offsets are only 16 bits wide, segments on the 80286 are limited to 64K in length. Although this is much larger than the size of the average memory page, in the case of the segment it is much more critical. When a data structure spans multiple pages, this causes no particular concern. The software calculates addresses as large as necessary to access the structure element. The hardware reloads the page table entries

as required to provide access to the entire structure. Since segment registers must be loaded from software, however, the software must calculate
which segment to use to access the element. In practice, it is very clumsy
to access a structure that does not fit entirely within a single 64K segment.

Figure 6.2—Logical to Physical Address Conversion Under a Segmented Memory Model

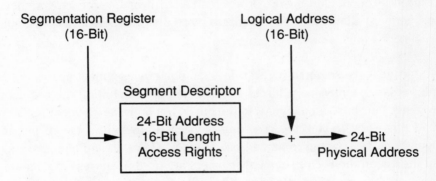

This is not usually as big a problem as it sounds. A program may have as
many different segments as it desires, either for code or data. Each function may be in its own segment, for example. Absolutely no one should
code a single function larger than 64K under any circumstance. Most
records and arrays are smaller than 64K as well. However, when a program needs to access very large arrays, it must resort to clumsy, perfor-
mance-robbing tricks.

The second problem is much worse. The 8086 and 8088 microprocessors'
segmentation model is completely different than that of the 80286 microprocessors. To understand why requires a little background.

Even though the 8-bit Intel 8080 had been a great success in its time, the
Z80 from Zilog took much of the wind from its sails. Intel had responded
with the electronically improved 8085. As this chip made no improve-
ments in the software arena, however, it did nothing to slow Intel's slide
from the number one position. Intel needed a sword with which to se-

cure the lead position in the newly developing 16-bit processors.

The story goes that Intel wanted to build the 16-bit 80286 with its segmented memory model. A count of the number of transistors it would take, however, showed that the technology had not advanced far enough to build this chip on a single wafer of silicon. So instead, Intel built the interim 8086. This processor had the same register structure and, for the most part, the same instruction set as the 80286. It did not have the advanced segmentation model, however. Instead it had a simplistic kludge, primarily to allow the 8086 to address more than the 64K which its 16-bit registers would indicate.

In the 8086, the segment register does not point to a segment descriptor at all. Instead, a physical address is calculated by left-shifting the segment register four bits and adding it to the offset. As both the segment register and offset are 16-bits, the resulting physical address is some 20 bits in length, corresponding to an address range of 1MB. In addition, since all of the bits of the 8086's segment registers are used in address calculation, none are leftover for access flags. Thus, the 8086 offers no memory protection features at all.

Figure 6.3—Segmentation on the 8086

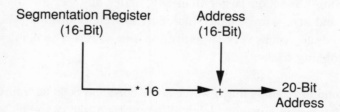

When IBM built their PC in 1982 (actually the third PC built by IBM), they considered several base processors. They first considered basing it on the 8-bit Z80 as they wanted to avoid the extra cost of 16-bit data lines. However, they decided on the 8088 as it had some particular advantages. The 8088 was a true 16-bit processor, being internally identical to the slightly older 8086. An 8088 computer hardly costs more than a Z80 to build, however, as the 8088 sported the same 8-bit data bus.

By the time the 80286 was in production, the 8086/88 software era was in full swing. DOS had been accepted as a de facto standard in personal operating systems. Before long, Wordstar had been ported over from CP/M and the 1-2-3 and dBase revolutions were both under way. By this time the tables had turned. No longer was the 80286 segmentation model the standard with the 8086's kludge the aberration, but rather the other way around.

For whatever reason, Intel designed two modes of operation into the 80286. There is the normal mode, known as *Native* or *Protected Mode*, and an 8086 emulation mode known as *Real Mode*. In Protected Mode, the 80286 operates as described above. In Real Mode, however, the 80286 mimics the operation of the 8086. Since DOS and its applications were written around the memory model of the 8086, the 80286 can only execute DOS programs in this Real Mode. (Switching from Real Mode to Protected Mode only requires a single instruction, but Intel made switching back quite difficult. If an application could easily switch to Real Mode, it could circumvent the detailed protection mechanisms designed into the segment descriptors.)

By the time the 80386 microprocessor was designed, the DOS revolution was well documented. The 80386 more or less supported the same Real and Protected Modes as did the 80286. It was clear that the 80386 would also have to support a mode of operation that obeyed the 8086 segmentation rules. To supplement this, Intel added a more or less conventional memory-paging model between the segment registers and physical memory. The 80386's paging is based on a two-tier scheme very similar to that described above. In addition, the 80386 forces pages onto 4K boundaries, freeing up the lower 12 bits of the page-table entry for protection and maintenance flags.

Even though some might consider paging in addition to segmentation as redundant, it is, in fact, quite clever. The paged memory model is much more common than segmented memory. Common, general-purpose applications can be ported to the 80386 with its conventional paged memory model much more easily than its predecessors. But the real advantage is that the true segmentation memory model cannot be utilized by DOS programs. Since the paging underneath is invisible to the application software, however, a DOS program can execute in a paged environment on the 80386 without change.

Memory Under DOS

The 20 bits of address resulting from the 8086's segmentation calculation give the chip a memory space of 1MB. At sixteen times the address range of the 64K CP/M systems that preceded it, this seemed like a virtually inexhaustible supply of memory when the IBM PC was first introduced.

Of course, not all of the 1MB of memory space is available to the user program. ROMs (Read Only Memories) containing the initialization code, the BIOS (Basic Input/Output System), and BASIC were located at very high memory. In addition, the video adapter for the PC is memory mapped to increase the speed with which it can be written. That is, the video adapter contains memory of its own. Up to 128K of the addressing range was earmarked for such memory. To allow for future expansion of the ROM area, this memory was placed at 0xA0000 (and extends through 0xBFFFF).

Since user memory must be contiguous, video memory becomes the upper boundary of where DOS applications can reside. It is the placement of this video memory that forms the famous 640K limit of application memory. The lower 640K of memory has been given the name *conventional memory* while the area above video RAM is known as *high memory*. Even the entire 640K in conventional memory is not available to the user program. DOS plus any File Control Blocks, device drivers, or buffers must also be carved out of this space. Overall the memory map for the PC looks like that in Figure 6.4.

Like clothes on a growing child, what once seemed more than sufficient soon became confining. Before long the search for more memory was on. As noted, the 24-bit Protected Mode physical address of the AT's 80286 raises the total address space up to 16MBs, a sizable increase. AT users are free to add megabytes of memory in addition to DOS's measly 640K. This memory beyond 1MB is known as *extended memory*.

Of course, since DOS cannot execute under Protected Mode, this memory cannot be used by conventional DOS applications. Special drivers have been written to implement RAM disks and printer spoolers with this memory, so it's not entirely useless. These programs switch the 80286 into Protected Mode to access extended memory, but they must then switch the chip back into the 8086-emulating Real Mode before returning to DOS.

Figure 6.4—Memory Map of the PC

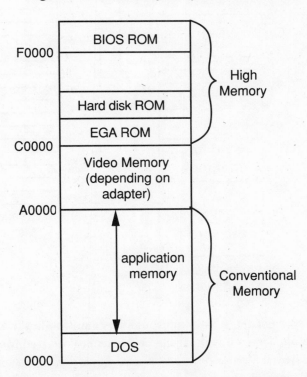

An application in need of large amounts of memory is free to pull the same trick, but there is a lot to dissuade it. An application that does so can only execute on an 80286-based machine. In addition, while going from Real Mode to Protected Mode is straightforward, switching the 80286 back in the other direction is very time consuming. This slows the application down considerably. This switch must be made often, however, since it is required before making any DOS or even video BIOS calls.

Figure 6.5—EMS 3.2 Bank Switching Memory

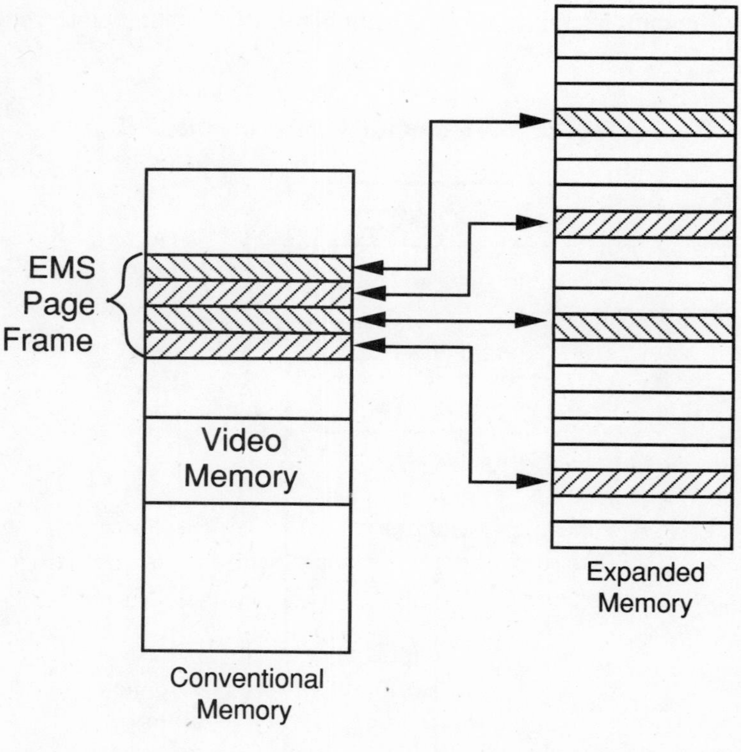

Something was needed to fold more memory into the lower 1MB where programs could access it without the problems of Protected Mode. Lotus, Intel, and Microsoft agreed on a standard bank switching specification, called the Expanded Memory Specification (EMS), the most popular version of which was Version 3.2. (The term expanded memory was adopted to differentiate this memory from extended memory.) Under EMS 3.2, a 64K block that normally goes unoccupied in the area between video RAM and the BIOS ROM is used to bank switch up to 8MBs of RAM.

To use EMS memory, a program first requests the number of 16K blocks of expanded memory desired (these blocks are known as pages). Once granted, the program specifies which page it wishes to access. This page is mapped into the 64K window in upper memory, known as the *page frame*. Up to four pages can be mapped into the 64K space available at any one time. If access to a fifth page is desired, it must replace one of the four pages already mapped into the page frame.

Bank switching was a technique already well-known to the CP/M machines of by-gone years. What made EMS so much more successful than the bank-switching schemes preceding it was that EMS was a software and not a hardware specification. EMS defined a software interface similar to the interface to the BIOS routines. It said almost nothing about the hardware. What it did say was uncharacteristically charitable. For example, the 64K page frame could be anywhere above the video memory desired. No fixed address is called out. Manufacturers already offering bank switched memory often had only to write a new software interface to be EMS compatible. Others could generally comply with only small changes to their memory boards.

When the remapping of expanded memory blocks is handled in hardware, it is usually accomplished in just a few CPU instructions. This is so fast that no noticeable overhead time is incurred. However, the mapping and remapping of memory pages is much clumsier than accessing memory directly. In addition, since this memory is above the 640K boundary, its use is limited to data. Programs cannot generally fit their code into the EMS pages. The EMS 3.2 specification had been written to aid application programs in the storage of large amounts of *data*.

The ink had barely dried on the EMS 3.2 specification when AST, Quadram, and Ashton-Tate jointly introduced Extended EMS or EEMS memory (although, technically, this made it enhanced expanded memory, this gyration in terminology was too much even for the PC world). The EEMS specification is a proper superset of the EMS 3.2 specification. Every service call in the EMS 3.2 specification is also present in the EEMS standard. Software written for EMS 3.2 will work properly under EEMS memory.

What EEMS adds, however, is the ability to have more than one page frame. Another page frame can be defined below video memory in conventional memory. This lower page frame may also be larger than 64K in length. This, plus a few extra additions, allow programs to bank switch code as well as data. DESQview is one of the few programs to ever make full use of the extended abilities of EEMS memory.

Much ill will was generated by the introduction of EEMS. Although EEMS was clearly superior, the majority of the PC community stuck with the EMS 3.2 subset until August 1987, when all parties agreed on the new specification, EMS 4.0. EMS 4.0 is also a proper superset of 3.2. Any program designed to execute with 3.2 will run with 4.0 memory. EMS 4.0 is not a proper superset of EEMS. Changes may be required to EEMS programs before they will execute properly in the 4.0 environment. However, EMS 4.0 is very similar to the EEMS specification. EMS 4.0 clearly represents the capitulation of the rest of the world to the supporters of EEMS.

EMS 4.0 raises the amount of memory that may be bank switched from 8MBs to 32MBs, an appreciable sum even by today's standards. In addition, EMS 4.0 allows memory to be mapped into any unused areas in the address space, including the conventional memory area below 640K. This significantly enhances the ability of the programs to execute out of 4.0 memory.

Not entirely by accident, the bank-switching capabilities of EMS memory are a subset of the paging capabilities of the 80386. Several drivers are commercially available that emulate EMS 4.0 memory using the paging features of the 80386. All of the 80386's memory becomes EMS 4.0 memory! DESQview users should use Quarterdeck's driver, QEMM386. This driver allows the 80386's extended memory to appear as 4.0 expanded memory to DOS programs that look for it. In addition, however, this driver has further capabilities expressly designed to operate with DESQview.

It is important to remember that programs can execute out of EMS 4.0 even if they know nothing about 4.0 memory! DESQview, being familiar with EMS 4.0 or 80386, can page blocks of memory in and out of conventional memory before allowing a program to execute. To the program itself, this memory will continue to look like standard, non-paging memory.

Memory Under DESQview

As with any program, DESQview requires memory to run. On a machine equipped with 640K or less of RAM, DESQview requires some 160K of conventional memory in addition to that used by DOS alone. On a machine with RAM installed in the high memory range, such as is usually the case on 80286/80386-equipped machines or machines containing EEMS or EMS 4.0 memory, the XDV loader may be used to load DESQview into high memory. In this case, DESQview may not use any conventional memory.

In addition to its code space, DESQview requires a certain amount of data space as well. This area of RAM is known as *common memory*. The objects that we have been studying in previous chapters are allocated from this common memory. Common memory is allocated during DESQview initialization. The default of 17K is suitable for about nine processes, but this depends upon how many objects each process opens. The size of common memory is adjustable using the SETUP program.

Figure 6.6—Memory Map with DESQview

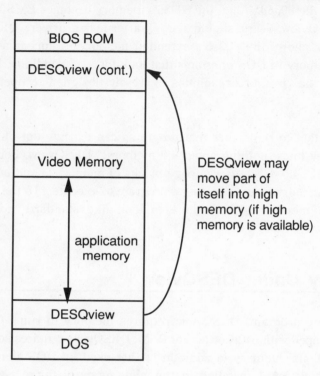

Each application program executes out of its own conventional memory. DESQview calls this *process memory*. Normally, applications load immediately above DOS or above the last Terminate and Stay Resident (TSR) to execute. A program must assume that any memory between the beginning of memory and itself contains DOS, device drivers, TSRs, etc., and should be left alone. However, since only one program executes at a time under DOS, the program may assume that all of the memory between itself and the end of memory is available for use.

In a multitasking environment, it is important that a program be allocated the amount of process memory it requires and no more. DESQview loads the program as high as possible in conventional memory—consistent with its memory requirements. For future programs, it then moves the *end of memory* down to immediately prior to the loaded program.

Take, for example, the following case:

Figure 6.7—A Typical Conventional Memory Configuration

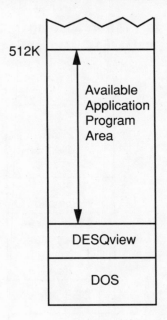

Now assume that DESQview is asked to load a program that requires 256K of RAM to execute. DESQview loads such a program starting at address 256K (0x40000 hex). This leaves the memory the program needs in the range of 256K to 512K. If the next program requires only 64K to execute, it would then be loaded at address 192K (0x30000 hex). Every time DESQview schedules this second program to run it sets the *top of memory* to 256K so that the program will not attempt to overwrite the first program by erroneously believing the memory from 256K to 512K to be free.

The amount of conventional memory allocated to a program at startup is set by the user in the .DVP file by executing the *Add a Program* or *Change a Program* command under the *Open Window* option of the

DESQview window. The *Memory Size* field on the first page of the *change a program* window indicates the minimum amount of conventional memory that the program *must* have in order to execute. The program will be allocated at least this amount or else it will not be started.

Figure 6.8—Memory After Loading a 256K Application and a 64K Application

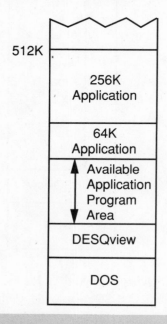

On the *advanced options* page of the *change a program* window (accessed by tapping the F1 key) is a field labeled *Maximum Program Memory Size*. If this field is set, then the program is allocated up to the *Maximum Memory Size* amount of conventional memory, if available, but no more. If the full *maximum memory size* is not available, then the remainder of available conventional memory is allocated to the program.

For example, assume that 512K of memory is available. A program with a *Memory Size* of 256K will receive 256K when started. If the same program had a *memory size* of 256K but a *maximum memory size* of 640K, then this program would receive the full 512K.

A program without a *maximum memory size* can be assured of receiving the *memory size* amount of memory. A program with the *maximum memory size* specified will receive somewhere between this amount and the *memory size* amount of memory. Specifying an unattainable amount as the *maximum memory size* (such as 640K) will assure a program of receiving the remainder of available conventional memory, in a nonmapped system.

When a program requests the amount of expanded memory available in the system, DESQview normally reports the entire amount of expanded memory available. For some especially unfriendly programs this may be dangerous, however. Assuming themselves to be the only programs on the system, some programs will automatically allocate all available expanded memory to themselves, whether they need it or not. Not only does this preclude other programs that may be running at the same time from allocating any expanded memory for their own needs, but it prevents DESQview from using it for its own needs. To thwart such antisocial behavior, the user may specify a *Maximum Expanded Memory Size*, also on the advanced options field. When set, DESQview will not report nor allocate any more expanded memory than this amount to the application.

Under DESQview, each program is also allocated a block of memory known as *system memory*. This memory, which is handled by DESQview as part of process memory, is used for the storage of logical window buffers and other DESQview tables that are only used by a single process. System memory is allocated with the process to save common memory, since system memory can be mapped together with the process to which it belongs.

A program specifies the amount of system memory desired in the *.DVP* file using the *Change a Program* menu as well. The amount of system memory required for an application is the first field under the advanced options window. The amount of system memory to assign can be determined emperically. When too little is allocated, DESQview admonishes the user to increase the allocation.

Memory Beyond the 640K Barrier

What happens when an application requires more conventional memory to execute than is currently free? Under DOS, the user receives a *Not enough memory* message and the request terminates. Under DESQview, there are several other possibilities, however.

The first option is to write one of the programs that is already loaded out to disk. This frees up the memory occupied by the program for use in loading the new program. This is known as *swapping an application to disk*. By swapping an application to disk, the operating system can free up internal memory for the program being loaded.

If DESQview receives a request to initiate an application and there is not enough memory, it swaps out one of the applications already loaded and then checks again. It continues to swap applications to disk until sufficient memory is available to load the requested application or until all swappable applications have been unloaded. Of course, once an application has been written to disk it cannot execute. It will not receive any time slices during the normal task scheduling until it is reloaded into internal memory.

Since personal computer disks are such slow devices, it may take up to several seconds to reload such an application into RAM. Therefore, it is not desirable to swap an application back into RAM until someone expresses an interest in seeing it execute. DESQview does not reload an application that has been swapped out until it is made the foreground application. Usually this is the result of the user selecting it from the DESQview Switch menu.

Swapping an application back into RAM is similar to loading it the first time. If sufficient memory is not available to hold the application, other applications are swapped out to disk repetitively until sufficient RAM is freed. (There may be other considerations as well. For example, an application generally must occupy the same memory range as it did when it was first loaded.)

Applications servicing interrupts may not be swapped out. (These are most often programs that perform serial communication.) To do so would be fatal: the program might install itself on the interrupt and then wait for input. Once it is swapped out, however, the memory it once occupied becomes filled with a new application. The interrupt vector now points at a program that is not expecting to receive an interrupt. If the interrupt occurs, the system will crash.

A program may also be swapped out by selecting the *Put Aside* option under the *Rearrange* selection of the DESQview menu.

A program that is swappable to disk need not take special precautions. However, the system designer might not want a particular application to be swappable as all tasks within the same process become suspended while the application is on disk. A program may be marked as non-swappable in one of two ways. In the *Advanced Options* menu of the *Change a Program* utility is the option *Can be swapped out (Y, N, blank)*. Selecting an *N* in this case marks the application as unswappable. Such an application may not be *Put Aside*. If a blank is entered, which is the default condition, then the application is still not swappable if the question *Uses serial ports* on the *Basic Options* menu of *Change a Program* is answered with anything but *No*. If both of these conditions are met, then the application is swappable.

Of course, disks are fairly slow devices. Although RAM disks make better swap devices, EMS 3.2 memory is even better yet. DESQview can also swap an application into EMS 3.2 memory to free up conventional memory for other applications. DESQview brings empty page blocks into the page frame, fills them with the program to be swapped out, and then pages them back out again to make room for fresh pages. The effect here is akin to a shovel with each page taking a 16K scoop.

The paging operation is quite fast. The main overhead in swapping to EMS 3.2 memory is the copying of program from conventional memory to the expanded memory blocks in the page frame. Since this occurs at CPU speeds, it is much faster than copying to disk, but nevertheless the time may be noticeable.

**Figure 6.9—Swapping an Application
Out to EMS 3.2 Memory**

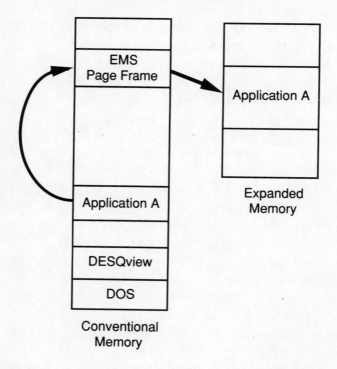

Once in EMS 3.2 memory, the application must be copied back into the conventional memory it previously occupied before it may be allowed to execute again. Since the page frame is in high memory, DOS programs cannot be executed there. Even if they could, the EMS 3.2 page frame is limited to 64K in length. Since the entire program must be mapped into the 1MB address space at one time before it may be given control, only programs of 64K or less can execute from EMS 3.2 memory anyway. Therefore, programs must be swapped back into the conventional memory before they can be executed again.

DOS programs can be executed out of EMS 4.0 (and EEMS) memory with its larger page frame in conventional memory, however. This makes memory management under DESQview much more flexible. Instead of copying a program out of conventional memory to make room, pages of conventional memory are paged out and new memory blocks are paged into the page frame for each new application.

When it becomes time to return to the old application, DESQview need only to swap the EMS pages it occupies back into their original positions within conventional memory. If the application is larger than the page frame size, then whatever sections that do not fit must be swapped out exactly as in the EMS 3.2 case. But if the application fits entirely within the page frame, then no swapping is necessary.

Since paging EMS memory requires just a few instructions, applications may be paged in and out of memory very rapidly. Applications that are paged (and not swapped) continue to be multitasked and to receive CPU time. DESQview knows to page these applications back into memory before giving them control of the CPU as a routine part of the task-switch process.

Notice that providing a swap disk in the DESQview *SETUP* program might defeat this feature. Leave this field blank if you have EMS or QEMM386 memory. Only fill this field in if you plan to use a RAM disk other than C: as the swap device.

The algorithm for placing applications in memory is slightly different in a machine equipped with EMS 4.0 memory. It is no longer advantageous to pack applications in memory as with a non-4.0 system. Instead, it is more advantageous to load each program with its own EMS 4.0 virtual memory pages. That is, each application is loaded ending at the end of conventional memory. This is to allow as much of each application to fit within the 4.0 page frame as possible.

Figure 6.10—Mapping Applications In and Out of Conventional Memory in a System Equipped with a Very Large EMS 4.0 Page Frame or on an 80386-Based PC

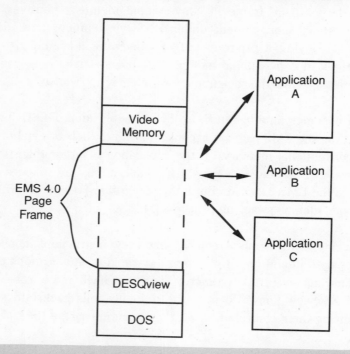

While it is possible to execute DESQview on an 80386-based PC without the QEMM386 device driver, doing so is a waste of the machine's impressive capabilities. In fact, the performance enhancements are so significant that Quarterdeck gives the combination of QEMM386 and DESQview 2.2 (or above) a new name, calling it DESQview386. Although partially the result of marketing pressure, the new name is not completely unjustified. Throughout this book, I assume that all 80386-based machines are equipped with QEMM386 or, at least, an EMS emulator from some other company. If not, the 80386 PC has no capabilities above those of simple PCs and ATs.

QEMM386's memory has advantages over EMS 4.0. For one thing, the page range is unlimited, stretching over the entire conventional memory range. Almost any block of memory may be switched in or out of the lower 640K of logical memory (DOS is not swapped out, nor is DESQview itself). No application that fits in conventional memory is too large to fit entirely within the page frame. Even applications that fill the 640K range of conventional memory can be paged entirely out of memory with no need for any part to be swapped out using the time consuming memory-to-memory copy operation.

So What?

On systems equipped with EEMS, EMS 4.0, or an 80386, multitasking under DESQview allows the programmer to make reasonable use of large amounts of extended memory. The upper megabytes of RAM space are no longer confined to oversized RAM disks or expansive printer spoolers. For the user, this means as many programs as will fit in available memory may be loaded and continue to execute simultaneously. For the program designer, this has a much greater significance: the fall of the 640K barrier.

A given problem may be divided into several tasks that are then assigned to different processes. Although each individual process is limited to the 640K limit of DOS itself, there is no limit to the size of a program divided in this manner. As each process is scheduled to execute, its memory is paged into the lower 640K of logical memory and allowed to execute. (Even the amount of RAM in the host machine is not an absolute limit as DESQview allows the swapping of processes to and from disk—with reduction in performance, admittedly.)

This does, however, carry with it some programming considerations. When I discussed using global variables to communicate between processes back in Chapter 4, I spoke of the possibility that one process might not have access to another process's memory. At that time, I did not really define how that might be the case. We can see now that this is almost always the case on systems equipped with EMS 4.0 memory or an 80386 processor.

When one process is paged into conventional memory, other processes must be paged out since they occupy the same logical address space. Independent processes are almost mutually exclusive in conventional memory on a paged system. Thus, on these systems a process *cannot* access the memory of another process. Two such processes cannot communicate via locally defined global variables, even if they were to pass the address of such a variable in a message between them.

Even on systems without memory-mapping capabilities, it is always possible, although perhaps unlikely, that the receiving process has been swapped out to disk when communication is attempted. A sending application that attempts to store information directly into the memory of a swapped application will overwrite an unsuspecting application occupying the same memory with an ensuing crash of the entire system.

It is possible to disable swapping either temporarily in the *Tune Performance* menu or permanently in the DESQview *SETUP* program. In a system in which swapping has been disabled and which contains neither EMS 4.0 memory nor an 80386 processor, much of the remainder of this section is irrelevant. In such simple systems, processes are not dynamic and, therefore, do have reliable access to each other's memory. However, to write programs with this assumption automatically precludes them from executing on more advanced systems. This may prove extraordinarily unwise when the program begins to exceed the available 640K conventional memory space.

Of course, separate tasks within the same process do not suffer this memory-mapping problem. It is the process that is paged or swapped into and out of memory, not the task or the application. If a task is executing, it is assured that any other tasks in the same process are loaded and accessible in memory. The programs presented in Chapter 4 that communicated between tasks in the same process via global variables were completely justified.

DESQview stores messages sent between two tasks in the same process in system memory. As noted, a process's system memory is swapped and paged together with its process memory. However, all tasks within the same process have simultaneous access to the same system memory. Since window information is also stored in system memory, tasks within the same process also have access to each other's windows (provided, of course, that they can get the window's handle).

When a task sends a mail message using *mal_write()*, DESQview examines the sending task and the task that owns the target mailbox. If the receiving task is in the same process as the sending task, then DESQview uses the process's system memory to hold the message. The reading task receives the address of the message in system memory.

The size of system memory is specified in the *.DVP* file and is set by the *System Memory (in K)* field in the *Advanced Options* menu of *Change a Program*.

Data may only be passed from one process to another in memory that is not paged or swapped out during a task switch, and to which both processes have access. In Chapter 4, I used a small section of video RAM, but I admitted even then that this was neither a safe nor a reasonable solution. There are other sections of memory that are never moved. For example, DOS and DESQview are omnipresent. DESQview's common memory pool is also present in memory at all times.

DESQview uses the common memory pool to store messages between tasks in different processes. No matter how many times or in what way processes are paged and swapped in and out, DESQview does not move the common memory pool. Messages stored there may be accessed at any time.

When asked to send a message to a mailbox owned by a different process, *mal_write()* copies the caller's message into common memory. The reading process then receives a pointer to the message in common memory.

Communicating via the common memory pool has several problems, however. First, it is somehow unpleasant to have an application's memory mixed up with DESQview's memory buffers. Debugging such applications may be made slightly more difficult by finding the user's message stuck in the middle of memory whose purpose is both unclear and changing. Worse than this, however, is the fact that the common memory pool is not very large in most systems. Since it is static in size, any memory devoted to common memory detracts from the size of the conventional memory pool available to all applications. Generating a large common memory pool just on the off chance that some applications might need it is not very memory efficient.

The size of the common memory pool may be increased by using the DESQview SETUP if many large messages are to be passed between processes. DESQview must be terminated and restarted before the new settings for the common memory pool take effect.

Sharing system memory between processes is more desirable. To share system memory with other processes, the programmer merely places a * in the *Shared Program Pathname* field of the *Advanced Options* window of the *Change a Program* menu.

Shared system memory is allocated immediately above common memory. Unlike common memory, however, shared system memory is dynamic. With the start of each application that requires it, shared system memory grows by the amount of system memory specified in the *.DVP*. Shared system memory shrinks as much possible when applications are terminated.

When *mal_write()* is asked to pass a message between two processes, both of which use shared system memory, DESQview copies the message into shared system memory. The address received by the reading process is the address of the message in shared system memory.

Figure 6.11—Shared System Memory

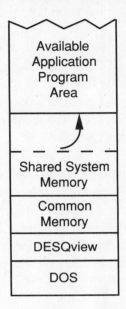

Since system memory is also used for window storage, processes sharing system memory may access each other's windows. A process may send its window handle to another process and that process may then write to it, for example. (Remember, this is true only if both processes use shared system memory.)

Shared system memory can also be used for passing messages by reference between tasks in different processes. When we first discussed passing by reference in Chapter 4, it was presented as a means for communicating large blocks of data between tasks of the same process. Passing by reference is potentially quicker since it avoids the copy step—instead the address of the sender's message is sent to the receiving task and not a copy.

Normally messages may not be passed by reference between different processes due to the memory-mapping problems mentioning earlier. A process that receives the address of a message contained within another process will not be able to access that message on a mapped system. The shared system memory pool, which is accessible by all processes with shared system memory, is used to contain messages whose address may then be communicated in a conventional message.

To send such a message, the sending task first requests a block of system memory from DESQview. It then builds the message it intends to send in this block. Finally it sends the address of this block to the receiving task in a conventional message. If both tasks use shared system memory, the receiving task is able to access the memory block directly using the address received from the mailbox read.

No time is saved if the sending task gets a block of memory and then copies the already built message into it before sending its address. In this event, the user program is essentially doing what DESQview would handle automatically when passing by value. Time is saved, however, if the program can request the block of memory early and then use this dynamically allocated block to save data instead of a locally declared structure.

System memory is requested via the *api_getmem()* API call. The caller passes a single argument indicating the size of the block requested and receives the address back of the block to use. This is much like the C library function *malloc()*. For example, the following code fragment defines a structure, allocates it out of system memory, and stores data into it.

```
struct data_type {
                    int type;
                    char datablock [512];
                    } *dataptr;

/*line 1*/
dataptr = (struct data_type *) api_getmem (sizeof (struct data_type));

/*line 2*/
dataptr->type = 1;

/*line 3*/
read (FILEHANDLE, dataptr->datablock, sizeof (dataptr->datablock));

/*line 4*/
mal_subfrom (MALHANDLE, dataptr, sizeof (struct data_type), STATUS);
```

The declaration is for a structure *data_type* containing an integer field and a large block. Line one in the code segment allocates a block of memory from system memory. The size of the block allocated is sufficient to contain the structure. The resulting pointer is stored into the pointer variable *dataptr*. The type cast serves to avoid the warning of mismatched pointer types.

Line two demonstrates how individual fields are accessed. Line three shows that fields within the structure may be used just like normally declared variables. In this case, a file-read request is being made directly to the *datablock* field. Finally, the block containing the type and the data block just read are sent to the mailbox *MALHANDLE*. (This along with the *STATUS* and *FILEHANDLE* presumably have been declared and initialized somewhere else in the program.)

The receiving task looks exactly like those in Chapter 4 with the exception that once the task has finished with the message, it must return the shared system memory to DESQview with the *api_putmem()* API call. Unlike messages that it copies to its own memory buffers (passed by value), DESQview does not know where a message passed by reference is located and cannot be responsible for freeing it. However, this technique offers the advantage that multiple messages may be read and retained unlike conventional messages that *disappear* when the next *mal_read()* call is made.

Using blocks of shared system memory passed by reference in this fashion, the number of memory to memory transfers is minimized. The block is allocated, data is stored into it, and is then sent to the receiving task. Once it has been sent, the sending task no longer *owns* the block of memory. No further reference should be made to *dataptr* after line four (except for the unusual event that the sending and receiving processes have agreed to continue using this block as a memory communications path). The message receiver will likewise be able to access the data directly from the message until the block is freed.

Using EMS from the Application

Accessing EMS memory is not a privilege limited to DESQview. EMS memory was designed to be accessed by application programs as well. A program in need of memory in excess of what conventional memory can provide may request 16K blocks of memory from the EMS handler.

A list of the basic EMS function calls appears in Figure 6.12. EMS calls are made by executing an interrupt 0x67 with the registers set as specified. In every case, the error return is returned in register *AH*. If *AH* is equal to zero upon return, then all went well. Otherwise, a list of errors appears in Figure 6.13

Figure 6.12—The Basic User EMS Function Calls

Function	Input	Output
1) Get Status	AH = 40H	
2) Page Frame Addr	AH = 41H	BX = page frame segment
3) Free Page Count	AH = 42H	BX = number of unallocated pages
		DX = total number of pages in EMS
4) Allocate Pages	AH = 43H	DX = EMS handle for these pages
		BX = no. pages
5) Map Handle Page	AH = 44H	
	BX = page number	
	AL = frame slot	
	DX = page handle	
6) Deallocate Pages	AH = 45H	
	DX = page handle	
7) Get EMS Version	AH = 46H	AL = EMS version number

Figure 6.13—Errors Returned from Basic Calls

Value of AH	Error
0H	No error detected (all went well)
80H	Error in EMS software
81H	Error in EMS hardware
83H	Invalid page handle
84H	Undefined function code provided in *AH*
85H	All EMS handles in use
87H	Not enough EMS pages to satisfy request
88H	Not enough unallocated EMS pages to satisfy request
89H	Can't allocate zero pages
8AH	Logical page number out of range
8BH	Page slot out of range

To access expanded memory, the user program must first make sure that EMS memory is present. The EMS handler installs itself into interrupt 0x67; however, a program cannot execute an interrupt 0x67 until it is sure there is an EMS handler there to field the request. The most common technique for testing the presence of an EMS handler is to examine the address contained in interrupt 0x67. This address points to the EMS handler. The segment portion of this address points to the header field. If this header contains the string "EMMXXXX0" at offset 0xA then an EMS handler is present.

A function to test for an EMS handler is shown in the code section below.

```
/*EMS_present - return a 1 if EMS handler found to be present;
               0 otherwise*/
union {
      ulong lword;
      int   sword[2];
      } address;

typedef struct {
               char padding [0x0a];
               char name [8];
               } EMS_handler;
EMS_handler *EMS_ptr;
#define EMS_int 0x67
```

```
#define EMS_name "EMMXXXX0"

int EMS_present (void)
{
    int matches;

    address.lword = (ulong)getvect (EMS_int);
    address.sword [0] = 0;
    EMS_ptr = (EMS_handler *)(address.lword);
    matches = strncmp (EMS_ptr->name, EMS_name, 8);
    return !matches;
}
```

The function *getvect()* is used to return the address contained in interrupt 0x67. The union *address* is used to access the segment and offset portions of an 8086 address separately. The full address is first stored into the long word *lword*. The segment portion of the address is contained in sword [1]. The offset portion is then cleared by storing a zero into *sword[0]*. lword now points to the EMS header structure. The first eight characters of the name are compared with the string *EMMXXXX0*. If the two are equal, the function returns a one and if not, a zero.

Once the program is sure that an EMS handler is present, it should then check to make sure it is working properly using the *Get Status* function call.

To invoke interrupt 0x67, C programs should use the *int86()* or similar library function. This function allows C programs to perform 8086 software interrupts by first loading the registers into a structure and then performing the call. This function loads the registers from this structure, performs the interrupt, and then stores the returned registers back into this structure where they may be examined from the C program again.

The following function returns the status of the EMS handler. A zero indicates that all is working well. A list of the possible errors appears in Figure 6.13.

```
int EMS_status (void)
{
    union REGS regs;

    regs.h.ah = 0x40;
    int86 (EMS_int, &regs, &regs);
    return regs.h.ah;
}
```

To determine the address of the page frame within memory, the program may use the *Page Frame Address* EMS call. This is the address into which the EMS pages will be mapped and the address which the program should use in accessing them.

The following function returns the address of the page frame. In the event of error, it returns a zero.

```
void *EMS_frameaddr (void)
{
    union REGS regs;

    regs.h.ah = 0x41;
    int86 (EMS_int, &regs, &regs);
    if (regs.h.ah)
        return (void *)0;
    address.sword [1] = regs.x.bx;    /*load segment*/
    address.sword [0] = 0;            /*now offset*/
    return (void *)address.lword;     /*return address*/
}
```

Now the program is able to request as many pages as it requires up to the number available. Each request for pages is assigned a handle. Pages should be requested in blocks as there are a limited number of handles. The handle is presented by the program whenever it wants a particular page mapped into one of the physical slots in the page frame. Finally, the program must deallocate its EMS pages before exiting.

Functions to allocate and deallocate EMS pages are shown below.

```
unsigned EMS_allocate (unsigned pagecount)
{
    union REGS regs;
```

```
        regs.h.ah = 0x43;
        regs.x.bx = pagecount;
        int86 (EMS_int, &regs, &regs);
        if (regs.h.ah)
              return 0;
        return regs.x.dx;
}
unsigned EMS_deallocate (unsigned handle)
{
        union REGS regs;

        regs.h.ah = 0x45;
        regs.x.dx = handle;
        int86 (EMS_int, &regs, &regs);
        return regs.h.ah;
}
```

Some particularly ill-behaved programs begin execution by requesting all EMS memory in the system, whether they need it or not. While not harmful in a single-tasking system, this is disruptive in the DESQview environment. Not only does this preclude other programs that may be running at the same time from allocating any expanded memory, but it prevents DESQview from using it for its own needs. To thwart such antisocial behavior, the user may specify a *Maximum Expanded Memory Size*, on the *Advanced Options* menu of the *Change a Program*. When set, DESQview will not report nor allocate any more expanded memory than this amount to the application.

To access an EMS block, it must be mapped into one of the 16K slots of the page frame. In EMS 3.2 memory, the page frame is limited to 64K in length, so the slots are numbered from zero through three. In EEMS and EMS 4.0 memory, the page frames are somewhat larger, so more slots are defined.

Once the block of EMS memory has been mapped in, the program refers to it by the address of the slot it occupies. The same block of memory can be mapped into different slots at different times, and thus carry different physical addresses. Since the slots are of a fixed 16K size, the address of a slot within the page frame is simply its number multiplied by 16K.

A function to map EMS pages into the page frame is shown below.

```
unsigned EMS_map (unsigned page,
                  unsigned frameslot,
                  unsigned handle)
{
    union REGS regs;

    regs.h.ah = 0x44;
    regs.x.bx = page;
    regs.h.al = (char)frameslot;
    regs.x.dx = handle;
    int86 (EMS_int, &regs, &regs);
    return regs.h.ah;
}
```

The address of a page-frame slot can be calculated from the page-frame segment plus the knowledge that slots are 16K in length. The four slots are found at offsets of zero, 16, 32, and 48K, respectively. A function to calculate the address of a page-frame slot is shown below. Notice again that the address offset is stored into *sword[0]*, the segment into *sword[1]*, and the resulting address read from *lword*.

```
void *EMS_slotaddr (unsigned slotnum)
{
    unsigned frame_offsets [] = {0, 0x4000, 0x8000, 0xC000};

    if (slotnum > 3)
        return 0;
    address.sword [1] = EMS_frameaddr ();
    address.sword [0] = frame_offsets [slotnum];
    return (void *)address.lword;
}
```

A simple program that allocates a few blocks and maps them into different slots in the page frame is shown in EMSTST1.C. This program first checks for the presence of EMS memory, then allocates a few blocks, initializes the first word of each, and maps each block into a different page-frame slot.

```
 1[ 0]: /************************************************************************
 2[ 0]:    EMS Test #1 - check for the presence of EMS memory.  If present,
 3[ 0]:                 allocate a few blocks and access them in a simple
 4[ 0]:                 fashion just to prove that we can do it.  Note that
 5[ 0]:                 this program is not actually DESQview specific so the
 6[ 0]:                 EMS routines can be included in any C program which
 7[ 0]:                 wants access to EMS memory.
 8[ 0]: ************************************************************************
 9[ 0]:
10[ 0]: #include <stdio.h>
11[ 0]: #include <dos.h>
12[ 0]: #include "dvapi.h"
13[ 0]:
14[ 0]: /*define the EMS interrupt and device name*/
15[ 0]: #define EMS_int 0x67
16[ 0]: #define EMS_name "EMMXXXX0"
17[ 0]:
18[ 0]: /*prototype declarations for the EMS package*/
19[ 0]: void main (void);
20[ 0]: unsigned EMS_present (void);
21[ 0]: unsigned EMS_status (void);
22[ 0]: void    *EMS_frameaddr (void);
23[ 0]: unsigned EMS_pagecount (void);
24[ 0]: unsigned EMS_allocate (unsigned pagecount);
25[ 0]: unsigned EMS_map (unsigned page, unsigned frameslot, unsigned handle);
26[ 0]: unsigned EMS_deallocate (unsigned handle);
27[ 0]: void *EMS_slotaddr (unsigned slotnum);
28[ 0]:
29[ 0]: /*use the union 'address' to access the segment and offset portions
30[ 0]:    of an 8086 address seperately*/
31[ 0]: union {
32[ 1]:        ulong    lword;
33[ 1]:        unsigned sword[2];
34[ 0]:      } address;
35[ 0]:
36[ 0]: /*these globals are used to calculate the frame address*/
37[ 0]: unsigned frame_segment;
38[ 0]: unsigned frame_offsets [] = {0x0000, 0x4000, 0x8000, 0xC000};
39[ 0]:
40[ 0]: /*main - allocate 'N' blocks of EMS memory and then
41[ 0]:           map them about into different page frame slots and
42[ 0]:           access them (just to prove it can be done)*/
43[ 0]: void main (void)
44[ 0]: {
45[ 1]:     #define N 5
46[ 1]:     unsigned *ptr, slotnum, i, blocknum;
47[ 1]:     unsigned handle;
48[ 1]:
49[ 1]:     printf ("\n\nThis program accesses %d blocks of EMS memory\n"
50[ 1]:               "(if present) just to show how it is done\n",
51[ 1]:               N);
52[ 1]:     if (EMS_present ()) {
53[ 2]:         ptr = EMS_frameaddr();
54[ 2]:         if (handle = EMS_allocate (N)) {    /*allocate N blocks*/
55[ 3]:             for (i = 0; i < N; i++) {
56[ 4]:                 EMS_map (i, 0, handle);
```

```
 57[ 4]:                    *ptr = i;
 58[ 3]:                }
 59[ 3]:                for (i = 0; i < 10; i++)
 60[ 3]:                    for (blocknum = 0; blocknum < N; blocknum++) {
 61[ 4]:                        slotnum = (blocknum + i) % 4;
 62[ 4]:                        EMS_map (blocknum, slotnum, handle);
 63[ 4]:                        ptr = EMS_slotaddr (slotnum);
 64[ 4]:                        printf ("block %d mapped to frame %d "
 65[ 4]:                                "contains %d,   ",
 66[ 4]:                                blocknum, slotnum, *ptr);
 67[ 3]:                    }
 68[ 3]:                EMS_deallocate (handle);
 69[ 2]:            }
 70[ 1]:        }
 71[ 1]:        printf ("\nFinished! Enter any character to quit\n");
 72[ 1]:        getch ();
 73[ 0]: }
 74[ 0]:
 75[ 0]: /*EMS_present - return a 1 if EMS handler found to be present;
 76[ 0]:                 0 otherwise*/
 77[ 0]: typedef struct {
 78[ 1]:                char padding [0x0a];
 79[ 1]:                char name [9];
 80[ 0]:                } EMS_handler;
 81[ 0]: EMS_handler *EMS_ptr;
 82[ 0]:
 83[ 0]: #define getvect(x) (*(void * *)(EMS_int * 4))
 84[ 0]: unsigned EMS_present (void)
 85[ 0]: {
 86[ 1]:    unsigned matches;
 87[ 1]:
 88[ 1]:        address.lword = (ulong)getvect (EMS_int);
 89[ 1]:        address.sword [0] = 0;
 90[ 1]:        EMS_ptr = (EMS_handler *)(address.lword);
 91[ 1]:        matches = strncmp (EMS_ptr->name, EMS_name, 8);
 92[ 1]:        return !matches;
 93[ 0]: }
 94[ 0]:
 95[ 0]: /*EMS_status - return the status of the EMS handler*/
 96[ 0]: unsigned EMS_status (void)
 97[ 0]: {
 98[ 1]:        union REGS regs;
 99[ 1]:
100[ 1]:        regs.h.ah = 0x40;
101[ 1]:        int86 (EMS_int, &regs, &regs);
102[ 1]:        return regs.h.ah;
103[ 0]: }
104[ 0]:
105[ 0]: /*EMS_frameaddr - return the address of the page frame*/
106[ 0]: void *EMS_frameaddr (void)
107[ 0]: {
108[ 1]:        union REGS regs;
109[ 1]:
110[ 1]:        regs.h.ah = 0x41;
111[ 1]:        int86 (EMS_int, &regs, &regs);
112[ 1]:        if (regs.h.ah)
```

```
113[ 1]:          return (void *)0;
114[ 1]:       frame_segment = regs.x.bx;         /*save for future use*/
115[ 1]:       address.sword [1] = regs.x.bx;
116[ 1]:       address.sword [0] = 0;
117[ 1]:       return (void *)address.lword;
118[ 0]: }
119[ 0]:
120[ 0]: /*EMS_pagecount - return the number of unallocated pages*/
121[ 0]: unsigned EMS_pagecount (void)
122[ 0]: {
123[ 1]:       union REGS regs;
124[ 1]:
125[ 1]:       regs.h.ah = 0x42;
126[ 1]:       int86 (EMS_int, &regs, &regs);
127[ 1]:       if (regs.h.ah)
128[ 1]:            return 0;
129[ 1]:       return regs.x.bx;
130[ 0]: }
131[ 0]:
132[ 0]: /*EMS_allocate - allocate the number of pages specified. Return
133[ 0]:                 the page handle*/
134[ 0]: unsigned EMS_allocate (pagecount)
135[ 0]:       unsigned pagecount;
136[ 0]: {
137[ 1]:       union REGS regs;
138[ 1]:
139[ 1]:       regs.h.ah = 0x43;
140[ 1]:       regs.x.bx = pagecount;
141[ 1]:       int86 (EMS_int, &regs, &regs);
142[ 1]:       if (regs.h.ah)
143[ 1]:            return 0;
144[ 1]:       return regs.x.dx;
145[ 0]: }
146[ 0]:
147[ 0]: /*EMS_map - map an EMS page into one of the frame page slots. Return
148[ 0]:                 status returned from call*/
149[ 0]: unsigned EMS_map (page, frameslot, handle)
150[ 0]:       unsigned page, frameslot, handle;
151[ 0]: {
152[ 1]:       union REGS regs;
153[ 1]:
154[ 1]:       regs.h.ah = 0x44;
155[ 1]:       regs.x.bx = page;
156[ 1]:       regs.h.al = (char)frameslot;
157[ 1]:       regs.x.dx = handle;
158[ 1]:       int86 (EMS_int, &regs, &regs);
159[ 1]:       return regs.h.ah;
160[ 0]: }
161[ 0]:
162[ 0]: /*EMS_deallocate - deallocate the pages attached to a page handle*/
163[ 0]: unsigned EMS_deallocate (handle)
164[ 0]:       unsigned handle;
165[ 0]: {
166[ 1]:       union REGS regs;
167[ 1]:
168[ 1]:       regs.h.ah = 0x45;
```

```
169[ 1]:        regs.x.dx = handle;
170[ 1]:        int86 (EMS_int, &regs, &regs);
171[ 1]:        return regs.h.ah;
172[ 0]: }
173[ 0]:
174[ 0]: /*EMS_slotaddr - given a slot number, calculate its address.
175[ 0]:                     EMS_frameaddr() must be called first*/
176[ 0]: void *EMS_slotaddr (slotnum)
177[ 0]:        unsigned slotnum;
178[ 0]: {
179[ 1]:        if (slotnum > 3)
180[ 1]:            return 0;
181[ 1]:        address.sword [1] = frame_segment;
182[ 1]:        address.sword [0] = frame_offsets [slotnum];
183[ 1]:        return (void *)address.lword;
184[ 0]: }
```

Using EMS Memory from DESQview

There is no immediate connection between DESQview and EMS memory, even though DESQview makes use of EMS memory. Application programs that use EMS memory execute under DESQview just like any other programs. However, EMS does provide the capability of easily communicating large blocks of data between tasks.

Even though accessible from all tasks, common memory is very limited in size. In addition, it cannot be allocated through a *malloc()* like an API call. Shared system memory is both dynamic and allocatable through a DESQview API call, but it has the problem that it still comes from conventional memory. Large blocks of shared system memory take up room normally needed for program space.

By comparison, a single EMS page may hold a message of up to 16K in length. Messages up to 64K in length may be created from multiple EMS pages. Messages larger than this can simply be divided up among several pages. Of course, there is no way to tell DESQview to allocate a message directly out of expanded memory. Fortunately, however, this is not necessary.

The sending program merely needs to allocate the expanded memory itself. It may then use the expanded memory to hold the data desired. To send this block to another process, the program only needs to send a message containing the page handle and, perhaps, an indication of the number of pages in the message. The receiving process can then use the handle to map the data into its page frame and access it as desired. If the data is to be passed on to other processes for continued processing, the procedure is repeated: place the handle into a message and send it on.

Conceptually, this method is identical to passing messages that contain the address of shared system memory blocks, except that in this case the address has been replaced by an EMS memory handle. EMS blocks offer the advantage of very high communication bandwidth. The message size does not increase with the amount of data (since only the handle is transmitted).

Just as with messages passed via shared memory, the sending process normally forgets about the EMS handle once it had been sent to the receiving process. It is safest when only one process accesses the data at a time. It is possible, however, for two processes to communicate via flags defined within a block of EMS memory. Both processes simply map the EMS memory block into their page frames. The same protocols apply as those applying to communication through variables in conventional memory.

The added variable of which block is mapped where does not add any additional complexity. DESQview handles mapping pages properly during process switches. If, for example, one process has a given EMS page mapped into frame slot zero while another process has the same page mapped into frame slot three and a different page in slot zero, this causes no problem. As part of the process switch during scheduling, DESQview takes care to remap the pages into their proper slots before giving control to a process.

This communication path is not limited to different processes. Even tasks within the same process may use this communication path. However, here the sending task may not continue to access an EMS memory handle it has passed to another task in the same process without the protection of some type of semaphore. Otherwise, one task could remap a block of memory being accessed by another task.

The program EMSTST2.C gives an example of two tasks that communicate blocks of data via EMS memory. The outline is very similar to the message passing programs seen earlier. In this case, however, a single subtask is started. The main program allocates a block of EMS memory, maps it into slot zero, and writes data into it.

The block, along with an indication of the amount of data in it, is then sent to the subtask. The subtask maps the block into slot 3 and prints the contents into its window. Once finished, the subtask returns the block to the EMS handler. The message back to the main task signals that it is okay to allocate another block and repeat the process. The entire process is repeated fifty times with ever-decreasing amounts of data.

```
 1[ 0]: /***********************************************************************
 2[ 0]:    EMS Test #2 - check for the presence of EMS memory.  If present,
 3[ 0]:                 use the EMS blocks to communicate information between
 4[ 0]:                 a main and subtask.  (Send a message containing the
 5[ 0]:                 EMS handle of the block containing the data).
 6[ 0]: ***********************************************************************
 7[ 0]: #include <stdio.h>
 8[ 0]: #include <dos.h>
 9[ 0]: #include "dvapi.h"
10[ 0]:
11[ 0]: /* minimum API version required and actual API version */
12[ 0]: #define required 0x201
13[ 0]: int  version;
14[ 0]:
15[ 0]: #define EMS_int 0x67
16[ 0]: #define EMS_name "EMMXXXX0"
17[ 0]:
18[ 0]: /*prototype declarations for locally declared functions*/
19[ 0]: void main (void);
20[ 0]: void program_body (void);
21[ 0]: ulong fork (int, int, char *, int);
22[ 0]: int subtask (void);
23[ 0]: unsigned EMS_present (void);
24[ 0]: unsigned EMS_status (void);
25[ 0]: void    *EMS_frameaddr (void);
26[ 0]: unsigned EMS_pagecount (void);
27[ 0]: unsigned EMS_allocate (unsigned);
28[ 0]: unsigned EMS_map (unsigned, unsigned, unsigned);
29[ 0]: unsigned EMS_deallocate (unsigned);
30[ 0]: void *EMS_slotaddr (unsigned);
31[ 0]:
32[ 0]: /*use the union 'address' to access the segment and offset portions
```

```
33[ 0]:    of an 8086 address seperately*/
34[ 0]: union {
35[ 1]:        ulong    lword;
36[ 1]:        unsigned sword[2];
37[ 0]:        } address;
38[ 0]:
39[ 0]: /*these globals are used to calculate the frame address*/
40[ 0]: unsigned frame_segment;
41[ 0]: unsigned frame_offsets [] = {0x0000, 0x4000, 0x8000, 0xC000};
42[ 0]:
43[ 0]:
44[ 0]: /*main - start up the Desqview API*/
45[ 0]: void main (void)
46[ 0]: {
47[ 1]:   version = api_init();
48[ 1]:   if (version < required) {
49[ 2]:     printf ("This program requires DESQview version %d.02%d or later.\
50[ 2]:             required/256,required%256);
51[ 1]:   }
52[ 1]:
53[ 1]:   /* tell DESQview what extensions to enable and start application */
54[ 1]:   else {
55[ 2]:     api_level (required);
56[ 2]:     if (EMS_present ())
57[ 2]:         if (EMS_status () == 0) {
58[ 3]:             EMS_frameaddr ();
59[ 3]:             program_body();
60[ 3]:             api_exit();
61[ 3]:             exit (0);
62[ 2]:         }
63[ 2]:
64[ 2]:     win_disperor (win_me (),
65[ 2]:                   "Requires EMS memory or emulator", 31,
66[ 2]:                   0, 0, 1, 0);
67[ 1]:   }
68[ 0]: }
69[ 0]:
70[ 0]: /*program body - start up 2 tasks and let them communicate
71[ 0]:                 sequences of random numbers via a block of EMS memory
72[ 0]:
73[ 0]: struct message {                /*format of message to initiate child
74[ 1]:                 int xloc;       /*column of window*/
75[ 1]:                 int yloc;       /*row of window*/
76[ 1]:                 ulong parent;   /*handle of parent task*/
77[ 0]:                 };
78[ 0]:
79[ 0]: struct datamsg {
80[ 1]:                 unsigned handle;  /*EMS memory handle*/
81[ 1]:                 unsigned nowords; /*number of words of data present*/
82[ 0]:                 };
83[ 0]:
84[ 0]:
85[ 0]: void program_body (void)
86[ 0]: {
87[ 1]:   int i, j, *data;
88[ 1]:   ulong winhan, tskhan, mymail, hismail;
```

```
 89[ 1]:   struct datamsg msg;
 90[ 1]:   int *msgptr;
 91[ 1]:   int  msglngth;
 92[ 1]:   unsigned handle;
 93[ 1]:   #define STACKSIZE 1000
 94[ 1]:   char stacks [STACKSIZE];
 95[ 1]:
 96[ 1]:   winhan = win_new ("Main Program", 12, 15, 60);
 97[ 1]:   win_move (winhan, 1, 1);
 98[ 1]:   win_logattr (winhan, 1);
 99[ 1]:   win_attr (winhan, 1);
100[ 1]:   win_unhide (winhan);
101[ 1]:   win_top (winhan);
102[ 1]:
103[ 1]:   /*now start subtask as a seperate task*/
104[ 1]:   tskhan = fork (18, 8, stacks, STACKSIZE);
105[ 1]:
106[ 1]:   /*wait for subtask to indicate that it is finished and
107[ 1]:     then allocate a block of EMS memory and send it some
108[ 1]:     (more) random numbers 100 times in a loop*/
109[ 1]:   mymail = mal_me ();
110[ 1]:   hismail = mal_of (tskhan);
111[ 1]:   read (mymail, &msgptr, &msglngth);
112[ 1]:   for (i = 50; i; i--) {
113[ 2]:
114[ 2]:       /*allocate a block of EMS memory*/
115[ 2]:       handle = EMS_allocate (1);
116[ 2]:       EMS_map (0, 0, handle);
117[ 2]:
118[ 2]:       /*now write something into it and show user*/
119[ 2]:       data = EMS_slotaddr (0);
120[ 2]:       for (j = i * 2; j; j--) {
121[ 3]:           *data = j+i;
122[ 3]:           win_printf (winhan, "%x, ", *data++);
123[ 2]:       }
124[ 2]:       win_printf (winhan, "\n\n");
125[ 2]:
126[ 2]:       /*send the block in a message to the subtask and wait until
127[ 2]:         he's finished with it before continuing*/
128[ 2]:       msg.handle  = handle;
129[ 2]:       msg.nowords = i * 2;
130[ 2]:       mal_write (hismail, &msg, sizeof (msg));
131[ 2]:       mal_read (mymail, &msgptr, &msglngth);
132[ 1]:   }
133[ 1]:
134[ 1]:   /*now send termination message and await acknowledgement before quit
135[ 1]:   msg.nowords = 0;
136[ 1]:   mal_write (hismail, &msg, sizeof (msg));
137[ 1]:   mal_read (mymail, &msgptr, &msglngth);
138[ 1]:   win_free (winhan);
139[ 0]: }
140[ 0]:
141[ 0]: /*fork - fork a new task*/
142[ 0]: ulong fork (x, y, stack, stacksize)
143[ 0]:   int x, y;
144[ 0]:   char *stack;
```

```
145[ 0]:    int stacksize;
146[ 0]: {
147[ 1]:    ulong tskhan;
148[ 1]:    struct message msg;
149[ 1]:
150[ 1]:    /*start the subtask*/
151[ 1]:    tskhan = tsk_new (  subtask,  stack, stacksize,
152[ 1]:                        "Subtask",     7,      15,     60);
153[ 1]:
154[ 1]:    /*now send it a message containing its location information*/
155[ 1]:    msg.xloc = x;
156[ 1]:    msg.yloc = y;
157[ 1]:    msg.parent = tsk_me();
158[ 1]:    mal_write (mal_of (tskhan), &msg, sizeof(msg));
159[ 1]:
160[ 1]:    /*finally return the task handle*/
161[ 1]:    return tskhan;
162[ 0]: }
163[ 0]:
164[ 0]: /*subtask - an example subtask which receives data in EMS memory
165[ 0]:                blocks.  This task merely prints the data so the user
166[ 0]:                can compare it with the original*/
167[ 0]: int subtask (void)
168[ 0]: {
169[ 1]:    int i;
170[ 1]:    ulong winhan, parenthan;
171[ 1]:    struct message *msgptr;
172[ 1]:    struct datamsg *dataptr;
173[ 1]:    int   msglngth, *data;
174[ 1]:
175[ 1]:    /*wait for an initiation message with location information
176[ 1]:       and set up window to match*/
177[ 1]:    mal_read (mal_me(), &msgptr, &msglngth);
178[ 1]:    winhan = win_me();
179[ 1]:    win_move (winhan, msgptr->yloc, msgptr->xloc);
180[ 1]:    win_logattr (winhan,1);
181[ 1]:    win_attr (winhan, 2);
182[ 1]:    win_unhide (winhan);
183[ 1]:    win_top (winhan);
184[ 1]:
185[ 1]:    /*now send a message indicating we are ready for data.  Continue
186[ 1]:       receiving data until a data count of zero is received.*/
187[ 1]:    parenthan = mal_of (msgptr->parent);
188[ 1]:    for (;;) {
189[ 2]:        /*read message with EMS handle*/
190[ 2]:        mal_read (mal_me (), &dataptr, &msglngth);
191[ 2]:
192[ 2]:        /*if no data, exit loop*/
193[ 2]:        if (!dataptr->nowords)
194[ 2]:            break;
195[ 2]:
196[ 2]:        /*map page EMS into frame slot 3*/
197[ 2]:        EMS_map (0, 3, dataptr->handle);
198[ 2]:
199[ 2]:        /*print data to window*/
200[ 2]:        data = EMS_slotaddr (3);
```

```
201[ 2]:          for (i = dataptr->nowords; i; i--)
202[ 2]:              win_printf (winhan, "%x, ", *data++);
203[ 2]:          win_printf (winhan, "\n\n");
204[ 2]:
205[ 2]:          /*deallocate EMS page and acknowledge completion*/
206[ 2]:          EMS_deallocate (dataptr->handle);
207[ 2]:          mal_write (parenthan, "", 1);
208[ 1]:     }
209[ 1]:
210[ 1]:     /*acknowedge termination*/
211[ 1]:     mal_write (parenthan, "", 1);
212[ 1]:     win_free (winhan);
213[ 0]: }
214[ 0]:
215[ 0]: /*EMS_present - return a 1 if EMS handler found to be present;
216[ 0]:                     0 otherwise*/
217[ 0]: typedef struct {
218[ 1]:                  char padding [0x0a];
219[ 1]:                  char name [9];
220[ 0]:                  } EMS_handler;
221[ 0]: EMS_handler *EMS_ptr;
222[ 0]:
223[ 0]: #define getvect(x) (*(void * *)(EMS_int * 4))
224[ 0]: unsigned EMS_present (void)
225[ 0]: {
226[ 1]:     unsigned matches;
227[ 1]:
228[ 1]:     address.lword = (ulong)getvect (EMS_int);
229[ 1]:     address.sword [0] = 0;
230[ 1]:     EMS_ptr = (EMS_handler *)(address.lword);
231[ 1]:     matches = strncmp (EMS_ptr->name, EMS_name, 8);
232[ 1]:     return !matches;
233[ 0]: }
234[ 0]:
235[ 0]: /*EMS_status - return the status of the EMS handler*/
236[ 0]: unsigned EMS_status (void)
237[ 0]: {
238[ 1]:     union REGS regs;
239[ 1]:
240[ 1]:     regs.h.ah = 0x40;
241[ 1]:     int86 (EMS_int, &regs, &regs);
242[ 1]:     return regs.h.ah;
243[ 0]: }
244[ 0]:
245[ 0]: /*EMS_frameaddr - return the address of the page frame*/
246[ 0]: void *EMS_frameaddr (void)
247[ 0]: {
248[ 1]:     union REGS regs;
249[ 1]:
250[ 1]:     regs.h.ah = 0x41;
251[ 1]:     int86 (EMS_int, &regs, &regs);
252[ 1]:     if (regs.h.ah)
253[ 1]:         return (void *)0;
254[ 1]:     frame_segment = regs.x.bx;          /*save for future use*/
255[ 1]:     address.sword [1] = regs.x.bx;
256[ 1]:     address.sword [0] = 0;
```

```
257[ 1]:      return (void *)address.lword;
258[ 0]: }
259[ 0]:
260[ 0]: /*EMS_pagecount - return the number of unallocated pages*/
261[ 0]: unsigned EMS_pagecount (void)
262[ 0]: {
263[ 1]:      union REGS regs;
264[ 1]:
265[ 1]:      regs.h.ah = 0x42;
266[ 1]:      int86 (EMS_int, &regs, &regs);
267[ 1]:      if (regs.h.ah)
268[ 1]:           return 0;
269[ 1]:      return regs.x.bx;
270[ 0]: }
271[ 0]:
272[ 0]: /*EMS_allocate - allocate the number of pages specified. Return
273[ 0]:                 the page handle*/
274[ 0]: unsigned EMS_allocate (pagecount)
275[ 0]:      unsigned pagecount;
276[ 0]: {
277[ 1]:      union REGS regs;
278[ 1]:
279[ 1]:      regs.h.ah = 0x43;
280[ 1]:      regs.x.bx = pagecount;
281[ 1]:      int86 (EMS_int, &regs, &regs);
282[ 1]:      if (regs.h.ah)
283[ 1]:           return 0;
284[ 1]:      return regs.x.dx;
285[ 0]: }
286[ 0]:
287[ 0]: /*EMS_map - map an EMS page into one of the frame page slots. Return
288[ 0]:            status returned from call*/
289[ 0]: unsigned EMS_map (page, frameslot, handle)
290[ 0]:      unsigned page, frameslot, handle;
291[ 0]: {
292[ 1]:      union REGS regs;
293[ 1]:
294[ 1]:      regs.h.ah = 0x44;
295[ 1]:      regs.x.bx = page;
296[ 1]:      regs.h.al = (char)frameslot;
297[ 1]:      regs.x.dx = handle;
298[ 1]:      int86 (EMS_int, &regs, &regs);
299[ 1]:      return regs.h.ah;
300[ 0]: }
301[ 0]:
302[ 0]: /*EMS_deallocate - deallocate the pages attached to a page handle*/
303[ 0]: unsigned EMS_deallocate (handle)
304[ 0]:      unsigned handle;
305[ 0]: {
306[ 1]:      union REGS regs;
307[ 1]:
308[ 1]:      regs.h.ah = 0x45;
309[ 1]:      regs.x.dx = handle;
310[ 1]:      int86 (EMS_int, &regs, &regs);
311[ 1]:      return regs.h.ah;
312[ 0]: }
```

```
313[ 0]:
314[ 0]: /*EMS_slotaddr - given a slot number, calculate its address.
315[ 0]:                   EMS_frameaddr() must be called first*/
316[ 0]: void *EMS_slotaddr (slotnum)
317[ 0]:     unsigned slotnum;
318[ 0]: {
319[ 1]:     if (slotnum > 3)
320[ 1]:         return 0;
321[ 1]:     address.sword [1] = frame_segment;
322[ 1]:     address.sword [0] = frame_offsets [slotnum];
323[ 1]:     return (void *)address.lword;
324[ 0]: }
```

In this example program, the memory blocks being passed are largely empty. However, neither the program complexity nor the time to send the blocks increases as the amount of data increases.

Actually, the time to print the contents of the blocks is considerably longer than the time to transmit them between tasks. To get a feel for the actual transmission time, rerun the programs with the *win_printf()* calls commented out.

Sharing Code

As previously noted, entering a * in the *Shared Program* pathname field of the *Advanced Options* menu allows programs to share data in the shared system memory area. This, of course, is not the only use for this field. It is also possible for programs to share code.

When DESQview starts a new process, it begins by loading the specified program into memory. A check is then made of the *Shared Program* field of the *.DVP* file. If a file name is present in this field, then DESQview checks to see if this *shared program* is already in memory. If not, DESQview loads it into shared system memory. DESQview passes control to the shared program immediately prior to giving control to the user program itself.

The shared program is also passed control after the program terminates, but before DESQview removes it from memory. The shared program itself remains in shared system memory as long as one or more programs referencing it are active. As soon as the last program referencing a shared program terminates, the shared program is removed from memory as well.

A single program may have more than one shared program. To do so, a file name preceded by a + is provided in the *.DVP* file. With the plus sign, DESQview assumes that the file contains a list of filename pairs. Each pair is a shared program with a corresponding shared data file. The shared programs are loaded independently into shared system memory. They are then called by DESQview in the order in which they appear in the *plus-file* immediately prior to giving control to the user program.

There are several reasons for this feature. The first is simply to allow a DESQview-incompatible program to be made DESQview-aware. A special shared program called a loader is specified in the *.DVP* file for such a program. DESQview automatically loads these loaders when the user attempts to execute the application. Since the shared program gets control before the application, it can *reach* into the application and patch an offending section of code to make the program more DESQview-tolerant. For example, the loader for many applications causes them to write to virtual screen memory instead of directly to the screen so that they may be properly windowed.

This patch may take the form of actually editing a particular section of code or it may be merely a matter of installing itself into an interrupt, much like a TSR-type utility. A shared program that has installed itself into an interrupt need not worry about confusing other processes. DESQview keeps the interrupt vectors for different processes separate by replacing all 0x100 hex interrupts upon task switches. Thus, a TSR established for one process has no effect on other processes. A shared program may remove itself from an interrupt when it receives control at termination.

Developers may also use this feature when attempting to integrate an existing program into their system. It is always preferable to address any problems in the source code and recompile. If, however, the source code is not available, a shared program may make whatever changes desired to the operation of the program in the same way that DESQview's loaders do.

As important as it might be, the ability to patch programs is not the most important aspect of this feature to developers using the DESQview API. More important is the *shared* aspect of shared programs. Before a shared program is loaded, DESQview checks to see if the program is not already present in memory. If so, the copy already present is given control. Duplicate copies of the shared program are not loaded.

Programs developed together always shared large sections of code. For example, the C library containing such mundane functions as *printf()* must be linked together with the compiled C object to generate the executable file. Although the entire library is not necessarily loaded into every program, the sections that are loaded are identical with the sections loaded into every other program developed with the same compiler. It is a waste of RAM to load a new copy of the C library into RAM every time a program is executed.

It could save a large amount of memory to include common functions as a shared program. Since shared programs are only loaded once, each subsequent program that is started would simply use the copy of the C library program already in memory. When fully developed, this concept is known as *Dynamic Link libraries*.

DESQview's shared programs are not complete Dynamic Link libraries. The user cannot simply select a particular C library to be dynamically linked at execution time. The user can implement different forms of shared libraries, however.

The program may decide to include common functions (for example, a database library) into a shared program and make them accessible through an interrupt, much like the PC's BIOS routines. During initiation, the shared program simply inserts its own address into an interrupt. To access this library, the application program loads its registers and then invokes the proper software interrupt, perhaps via the *INT86()* library call seen earlier.

Software interrupts are not the only means for C programs to communicate with shared programs. Shared programs are allowed to perform DESQview calls. A shared program may also load up the addresses of its entry points and send them in a message to the process mailbox. The application process can then read that mail message upon starting to find the address of the routines to invoke.

In the extreme case, the entire program might actually be in the shared program, the application itself being nothing but a stub. Once the shared program was given control, it would not actually return it until it was time to terminate. The main program would then be executed and then immediately terminated, passing control to the shared termination routine before eventually unloading the entire thing from memory. This would allow the user to execute as many copies of a program as desired with very little memory overhead. Just as multiple tasks within the same process share the same code segment, processes executing entirely out of shared programs utilize the same memory. Only the data and stack segments would be unique to the process.

For example, assume an application that must simultaneously monitor several serial ports. It is possible to write one program to monitor all available serial ports. It is easier, however, to write a single process to monitor a single, user-selectable port. The user can execute the process separately for each port. Although this is a superior solution since it is both easier to write and debug, and it allows more control of which ports are monitored at execution time, in a normal environment the code for this process must be duplicated for each port being monitored, resulting in some wasted memory. If written entirely as a shared program, however, all ports would be monitored by the same code segment executing as different processes.

Several unique requirements are placed upon shared programs. The format of a shared program must be that of a *.COM* file. That is, the file must contain a straight binary image of the program in memory. No conversion is done during the loading of the program. This effectively limits a shared program to 64K in length.

Unlike a *.COM* file, however, execution of a shared program begins at offset zero. When called at initialization, DESQview passes the address of the application's Program Segment Prefix, the application's window handle, and the drive and path of the DESQview directory to the shared program. DESQview also passes a zero in the *CX* register. When called at termination, DESQview returns many of the registers to it by the shared program. It also passes a value of one in the *CX* register. Figure 6.14 shows this in tabular form.

The shared program executes a *RET FAR 12* to return to DESQview. If the Carry Flag is clear, it is assumed that no error occurred. If the Carry Flag is set and *AX* contains a zero, then DESQview terminates the application without a message. If, however, the Carry Flag is set and *AX* is non-zero, the application is terminated and an error message generated.

Figure 6.14—Arguments to a Shared Program

At initialization:

```
CX          contains a 0
DX          Program Segment Prefix segment
            (offset is 0)
SS          upper 16 bits of task's window handle
            (lower 16 bits are 0)
SP          points to:
               return address            [4 bytes]
               length of shared data string [4 bytes]
               address of shared data string [4 bytes]
               address of DESQview directory [4 bytes]
```

At termination:

```
CX          contains a 1
SS          upper 16 bits of task's window handle
BP,DS,SI,ES,DI values returned at initialization
```

Because of the strict requirements placed on shared programs by this interface with DESQview, shared programs are almost always written in assembly language.

Other Uses for Shared Programs

DESQview does not execute a shared program until immediately before giving control to the process. Since the entire process is *ready to run*, the shared program may make DESQview calls. When doing so, the shared program is making calls as if it were the process being started (which it is).

Shared programs may execute DESQview calls when terminating as well. This provides several interesting capabilities. For example, a process may start other processes using the *app_start()* API call. DESQview does not provide notification to the original process when the new process actually starts, nor when it terminates. This problem is easily solved by attaching a shared program to the new process. Upon initialization, the shared program sends a *starting* message back to the original process, letting it know that the process has now started. Upon termination, the shared program sends a notification message as well, letting the original process know that the new process is no longer executing.

Shared programs can take on more challenging tasks, such as creating tasks of their own that continue to execute even after the application is allowed to start. For example, a shared program might establish *Help* notification on the default-process window. The shared program might then spawn a subtask to read the process's mailbox for notification messages. The shared program would allow the application to execute unaffected. With *Help* notification enabled, however, the user could select *Help* from the DESQview menu at any time. The resulting notification message would wake up the shared program subtask from its read. The subtask could then open a window to provide help information on the application.

A shared program can establish a pointer handler to add mouse capabilities to an application that is otherwise mouse oblivious. Here again, the shared program would spawn a subtask to read the pointer object for notification of mouse movement. Mouse movement would then be reported to the normal application by mailing the proper keystrokes to the keyboard object. Likewise, selecting fields defined by the application could also be interpreted, albeit with somewhat more difficulty. The application program would then perceive mouse movements as the user entering commands from the keyboard.

One could envision an object-oriented system built around shared programs and the DESQview message-passing system. Each different object class would be contained within a different shared program. Applications only include objects which they access by including the required shared programs in their *.DVP* files. As each shared program is executed at initialization, each class would be offered the chance to initialize itself (constructors, to use object-oriented terminology). Each class would establish a named mailbox when first executed to handle methods of that class. For example, a database class might define mailbox *DATA*.

Simple functions within each of the applications would then convert calls to the classes into messages for the appropriate-named mailbox. Just as the messages examined earlier, these messages would contain the mailbox handle of the caller to allow the class to respond properly. A properly constructed set of such shared applications would result in a capable *Smalltalk-type* object-oriented system.

The advantages to implementing these concepts in shared images are:

- the programmer may add shared programs to applications to which he does not have the source code

- shared programs are not duplicated no matter how many applications use them at once

- in the case of an object-oriented system built around shared programs, individual classes can be updated, expanded, or replaced without changing the application program that accesses them (this is a primary attraction of object-oriented systems)

- the user may remove the shared program from the *.DVP* if the capability that it adds is either not needed or not worth the memory required

This latter capability is truly amazing. The user may decide at execution time whether the capability added by the shared program is worth the cost in memory. For example, a shared program that adds *Help* capability may be useful for the beginner, but may also reduce the amount of data the program can handle by consuming conventional memory. The user may choose to include the *Help*-shared program during the learning period. Once comfortable with the command structure, however, the user may choose to regain the memory by removing this shared program from the *.DVP* file. The user can make this decision at any time (and reverse the decision) merely by editing the *.DVP* file.

This level of control is typical of programs divided into multiple processes under a multitasking operating environment like DESQview. It is also typical of the level of control that DESQview allows both the user and the application software through the DESQview API.

chapter 7

Critical Sections and Semaphores

During our discussion of task switching in Chapter 3, we saw how allowing more than one task access to a given memory location may cause problems. We did not examine the problem in depth at that time, but rather just to the point of allowing the example tasks, applications, and processes to execute properly. In this chapter I will revisit the subject of data collisions and critical sections in more detail.

A data collision occurs when two tasks attempt to write the same location at the same time. In a multiple processor system (a system that actually has more than one CPU), this statement sometimes means exactly what it says. The two processors attempt to write to a given memory location at the very same time. In a conventional single-processor system, which includes all DOS machines, you might not think data collisions to be a problem. However, this situation can still arise in a multitasking environment like DESQview.

Take the following example: Suppose that the program that calculates balances at my bank executes as multiple independent tasks. There are several different tasks, but task A and task B, which handle different types of input, can both debit and credit my balance. Task A receives a deposit of $100 from an ATM machine across town. Before task A can add the $100 to my account, it must know how much is currently in my account, so it reads out the current balance of $1,000 and performs the addition with the expected result of $1,100.

Before it can write the balance back out, however, task A's time expires, i.e., the timer interrupt occurs and DESQview takes control of the CPU away from task A. Task B, being the next task in line, is then given control. Task B picks up an interbank deposit of $200 to my account and processes it, leaving a resulting balance of $1,200. Task B then completes and gives control back to DESQview.

Sooner or later task A gets control again and continues with the interrupted instruction; that is, it writes the previously calculated $1,100 balance to my bank account, overwriting the $1,200 balance already there. That $100 deposit I just made has ended up costing me $200!

Figure 7.1—Time Line for Data Collision Between Two Tasks

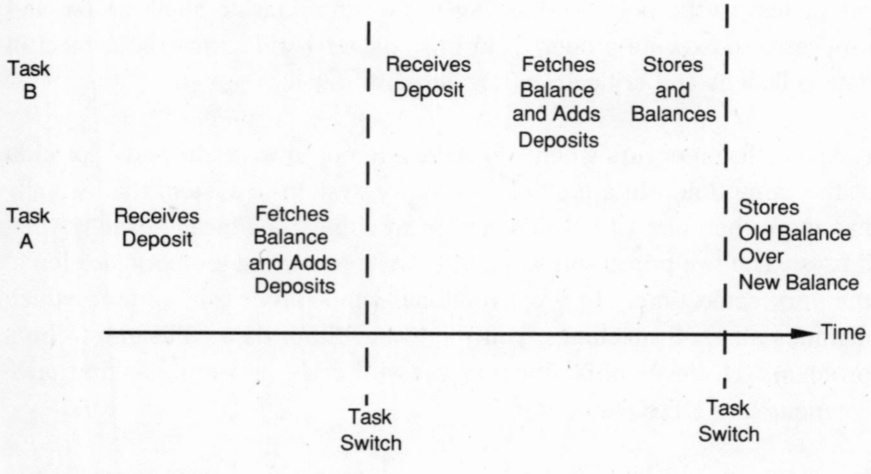

Data collisions may occur anytime two different sets of software execute asynchronously with respect to each other (in this context, *asynchronous* means that the timing between two events or tasks is not predictable). This may happen even in single-tasking systems with functions that service external interrupts. An interrupt can occur at any time, resulting in the immediate *scheduling* of the interrupt routine. The programmer can never be sure when the interrupt will occur. However, in a preemptive system like DESQview, the potential for these interactions exists between any two tasks as well.

In exactly the same way, collisions may occur on data contained within files. Assume that my balance is contained in a disk record (which I hope that it is!) and replay the example problem above. The same loss of data occurs whether the data is contained in RAM or on a disk somewhere. In fact, the problem is considerably worse when the data is disk resident. Since the time required to write a record to disk is so much longer than to simply write a variable to memory, the *window of vulnerability* is much larger, making the problem more likely to occur. (Locking of files, a feature implemented in DOS primarily to support LANs, can help reduce file collisions.)

Collisions may occur around hardware devices as well, although not usually with such serious consequences. Two tasks may simultaneously attempt to access the printer or serial port, for example. Generally, the results are a garbled mixture of output from the two tasks, but no real harm is done. The user recognizes the output as being in error and restarts the output request, presumably taking steps this time to keep the printer collision from occurring.

Some hardware devices are not so forgiving, however. For example, robots must be controlled with great dependability. The garbling of two movement commands that have been transmitted simultaneously may be disastrous.

It should be kept in mind that even though I might only discuss data collisions, other types of collisions can be just as dangerous. However, all collisions are prevented in the same way. The lessons from data collisions can be extended to cover the other cases as well.

Avoiding Collisions

An area of code in which a collision can occur is known as a *critical section* or *critical region*. In our bank example, task A was in a critical section of its program from the time it read my bank balance until the time it wrote the updated balance back out. Task B entered a mutual critical section when it read my balance to add the $200 interbank transfer and left the critical section when it wrote the bank balance back out. Collisions occur when two or more tasks are in mutually critical regions simultaneously.

Notice that a single task may have many critical sections. Every place where a task reads, manipulates, and then writes back a location in memory is a critical section if any other task can write to the same location.

Critical regions may be very small, sometimes containing only a few instructions. This is usually the case with critical regions centered around single-memory locations such as my RAM-resident bank balance. Yet no matter how small the region might be, it can not be overlooked. The size of an unprotected critical region is only an expression of the likelihood that a collision will occur. Given sufficient time, a collision is certain.

Protecting critical sections to avoid collisions without unnecessary loss in efficiency is a subject that has been studied in some detail by operating-system designers. Any solution addressing this problem properly should have the following five properties.[*]

1) No two tasks may be simultaneously in their mutually critical sections.
2) No assumptions may be made about relative process speeds or how long a process will continue to execute before being interrupted, nor about when a task will execute.

---

[*] Tanenbaum, Andrew S., *Operating Systems—Design and Implementation*. Englewood Cliffs, NJ: Prentice-Hall, Inc., 1987.

3) No process not within its critical section should affect other processes from entering their critical sections.
4) No process should be forced to wait forever under any circumstance to enter its critical section.
5) No process within its critical section should affect other processes that are not attempting to enter their critical section.

The first rule is simply the definition of a data collision. This a statement of what it is we are trying to avoid. We will use the next four rules as a guide in evaluating potential solutions to the collision problem.

Timing Solutions

When novice programmers first run into the collision problem, they are often tempted to take the *time it right* approach. In this approach, the programmer takes advantage of subtle timing considerations to make (reasonably) certain that a collision will not occur. In our banking example, suppose we knew that interbank transfers only occur at midnight. A programmer might, with some justification, assume the chances of a teller deposit being made at midnight are quite slim. Thus, the argument goes, there is no possibility of collision and the problem can be ignored.

The advantage to this approach is that it requires no extra programming. It does, however, conflict with rule two. The programmer has made an assumption that makes the possibility of a collision much smaller, but which does not exclude it entirely. In many ways this only makes the problem worse, since it makes the collision condition that much harder to find.

Relying upon such subtle timing effects hides another danger as well. The programmer is depending on facts over which the program has no control. Suppose a new bank president comes in and decides for whatever reason that it is more advantageous to run interbank transfers at noon during normal banking hours and not at midnight. The assumption upon which our solution rests is no longer valid and the program ceases to work for reasons that are not at all obvious. Programmers who made these decisions are likely to be long gone and, unless they have documented these limitations very carefully (which is unlikely), their successors will have a very difficult job finding the problem.

Generally, timing solutions involve shorter periods of time than hours. The programmer uses the relative timing between the tasks to avoid the collision. For example, assume that task A and B begin at the same time. The argument might go something like: "Task A and B start at the same time. Task A's critical region is right at the beginning of the task while task B's region is near the end. Task A should have plenty of time to finish its critical section before task B starts." This violates rule two as well. We cannot know that task A will not get suspended for a long period or that task A will not be given a large number of transactions to work, giving task B the chance to get ahead and cause the collision.

The objection mentioned above applies here as well. Someone may decide, for some reason, to rewrite task B so that it enters its critical region at the beginning of its processing rather than at the end. When task A no longer works, it will not be at all obvious what has caused the problem.

We must reject any solution that violates rule two. Such solutions are not deterministic. Even though the program might work now (at least, most of the time), small changes to the system might invalidate our timing assumptions in ways which may not be at all obvious, generating seemingly unrelated and bizarre effects. Systems based upon these types of interactions tend to be very fragile, breaking when even the smallest changes are made. Although it is theoretically possible that all of these interactions could be documented, in practice it never works this way. In fact, programmers may not even be aware of all of the fortuitous timing interactions that are protecting their otherwise unshielded critical sections.

Disabling Scheduling

A second approach is to simply disable rescheduling during the time that a task plans to be in its critical section. This ensures that no other tasks can get control of the system to execute their critical sections until rescheduling is reenabled after the task has exited its critical region.

Hardware interrupts can (and do) still occur; however, if (as is usually the case) the collision problem is only with other tasks, then they cause no problems. The task may be interrupted in the middle of its critical section, but only as long as the interrupt service routine does not execute a mutually critical section of its own. As soon as the interrupt is serviced, control returns to the interrupted task that completes its critical section.

In DESQview, the *api_beginc()* and *api_endc()* API calls disable and enable task rescheduling, respectively. These are named for *begin critical region* and *end critical region*, respectively.

This is probably the most widely used means of avoiding collisions between tasks. It is simple and can be applied as an *after the fact fix* to a program where timing solutions have not be designed in.

Unfortunately, this solution stands in violation of rule number five in the following way. If a task in its critical region has multitasking disabled, no other tasks are allowed time to be executed. This task keeps other tasks from running, even while they are not attempting to enter their critical region. In fact, even tasks that have no critical region at all are not allowed to execute.

The severity of this situation is largely dependent upon the size of the critical region. If, as in our bank example, the critical region is only a few instructions long, then usually no problem arises. But if the critical section is very large, or if it contains loops or operating system calls that may take a considerable time to execute, then the effects may be quite noticeable. Other tasks will appear to come to a sudden stop and the keyboard and mouse become unresponsive as the currently executing task enters its critical section and then just as suddenly resume execution when the task reenables tasking.

Even without the problem of time, disabling multitasking may not be possible. If an input is expected from other tasks or the operator while the task is within its critical region, then multitasking cannot be disabled. Take, for example, our multitasked banking application. Assume that, while in a critical section processing customer transactions, the teller task requests the customer's balance from the task that debits and credits accounts. If the teller task has multitasking disabled, the debit/credit task cannot execute to provide the teller task its answer.

This solution is also dangerous from another standpoint. System calls that suspend the calling task must reenable scheduling (otherwise the system would become *hung* with no one allowed to execute). Although it is usually obvious which system calls these are, it may not be so obvious that the system calls are being made.

For example, another programmer has written a perfectly nice library routine that reads a file from the floppy drive. If the floppy drive is not ready, the function prompts the user to install a new floppy and then hit any key at the keyboard to signal that it is ready. Since reading the keyboard suspends the calling task, this system call automatically reenables scheduling.

Now suppose that I come along with my critical section and decide to call this routine since, from its description, it looks like just the thing I need to solve my problem. The function works and all is fine until the first time the user forgets to put a floppy in the drive. When the library function gets suspended on the keyboard, scheduling is reenabled, leaving my critical region unprotected. The system crashes for a very nonobvious reason.

Such problems are made even more difficult to track down by the fact that it is usually impossible, or at least very difficult, to execute a task that has disabled rescheduling from a debugger. The debugger will attempt to perform system calls of its own (including reading the keyboard for user input) that will automatically reenable scheduling. The programmer must execute the entire critical section as one instruction, setting a breakpoint before and after it, but not within it. If the critical section itself contains a bug, the programmer must often go to extraordinary measures to locate it.

The DESQview API Debugger from Quarterdeck has several options for handling break points set in critical sections. The API Debugger can either: 1) ignore all break points set within the critical region, treating the entire region between the *api_beginc()* and *api_endc()* as a single instruction; 2) store any API calls made in this region until the *api_endc()* call, at which time the calls are displayed; or 3) ignore the *api_beginc()* and *api_endc()* calls. The user selects which of these options to take by selecting the *Critical* API Debugger command.

Thus, disabling rescheduling is only a reasonable solution for critical sections that are quite short. This is the way in which this solution was used in Chapter 3 to protect the single variable *TCOUNT* from being accessed by multiple tasks. This solution should be avoided if the critical region is either very long or makes function or system calls. If it cannot be avoided, the programmer must carefully document that the rescheduling is to be left off and make sure that all called functions agree.

Latches

Another solution is to guard the critical region with a flag, known as a *latch*. The latch flag indicates whether the critical region is occupied or not. If the flag is set, then the critical section is occupied and it is not safe for other tasks to enter their critical section. On the other hand, if the flag is cleared, then the task can assume that no other tasks are in their critical section and the coast is clear for them to enter. As a warning against other tasks, the task sets the flag upon entering the critical section. Of course, it must clear the flag upon exiting to allow other tasks to proceed.

When analyzed by our four rules, this solution has a lot going for it. No timing assumptions are required and no processes not within their critical sections either affect or are affected by the presence of this latch. Unfortunately, the latch solution has three problems.

First, the latch must be in a memory location accessible by all of the tasks with critical regions. If critical regions exist with more than one data item or piece of hardware, a separate latch may be allocated for each, or a single latch may be employed to lock all of the data items as a group (with the result that tasks will be suspended much more often). For multiple tasks within the same process, this creates no problem. However, if the tasks are to be in different processes, then one of the memory solutions discussed in Chapter 6 must be employed.

The best option in this case is for one process, probably the parent process, to allocate a block of shared-system memory from which all latches are allocated. Of course, the other processes do not automatically know where this latch is located. Thus, the parent process must place the address of the allocated block into a message and send this message to the other processes. Each process reads this message at start up and uses the address contained within the message to reference the latch variables. Blocks of EMS memory can be used as well.

Second, even a casual examination of this solution shows that the latch itself is susceptible to a data collision. Task A might examine the latch and decide that it is safe to set the flag and proceed, but before it can its time slice expires and it loses control. Task B is then started, which also examines the flag and decides it is safe to proceed. When task A is restarted, both task B and task A may be in their critical regions at the same time.

One might first attempt to solve the problem by adding a latch to the latch; this effort is futile. No combination of simple latches will solve the problem. One solution commonly suggested to this problem is the alternating latch. The idea is this: Assume that task A and task B both have a critical section. We can avoid a latch collision if we let the two tasks alternate. Let's just say that if the latch is zero, then it is A's turn, and if it is one, then it must be B's turn. Both tasks examine the flag before beginning their critical sections. As A finishes its critical section, it sets the flag to one to give B a chance, and when B finishes it sets it back to zero for A's benefit.

The simplicity of this solution is appealing. There is a class of problems to which this solution might work. However, it is not a good general solution to our problem as it violates rules three and four: If it is task A's turn, then task B cannot enter its critical region. If task A never attempts to enter its critical region, it effectively locks B out of its region. Task A is keeping task B from entering by *not* requesting entry.

We could avoid collision over the latch variable by disabling scheduling while it is being checked and set. First we disable rescheduling and then we check the latch. If the latch is clear, then we set it, reenable scheduling, and continue on into our critical region. This is a reasonable solution. Disabling scheduling only long enough to check and set a flag has no effect on system performance and no system calls are made that might inadvertently reenable scheduling.

This leads to the third problem of what to do if the latch is set. If a task checks the latch and it finds that it may not proceed into its critical section, exactly what should it do?

One option is to immediately check again in a tight loop, figuring that eventually the lock will be cleared. As soon as it is cleared, we want to be ready. This is known as *busy waiting* and is an extraordinarily bad idea. To DESQview, tasks that busy wait appear to be performing real work and therefore continue to get CPU time. However, programs that continually check a flag do not make very efficient use of the CPU time they receive. Not only do they slow down the rest of the system, they even slow down the program that has the latch and upon which they are waiting.

At the other extreme, the task might suspend itself for a second or two before checking again. Although this removes the strain from the remaining tasks in the system, it puts the task itself at a disadvantage. First, the task might continue to delay for some time even after the flag has been cleared before the timer expires and it checks again. Worse yet, the delaying task might never get the latch at all.

Suppose the task that had the flag in the first place is not so hospitable and does not delay but busy waits instead. This task is likely to give up the latch and then reacquire it before our task times out and checks again. Our task will continue to wait while the more aggressive task executes its critical region over and over in violation of rule four.

In order for our task to get the latch in such a situation, its delay would have to time out just in the instant between when the other task gave up the latch and when it requests it again. As long as this pushy task has work to do, our task will have a very small chance indeed of ever getting through its critical section. If the pushy task is of a higher priority, then this may be exactly what is desired. If the tasks are at all similar in priority, however, a more equitable division is more desirable.

The best compromise is to check the latch once every time the task gets scheduled and simply give control back to the scheduler if the latch is busy. The scheduler will find the next task to schedule and continue on. However, every time through the scheduling loop our task will get a chance to take a look and see if the latch is still set.

The API call *api_pause()* gives control back to the rescheduler. Giving up control with *api_pause()* does not end the critical section—when the task regains control, rescheduling will again be disabled. The proper code to test a latch is as follows:

```
api_beginc();              /*turn scheduler off*/
for (;;) {
    if (latch == 0)        /*if latch is clear...*/
        break;             /*...carry on;...*/
    api_pause();           /*...otherwise, let others try*/
}
latch = 1;                 /*set latch for us*/
api_endc();                 /*reenable scheduling*/
```

This is not a perfect solution. There is still a certain amount of wasted overhead involved with repeatedly scheduling a task just so that it can check a flag and give control up again. It would be much better if the task never got control in the first place until the flag was cleared. However, the overhead in this case is much less than with busy waiting.

Latches suffer from another problem briefly touched upon above. No arbitration is performed to make sure that access to the latch is granted fairly. Tasks that check once per time slice have a decided disadvantage getting the latch, relative to tasks that busy wait. Even if all tasks use the same algorithm for checking, the latch timing will often conspire against one task or another. One of the tasks will very often get the latch preferentially due to the inherent sequencing of tasks.

A simple semaphore program is shown in listing SEMTST1.C. In this example, a parent task starts several subtasks using the same model for starting subtasks as the programs in chapters 3 and 4. Each subtask is passed a message containing the handle of the parent's display window. All of the tasks attempt to write this window simultaneously. Although not technically necessary, access to this window is controlled by a latch function appropriately called *latch()*.

Each task calls *latch()* before attempting to write to the window. The function *latch()* does not return to the caller until the latch is won, preferring instead to wait in a loop, alternately requesting the latch and giving up control. Once the latch is won, the task proceeds to write out a message (in its favorite color) and then return the latch and loop back to try again. After 100 of these loops, the subtask calls it quits and signals its demise back to the parent task, which is waiting for signals from all the subtasks before quitting.

Notice that the way the program is written each task is using the exact same latch function. (Indeed, all of the code for the subtasks is the same.) No task should have an advantage over the others. Nevertheless, the sequencing of tasks is not at all fair. What tends to happen is that a task finishes printing, releases the latch, and then immediately cycles back to grab it again before any of the other tasks have a chance to gain control of the CPU and request it. Uncommenting the call to *api_pause()* in the *unlock()* function changes the timing between the tasks—in this case, giving them a more equal chance at the latch. Solving this sequencing problem in larger programs to give all tasks fair access is not always so easy, however.

Because of their simplicity, latches are probably the most common critical-region protection used between tasks within the same process.

```
 1[ 0]: /****************************************************************
 2[ 0]:    Latch Test #1 - create several tasks and arbitrate access to
 3[ 0]:                    the common window using a latch.
 4[ 0]: ****************************************************************/
 5[ 0]:
 6[ 0]: #include <stdio.h>
 7[ 0]: #include "dvapi.h"
 8[ 0]:
 9[ 0]: /*locally declared programs*/
10[ 0]: void main (void);
11[ 0]: void program_body (void);
12[ 0]: ulong fork (int, ulong, char *, int);
13[ 0]: int subtask (void);
14[ 0]: void latch (void);
15[ 0]: void unlatch (void);
16[ 0]:
17[ 0]: /*minimum API version required is DESQview 2.00*/
18[ 0]: #define required 0x200
19[ 0]:
20[ 0]: /*main - standard pattern for DESQview programs*/
21[ 0]: void main (void)
22[ 0]: {
23[ 1]:   int  version;
24[ 1]:
25[ 1]:   version = api_init();
26[ 1]:   if (version < required)
27[ 1]:       printf ("This program requires DESQview %d.%02d or later.\n",
28[ 1]:               required >> 8, required & 0xff);
29[ 1]:   else {
30[ 2]:       /*tell DESQview what extensions to enable
31[ 2]:         and start application*/
32[ 2]:       api_level (required);
33[ 2]:       program_body();
34[ 1]:   }
35[ 1]:   /*if DESQview present (even if wrong version), shut it down*/
36[ 1]:   if (version)
37[ 1]:       api_exit();
38[ 0]: }
39[ 0]:
40[ 0]: /*program body - start up 5 tasks and wait for them to quit*/
41[ 0]:
```

```
42[ 0]: struct message {                       /*format of message to child task*/
43[ 1]:                     int count;          /*task count*/
44[ 1]:                     ulong parent;       /*handle of parent task*/
45[ 1]:                     ulong window;       /*handle of parent window*/
46[ 0]:                 };
47[ 0]:
48[ 0]: struct response {                       /*format of response message*/
49[ 1]:                     ulong child;        /*return the child handle*/
50[ 1]:                     int   count;        /*and its count*/
51[ 0]:                 };
52[ 0]:
53[ 0]: void program_body (void)
54[ 0]: {
55[ 1]:    int tcount;
56[ 1]:    ulong winhan;
57[ 1]:    struct response *msgptr;
58[ 1]:    int            msglngth;
59[ 1]:    #define NUMTASKS    5          /*start up 5 subtasks*/
60[ 1]:    #define STACKSIZE 1000         /*allocate some stack space for each*/
61[ 1]:    char stacks [NUMTASKS][STACKSIZE];
62[ 1]:
63[ 1]:    winhan = win_new ("Common Window", 13, 10, 38);
64[ 1]:    win_move (winhan, 5, 10);
65[ 1]:    win_logattr (winhan, 1);
66[ 1]:    win_attr (winhan, 1);
67[ 1]:    win_unhide (winhan);
68[ 1]:    win_top (winhan);
69[ 1]:
70[ 1]:    /*now start subtask NUMTASKS number of times*/
71[ 1]:    for (tcount = 0; tcount < NUMTASKS; tcount++)
72[ 1]:        fork (tcount, winhan, stacks [tcount], STACKSIZE);
73[ 1]:
74[ 1]:    /*wait for them all to quit - show we are still alive
75[ 1]:     in meantime*/
76[ 1]:    do
77[ 1]:        mal_read (mal_me(), &msgptr, &msglngth);
78[ 1]:    while (--tcount);
79[ 1]:
80[ 1]:    /*now put the window away*/
81[ 1]:    win_free (winhan);
82[ 0]: }
83[ 0]:
84[ 0]: /*fork - fork a new task*/
85[ 0]: ulong fork (taskcount, winhan, stack, stacksize)
86[ 0]:    int taskcount;
87[ 0]:    ulong winhan;
88[ 0]:    char *stack;
89[ 0]:    int  stacksize;
90[ 0]: {
91[ 1]:    ulong tskhan;
92[ 1]:    struct message msg;
93[ 1]:
94[ 1]:    /*start the subtask - the task window will never be displayed*/
95[ 1]:    tskhan = tsk_new (subtask, stack, stacksize, "", 0, 1, 1);
96[ 1]:
97[ 1]:    /*now send it a message containing its location information*/
```

```
 98[ 1]:    msg.count = taskcount;
 99[ 1]:    msg.parent = tsk_me();
100[ 1]:    msg.window = winhan;
101[ 1]:    mal_write (mal_of (tskhan), &msg, sizeof(msg));
102[ 1]:
103[ 1]:    /*finally return the task handle*/
104[ 1]:    return tskhan;
105[ 0]: }
106[ 0]:
107[ 0]: /*subtask - an example subtask which opens a window, counts down
108[ 0]:                and then removes itself*/
109[ 0]: int subtask (void)
110[ 0]: {
111[ 1]:    int i;
112[ 1]:    struct message *msgptr;
113[ 1]:    struct response msg;
114[ 1]:    int    msglngth;
115[ 1]:
116[ 1]:    /*wait for an initiation message with handle of window to
117[ 1]:      which to write*/
118[ 1]:    mal_read (mal_me(), &msgptr, &msglngth);
119[ 1]:
120[ 1]:    /*request access to the window - treat this like a critical
121[ 1]:      section controlled by a latch*/
122[ 1]:    for (i = 100; i; i--) {
123[ 2]:      latch();
124[ 2]:      win_attr (msgptr->window, msgptr->count + 2);
125[ 2]:      win_printf (msgptr->window, "Task %d counting at %d\n",
126[ 2]:                                 msgptr->count, i);
127[ 2]:      unlatch();
128[ 1]:    }
129[ 1]:
130[ 1]:    /*now send a message back of our demise*/
131[ 1]:    msg.child = tsk_me();
132[ 1]:    msg.count = msgptr->count;
133[,1]:    win_write (mal_of (msgptr->parent), &msg, sizeof(msg));
134[ 0]: }
135[ 0]:
136[ 0]: /*Latch and unlatch - complementary functions to latch and
137[ 0]:                    unlatch access to a critical section*/
138[ 0]: int latchvar;
139[ 0]: void latch (void)
140[ 0]: {
141[ 1]:      /*keep trying until allowed through*/
142[ 1]:      api_beginc ();          /*turn off scheduling while checking*/
143[ 2]:      for (;;) {
144[ 2]:          if (latchvar == 0)   /*is it available?*/
145[ 2]:              break;           /*clear - grab it!*/
146[ 2]:          api_pause ();        /*set - wait again*/
147[ 1]:      }
148[ 1]:      latchvar = 1;
149[ 1]:      api_endc ();            /*okay to reenable scheduling now*/
150[ 0]: }
151[ 0]: void unlatch (void)
152[ 0]: {
153[ 1]:      latchvar = 0;
```

```
154[ 1]:     /*api_pause ();*/         /*uncommenting this call changes
155[ 1]:                                 drastically the order
156[ 1]:                                 in which the tasks are scheduled*/
157[ 0]: }
```

Semaphores

As noted, the latch solution suffers from the problem that a task waiting for the latch to clear repeatedly gets scheduled to execute, even when the latch is not yet cleared. It would be much better if the task never got control until the latch was cleared and the task was free to continue into its critical section. There is an operation that has this property: the *mailbox read operation*. A task that attempts to read a mailbox that is empty is suspended until a message appears. This suggests a solution that does not suffer from the reschedule problem.

Suppose that we used a message instead of a latch. A task might request the message before entering its critical section. If the message is present, the task is allowed to proceed. If the message is not present because another task has read it already, then the task is suspended until the message is returned. Once the task exits its critical section, it is obliged to return the message by sending it to the mailbox again, just as it was obliged to release the latch earlier. The next task waiting is then unsuspended, given the message, and allowed to continue into its critical section.

The semaphore message technique has several advantages over the latch scheme above. First, a task is not scheduled until it is ready to proceed into its critical section. No time is wasted scheduling tasks unnecessarily. This technique also preserves the order of the requests. If several tasks are waiting simultaneously, they are given permission to pass into their critical regions in the order in which they first requested it. Finally, there is no problem of access between tasks located in different processes. All processes can read and write messages from any mailbox.

There are a few minor problems with the approach, however. First, this semaphore message must exist before the first request for passage is made.

This is easily solved if, at system initialization, the parent application sends an empty message to the mailbox to "prime the pump."

Another problem is that the semaphore mailbox must be accessible to all tasks. This may be solved by sending its handle in a message to all of the tasks involved. This is more easily handled, however, by giving the semaphore mailbox a name. (Something like *SEMAPHORE* might be nice.) Other tasks can then find the semaphore mailbox by looking up its name.

A third problem is that DESQview only allows one task to have a mailbox open at a time. That is, the scenario we described is not actually possible under DESQview. Multiple tasks cannot have the same mailbox open and read it at the same time.

To solve this, the programmer could invent a background *traffic cop* task to read the control mailbox. This task would receive requests from other tasks. A task that wanted to enter its critical section might send a request message to the control mailbox and then suspend itself. If the coast is clear, the traffic cop task would immediately unsuspend the task and allow it to continue on. If, however, another task was already in its critical section, the traffic cop task would allow the requester to remain suspended until it was okay for it to proceed.

Fortunately, this added complexity is not really necessary. DESQview's API includes two mailbox operations that are similar to the read and write message, but are designed specifically to function as semaphores: the *lock* and *unlock* operations. Lock is similar to mailbox read and unlock is similar to mailbox write with a few exceptions.

First, no message is actually passed between tasks. This is acceptable since the semaphore message was empty anyway. Besides, since no message is actually involved, the mailbox need not be seeded with an empty message before it may be locked. Second, DESQview allows multiple tasks to lock the same mailbox simultaneously. The tasks are suspended in the order in which they locked. This obviates the extra complexity of a traffic cop-type demon task. (The traffic cop approach is still very useful when there are other considerations governing when a task should be allowed access to its critical region—the logic of the traffic cop can be as involved as desired in deciding who gets to proceed and when.)

Prototypes for the *mal_lock()* and *mal_unlock()* API calls appear in Figure 7.2 along with those for the mailbox name and lookup functions. Remember that a mailbox must not be *mal_open()*ed if it will be locked.

Figure 7.2—Prototype Declarations for the Semaphore Message API Functions

```
                            /*find the handle of a named mailbox*/
ulong mal_find             /*returns mailbox handle*/
        (char *name);      /*name of mailbox*/

                            /*lock a mailbox semaphore*/
void  mal_lock             /*returns nothing*/
        (ulong malhan);    /*handle of mailbox to lock*/

                            /*name a mailbox*/
void  mal_name             /*returns nothing*/
        (ulong malhan,     /*handle of mailbox to name*/
         char *name,       /*name to assign*/
         int   length);    /*length of name*/

                            /*unlock a mailbox semaphore*/
void  mal_unlock           /*returns nothing*/
        (ulong malhan);    /*handle of mailbox to unlock*/
```

The program SEMTST2.C shows the same problem presented before with a mailbox semaphore solution. This program is virtually identical to the previous version except for the calls creating a new mailbox (*mal_new()*) and giving it a name (*mal_name()*) and the latch functions themselves. The latch function uses the *mal_lock()* and the unlatch uses the *mal_unlock()* call to control access.

Notice when executing the program that the tasks are now executed more in order. Also notice that adding *api_pause()* calls do not materially affect the order in which the tasks are scheduled once all the tasks have been started. This demonstrates that once all of the tasks have been started, accidental timing no longer plays a role.

```
 1[ 0]: /***************************************************************
 2[ 0]:     Lock Test #2 - create several tasks and arbitrate access to
 3[ 0]:                   the common window using a semaphore mailbox.
 4[ 0]: ***************************************************************/
 5[ 0]:
 6[ 0]: #include <stdio.h>
 7[ 0]: #include "dvapi.h"
 8[ 0]:
 9[ 0]: /*locally declared programs*/
10[ 0]: void main (void);
11[ 0]: void program_body (void);
12[ 0]: ulong fork (int, ulong, char *, int);
13[ 0]: int subtask (void);
14[ 0]: void latch (ulong);
15[ 0]: void unlatch (ulong);
16[ 0]:
17[ 0]: /*minimum API version required is DESQview 2.00*/
18[ 0]: #define required 0x200
19[ 0]:
20[ 0]: /*main - standard pattern for DESQview programs*/
21[ 0]: void main (void)
22[ 0]: {
23[ 1]:   int  version;
24[ 1]:
25[ 1]:   version = api_init();
26[ 1]:   if (version < required)
27[ 1]:       printf ("This program requires DESQview %d.%02d or later.\n",
28[ 1]:               required >> 8, required & 0xff);
29[ 1]:   else {
30[ 2]:       /*tell DESQview what extensions to enable
31[ 2]:         and start application*/
32[ 2]:       api_level (required);
33[ 2]:       program_body();
34[ 1]:   }
35[ 1]:   /*if DESQview present (even if wrong version), shut it down*/
36[ 1]:   if (version)
37[ 1]:       api_exit();
38[ 0]: }
39[ 0]:
40[ 0]: /*program body - start up 5 tasks and wait for them to quit*/
41[ 0]:
42[ 0]: struct message {                  /*format of message to child task*/
43[ 1]:                 int count;        /*task count*/
44[ 1]:                 ulong parent;     /*handle of parent task*/
45[ 1]:                 ulong window;     /*handle of parent window*/
46[ 0]:                 };
47[ 0]:
48[ 0]: struct response {                 /*format of response message*/
49[ 1]:                 ulong child;      /*return the child handle*/
50[ 1]:                 int   count;      /*and its count*/
51[ 0]:                 };
52[ 0]:
```

```
53[ 0]: void program_body (void)
54[ 0]: {
55[ 1]:    int tcount;
56[ 1]:    ulong winhan, semaphore;
57[ 1]:    struct response *msgptr;
58[ 1]:    int        msglngth;
59[ 1]:    #define NUMTASKS    5        /*start up 5 subtasks*/
60[ 1]:    #define STACKSIZE 1000        /*allocate some stack space for each*/
61[ 1]:    char stacks [NUMTASKS][STACKSIZE];
62[ 1]:
63[ 1]:    winhan = win_new ("Common Window", 13, 10, 38);
64[ 1]:    win_move (winhan, 5, 10);
65[ 1]:    win_logattr (winhan, 1);
66[ 1]:    win_attr (winhan, 1);
67[ 1]:    win_unhide (winhan);
68[ 1]:    win_top (winhan);
69[ 1]:
70[ 1]:    /*initialize the semaphore mailbox by creating it and
71[ 1]:      naming it*/
72[ 1]:    semaphore = mal_new ();
73[ 1]:    mal_name (semaphore, "SEMAPHORE", 9);
74[ 1]:
75[ 1]:    /*now start subtask NUMTASKS number of times*/
76[ 1]:    for (tcount = 0; tcount < NUMTASKS; tcount++)
77[ 1]:         fork (tcount, winhan, stacks [tcount], STACKSIZE);
78[ 1]:
79[ 1]:    /*wait for them all to quit - show we are still alive
80[ 1]:      in meantime*/
81[ 1]:    do
82[ 1]:         mal_read (mal_me(), &msgptr, &msglngth);
83[ 1]:    while (--tcount);
84[ 1]:
85[ 1]:    /*now put the window and the locking mailbox away*/
86[ 1]:    win_free (winhan);
87[ 1]:    mal_free (semaphore);
88[ 0]: }
89[ 0]:
90[ 0]: /*fork - fork a new task*/
91[ 0]: ulong fork (taskcount, winhan, stack, stacksize)
92[ 0]:    int taskcount;
93[ 0]:    ulong winhan;
94[ 0]:    char *stack;
95[ 0]:    int stacksize;
96[ 0]: {
97[ 1]:    ulong tskhan;
98[ 1]:    struct message msg;
99[ 1]:
100[ 1]:   /*start the subtask - the task window will never be displayed*/
101[ 1]:   tskhan = tsk_new (subtask, stack, stacksize, "", 0, 1, 1);
102[ 1]:
103[ 1]:   /*now send it a message containing its location information*/
104[ 1]:   msg.count = taskcount;
105[ 1]:   msg.parent = tsk_me();
106[ 1]:   msg.window = winhan;
107[ 1]:   mal_write (mal_of (tskhan), &msg, sizeof(msg));
108[ 1]:
```

```
109[ 1]:   /*finally return the task handle*/
110[ 1]:   return tskhan;
111[ 0]: }
112[ 0]:
113[ 0]: /*subtask - an example subtask which opens a window, counts down
114[ 0]:                and then removes itself*/
115[ 0]: int subtask (void)
116[ 0]: {
117[ 1]:   int i;
118[ 1]:   struct message *msgptr;
119[ 1]:   struct response msg;
120[ 1]:   int   msglngth;
121[ 1]:
122[ 1]:   /*wait for an initiation message with handle of window to
123[ 1]:     which to write*/
124[ 1]:   mal_read (mal_me(), &msgptr, &msglngth);
125[ 1]:
126[ 1]:   /*request access to the window - treat this like a critical
127[ 1]:     section controlled by a latch*/
128[ 1]:   /*latch (msgptr->window);*/
129[ 1]:   for (i = 100; i; i--) {
130[ 2]:     latch (msgptr->window);
131[ 2]:     win_attr (msgptr->window, msgptr->count + 2);
132[ 2]:     win_printf (msgptr->window, "Task %d counting at %d\n",
133[ 2]:                                 msgptr->count, i);
134[ 2]:     unlatch (msgptr->window);
135[ 1]:   }
136[ 1]:   /*unlatch (msgptr->window);*/
137[ 1]:
138[ 1]:   /*now send a message back of our demise*/
139[ 1]:   msg.child = tsk_me();
140[ 1]:   msg.count = msgptr->count;
141[ 1]:   win_write (mal_of (msgptr->parent), &msg, sizeof(msg));
142[ 0]: }
143[ 0]:
144[ 0]: /*Latch and unlatch - complementary functions to latch and
145[ 0]:                       unlatch access to a critical section
146[ 0]:                       using a lock on a named mailbox*/
147[ 0]: void latch (winhan)
148[ 0]:   ulong winhan;
149[ 0]: {
150[ 1]:   ulong semhan;
151[ 1]:
152[ 1]:   if (semhan = mal_find ("SEMAPHORE", 9)) /*look up the mailbox*/
153[ 1]:       mal_lock (semhan);
154[ 1]:   else
155[ 1]:       win_disperor (winhan, "Can't read SEMAPHORE!", 21, 0, 0, 1, 0);
156[ 0]: }
157[ 0]: void unlatch (winhan)
158[ 0]:   ulong winhan;
159[ 0]: {
160[ 1]:   ulong semhan;
161[ 1]:
162[ 1]:   if (semhan = mal_find ("SEMAPHORE", 9))
163[ 1]:       mal_unlock (semhan);
164[ 1]:   else
```

```
165[ 1]:        win_disperor (winhan, "Can't write SEMAPHORE!", 22, 0, 0, 1, 0)
166[ 0]: }
```

There is a class of problems for which this is not quite sufficient. Let us take the example of the line printer again. Assume, as is normally the case, that the actual printing is handled by a background task. Other tasks simply send messages to the printer task for printing. A response message is generated each time a print request is finished.

A task that has a lot to print may send several messages in a row. Since the programmer does not want the output from different tasks mingled with each other, a semaphore will probably be set up to control access to the printer. Tasks that want to print must first get access to the semaphore. Once the response message comes indicating that the print is finished, they will then release the semaphore.

A problem arises here, however. Suppose that a task has sent several requests to the printer task for printing. The task must be careful not to attempt to attain the latch once it already has it. Attempting to do so would end in a deadlock as the task would wait on itself forever. However, once the first response arrives, the task is likely to release the latch, allowing other tasks to access the printer before the other messages have been printed.

Of course, by careful use of flags, this problem can be solved. However, DESQview's semaphore mailboxes offer a simple solution to this problem. A single task may lock the same mailbox as often as it chooses. Each lock operation simply credits to the task's account. The semaphore is not released to other tasks until the task's account has been zeroed by a matching number of unlock operations.

In our printing example, the requesting task can lock the printer semaphore mailbox once for each message that it sends to print. As each print response arrives indicating that the print is complete, the program simply calls unlock again. When a response has arrived for each print request, a matching unlock call will have been performed for every lock call and the printer is released for other tasks to access.

Like the UNIX semaphore, which also has this feature, multilocking can also be used as a counting device. For example, assume that printer messages were to be sent out in groups of five. The first task could lock the semaphore mailbox five times in quick succession. As each print is finished, the response routine might unlock the semaphore until eventually the printer is available for use by other programs. Unlike UNIX, however, unlocking an already unlocked semaphore has no effect (i.e., the *unlock credits* do not accumulate).

Conclusion

The semaphore facility provides an efficient means of protecting critical regions and avoiding the collision of tasks over RAM, disk, or other external devices. Not only does it provide fair access to the asset, but also presents a minimal load on the operating system. This technique should be built into every program where collisions are a possibility.

```
┌─────────────────────────────────────────────┐
│                                             │
│  c  h  a  p  t  e  r      8                  │
│                                             │
└─────────────────────────────────────────────┘
```

Streams, Panels, and the Panel Design Tool

Streams

You may remember from Chapter 1 that there are actually three ways to access the DESQview API. So far we have only spoken of the C interface. Since the assembly language interface offers no new capabilities, we won't discuss it in this book; however, the third interface, the so-called stream interface, does offer some interesting capabilities, even to the C programmer.

In the stream interface, DESQview commands are embedded into the data being written to a window. This concept is familiar to anyone who has worked with ANSI (VT100 style) or HP terminals. A particular escape sequence might flip the terminal into inverse video while another might place the cursor at some particular coordinates on the screen. In fact, even DOS has this ability with its *ANSI.SYS*. Many programmers use *ANSI.SYS*-escape sequences, patterned after the ANSI standard.

DESQview's stream commands offer more capabilities than these terminal-escape sequences. Stream commands can be used to open a window, place it on the screen, set its color, give it a name, and redraw it. In short, stream commands can be used to perform most of the DESQview output functions that we have examined so far. In fact, most of the C API interface functions do nothing more than formulate a stream and then output it.

(You will notice this right away if you attempt to test your programs using the DESQview API Debugger, a separate product available from Quarterdeck. The majority of API C calls appear as nothing more than a stream write to the debugger. This can be quite confusing to the C programmer and somewhat reduces the effectiveness of the API Debugger. Fortunately, DESQview is compatible with standard debuggers such as CodeView and Turbo C 2.0's built-in debugger, so the API Debugger is not generally needed.)

What purpose do streams serve? For one thing, streams allow user code to be linked together with the operating system functions without either knowing the address of the other. User programs simply send their Escape commands and DESQview picks them up without knowing from which address they come. This reduces the problem of linking the two together as referred to in our discussion of shared code in Chapter 6: Memory Management. However, this cannot be the complete story as there are calls, such as *api_beginc()* and *api_endc()*, that are not handled via streams.

In fact, streams offer another advantage: the ability to completely divide the code from the data. Think of the output windows, including any text that is written to them, as data. The code is the framework that puts up and takes down these settings. Consider a program that displays questions and retrieves their answers. In a standard program, the code must perform a series of write statements just to get the questions to the screen. But the code logic is not truly concerned with the details of what the questions are, where they are, what language they're in, etc. The code logic is only concerned with the answers and what it should do with them.

Streams allow the output details to be combined with the text of the question itself. The code no longer needs to perform multitudes of window operations. A single write opens the window, positions it, colors it, and poses the proper questions. The format of the output displays can be modified without changes to the code. The data describes the form of the program while the code determines its function. This programming paradigm requires a slightly different way of looking at program output. As you will see as you work your way through this chapter, however, this form vs. function paradigm is exceedingly powerful.

Panels and Panel Files

A stream is a single series of commands beginning with an *ESCAPE*, a stream type (there are three different stream types), and a byte count. A stream may have as many commands as desired with the single proviso that its entire length is limited to 64K. It is not difficult to imagine that a very large stream may get quite confusing, so it is common to see a long stream broken up into a series of shorter streams.

All of the streams that deal with one window may be combined into what is known as a *panel*. While this is a somewhat arbitrary grouping, there is good justification for it. The programmer can think of a panel as a window, its attributes, and any text it contains.

For example, it would normally take several commands to create a drop-down menu. First the window must be opened with a logical size and a title. It must then be positioned, written to, unhidden, and redrawn before the user can see it. The window streams to do all of these things can be combined into a single panel. In the programmer's mind, the panel is synonymous with the drop-down menu.

Not that more than a couple of windows are ever visible at one time, but over the course of executing a program many different windows are created and removed. The programmer creates a different panel for each of these windows. To make the job of keeping track of these panels easier, DESQview allows multiple panels to be combined into a single file known as a *panel file*.

A panel file may contain 1 to 256 panels. The individual panels within the panel file carry an eight-character name to which the software can refer. To access a panel, the program points to the panel file and refers to the panel by name. Thus, the program simply invokes a panel with a name like *FILEMENU* to drop down the menu of file-related commands.

When panel files are referenced, DESQview looks up the specified panel in the panel file's directory. Once found, DESQview locates the panel and begins executing the stream commands it contains. In the case of *FILEMENU* this would presumably open up a menu containing entries such as *Save*, *Save As*, *Delete*, *Quit*, etc., depending upon the details of the application.

Panel files may be RAM resident, like an array, or disk resident. In either case, the format is the same. In the case of RAM-resident panel files, DESQview uses them directly. With disk-panel files, DESQview must first load the file into memory where it then uses it exactly like the RAM-resident panel file.

Fields

If we look back at our paradigm of dividing code and displays, we can see that output is only part of the problem. A program usually opens a window or places a menu on the screen to prompt the user for input of some kind. Users are no longer accepting of the single prompt-answer format for user input. They want the flexibility of pointing and selecting choices while filling in answers in any order. Manipulating the cursor between fields and inputting characters while allowing mistakes to be deleted can take a considerable amount of code.

This can be done. The user program can read individual key strokes via the *key_read()* API call and track the mouse by reading the pointer object. In addition, there are *qry_* API calls to read most of the window details that can be set with the *win_* calls we saw in earlier chapters. However, this manipulation takes a detailed and accurate knowledge of exactly how the screen is laid out. The code must know exactly where all the input fields are located, what color they are, etc.

This ruins our division of labor. There is little point in storing all of the window-building information in a panel file, only to hard code the window structure in the input functions. The code and data become so intertwined that it becomes impossible to change the form of the windows without changing the code as well.

What is needed is some way to define input areas within a panel. DESQview provides the programmer with just such a mechanism. Panels may define areas of input known as fields. The user code simply reads the field. The mundane details of responding to cursor commands, mouse clicks, and insert and delete keystrokes are handled by the DESQview operating system.

We will define and use fields in this chapter, but if you would like a sneak preview of what fields look like, just look at DESQview itself. The windows that DESQview displays are undoubtedly panels themselves, and input into these windows is through fields. Pop up the DESQview menu and notice how the options change colors as they are pointed at. Open up the *Change a Program* menu and notice how fields are handled when text is entered. This is the same feeling that programs using panel fields have.

There are four types of fields: *select fields*, *input fields*, *output fields*, and *inactive fields*. Let's consider each one in turn.

A *select field* is a field that has two states. The field may either be selected or not selected. The attribute (color) of a select field changes to indicate whether it is selected or not. In addition, a special character may be added to the front of a field when it is selected and removed when it is not (this is particularly useful for monochrome monitors).

The user may select a field in one of two ways. He may either point at the field with the mouse pointer and click on it or he may enter the *Keystroke*

Select Character for that field. For example, in the DESQview menu users may either point at *Open Window* and click it or they may simply enter an *O*. The effect is identical. A select field may have either one *Keystroke Select Character* or two (an example of the latter is the program selections in the *Open Window* menu).

In the absence of a mouse, the user may *point* at a select field from the keyboard. Home points to the first field. The tab key cycles through the fields, pointing at each one in turn. Shift-tab cycles in the reverse direction. Entering a space or Gray-Plus key selects the select field currently pointed at.

Select fields also have what is known as a pointing attribute. The field assumes this color when the pointer is currently pointing at it. In this way, the user knows specifically which field he is about to select. He also knows that the field is *selectable*, since fields that cannot be selected do not change their attribute when pointed at. The pointing and selected attribute for all select fields in a given panel are the same.

Notice that the user may not actually see the selected state of a select field— selecting a field may cause the program to display a new panel immediately. (This is the case with all of the fields in the DESQview menu.) Thus, select fields have three purposes: 1) a field that is binary (that is, has two states: on and off), 2) fields that have a limited number of enumerated states (the baud rate of a COM: port may consist of a short list of possible rates—only one of which is selected), or 3) a command that is to be carried out immediately.

The second type of field is an *input field*. Input fields are small areas of the panel into which the user can type any characters desired, such as the user's name or the name of a file or directory. Input fields do not have the property of being selected or not. They do have other properties, however.

For example, an input field may be uppercase only. That is, all input is automatically converted to uppercase in such a field. Another property is

Auto Carriage Return in which case a carriage return is entered as soon as the user enters the last character in the field (normally the cursor just stays on the last character in the field until a carriage return is entered). A third property is *Right Justify*. In this mode, the cursor stays at the right boundary and pushes characters to the left. This is useful when entering numbers. These and other such properties allow programmers to exactly specify their preferences for input to make the user's data-entry job as easy as possible.

Once again, look to DESQview itself to see examples of input fields. The *Change a Program* menu under the *Open Window* menu uses almost all input fields, some with different properties specified. Experimental entering of data will show the subtle affect these preferences have upon data entry.

The third case is that of the *output field*. Obviously, this is not an input field at all. If we reconsider our input problem again, however, we can see the need for such a field. It is often the case that the programmer would like to write to the displayed panel. For example, a panel-oriented spreadsheet might display a *WORKING* when the ReCalc select field is selected, followed by a *DONE* when the ReCalc had finished. To do so with a simple *win_printf()* the program must know how the window is laid out to avoid overwriting some key information displayed there. In reality, this is the same problem as our input problem earlier.

All fields carry a unique number. Output fields are written to by this number. In the above problem, our spreadsheet program need only write the word *WORKING* to the status output field and then later write the word *DONE*. Once again, the form has been divided from the function. The spreadsheet does not know or care where (or even if) the status is positioned within the panel or what it's attributes are. Output fields do not have any of the programmer-selectable properties of select and input fields.

(In fact, programs may write to a select or input field as well, just as if it were an output field.)

The last category of field is the *inactive field*. An inactive field is actually one of the other three types of fields that has been *turned off* or deactivated. An inactive field cannot be selected or read from, so the question arises, why have it?

Inactive fields have several important uses. First, a field may be deactivated if its selection no longer makes sense. For example, our spreadsheet may allow periodic automatic backups to be performed so that little data is lost in the event of power failure. The menu to control this would have a select field *Enable Auto Backup* and an input field for the name of the file to write; however, if the *Auto Backup* feature were not enabled, the filename field has no meaning. Thus, the spreadsheet program should deactivate the *Filename*-input field when the *Enable Auto Backup* select field is deselected.

Figure 8.1—Hypothetical Auto-Backup Control Menu

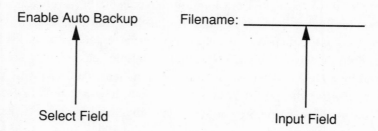

Deactivated fields can also serve as place holders. C programs can edit fields, turning them into any other type desired, but they cannot add them to an existing panel. Thus, it can be useful to include several deactivated fields that the application program can then convert into other types of fields as it desires.

Finally, deactivated fields may serve as place markers. The location of a field may be queried by the user code via the *qry_entry()* API call. Programmers may place deactivated fields where they want submenus to be opened by the program. (This is better handled, however, using several layers of panels, assigning a different panel for each submenu. Users can place the panel containing the submenu wherever they want, as well. A program may have multiple panels open at one time.)

Implementing a Panel File

A panel file consists of two distinct parts: the panel directory and the panels themselves. The format of the panel directory is shown in Figure 8.2.

Figure 8.2—Format of Panel File Directory

Field No.	Size(Bytes)	Meaning
1	2	0xC3C0—signature of a panel file
2	1	number of panels in file (0—> 255)
3	8	name of panel (8 ASCII characters)
4	4	offset of beginning of panel in panel file
5	2	length of panel

(fields 3 through 5 repeated for each panel)

The panels themselves are open to almost any stream commands with the proviso that the first stream must be an E5 Window Stream. The E5 command tells DESQview whether this panel will open a new window or whether it simply modifies an existing one. Its format is shown in Figure 8.3.

Once the E5 preamble is out of the way, the remainder of the panel is free form. Any valid stream commands may follow. These are the commands that create the panel window. (I realize that the reader does not know what the valid stream commands are. This book attempts to introduce the C programmer to the concepts of DESQview via the most natural interface from C, the API C Library. As soon as the reader feels comfortable with these concepts, the stream commands are documented in the *DESQview API Reference*.)

Figure 8.3—Format of First Stream in a Panel

Byte	Bits	Meaning
0	11100101	E5—begins an E5 Window Stream
1	11xxxxxx	creates a new window
	10xxxxxx	creates new field table for existing window
	01xxxxxx	uses existing field table and window
	xx1xxxxx	stream contains a field table
	xxx1xxxx	contains input fields
	xxxx1xxx	contains select fields but no input fields

Defining fields to DESQview is handled with the *FF* window-stream command (all of the field-related stream commands are in the range 0xF0 to 0xFF). Following the *FF* command is known as the *field table*. The field table is divided into two parts: the *field-table header* and the *field-table entries*. The field-table header is a six-byte table that describes the number and type of fields that are to follow. Its format is shown in Figure 8.4.

The first byte in the field-table header contains a count of the number of field-table entries to follow. The second byte, the format byte, describes the field table in general terms. As we will see later, panels generate four different types of messages to the user program, depending upon the value of the last two bits of this byte. (Any bits not listed are reserved and should be left at zero.)

The next two bytes, the *current-input field* and *current-select field*, are supplied by DESQview. They may be read by the user program but should not be written. The last two bytes are then pointed at and select attributes for any select fields within the field table. (The normal attribute, assumed when a select field is not pointed at and deselected, is in the field entry itself.)

Following the field-table header are the individual field entries. The format of the field-table entries is given in Figure 8.5. A separate field entry is present for each field within the panel. The number of the field is a result of the position of the field-table entry within the table. The first entry describes field one, the next entry describes field two, etc.

Figure 8.4—Format of Field Table Header

Byte	Bits	Meaning
0		number of field table entries to follow
1	x1xxxxxx	field contains keystroke selectable fields
	xx1xxxxx	if set, report button 1 clicks anywhere within panel (whether in select field or not)
	xxx1xxxx	same for button 2
	xxxx1xxx	if clear, report only *Y* and *N* when select fields selected; if set, report entire contents of field when selected and blanks when deselected
	xxxxx1xx	clear modified bits automatically; else, leave modified bits for *app* to clear
	xxxxxx00	return no data when field selected or data input—just an empty message
	xxxxxx01	return data from all fields w/o field numbers if any field changes
	xxxxxx10	return all data with field numbers
	xxxxxx11	return only modified fields with numbers
2		current input field (don't write this field)
3		current select field (don't write this field))
4		attribute to use for select fields when they are pointed at
5		attribute to use for select fields that are selected

Figure 8.5—Format of Field Table Entries

Byte	Bits	Meaning
0		starting logical row of field in window
1		starting logical column of field in window
2		ending logical row of field in window
3		ending logical column of field in window
4	00xxxxxx	inactive field
	01xxxxxx	output field
	10xxxxxx	input field
	11xxxxxx	select field
	xx1xxxxx	field can be filled with a broadcast write (broadcast write not accessible from C)
	xxxxxx1x	field selected
	xxxxxxx1	field modified
5		(select fields only) keystroke select character
5	1xxxxxxx	(input fields only) enter carriage return automatically when last character of field is entered
	x1xxxxxx	skip to next input field when this field is done
	xx1xxxxx	right justify input (number field)
	xxx1xxxx	convert input to upper case
	xxxx1xxx	clear field when first character is entered
	xxxxx1xx	send message to application whenever cursor leaves field (normally only sent when carriage return entered)
6		(select field only) normal attribute
7(opt)		(select field only) second keystroke select character

The first four entries in the field-table entry describe its upper, lower, left, and right boundaries. These values are zero relative from the upper left-hand corner of the panel's window. The next byte describes the field type. The meaning of the remaining bytes is dependent upon the field type. For inactive and output fields they have no meaning (they are still present so that all fields can be the same size). For select fields, byte five specifies the first keystroke select character, byte six specifies the attribute to use for the field when it is not selected or pointed at, and byte seven specifies the second keystroke-select character.

In actuality, byte seven is optional. Byte seven is only present if the window-stream command *E5,18* precedes the *FF* command that defines the table. If a select field is to have no keystroke-select characters, both byte five and byte seven (if present) should be zero. Such a select field can only be selected by being pointed at. If a field has only one select character then it should be in byte five, and byte seven (if present) should be zero. If the programmer wishes to use a non-ASCII select key, such as a function key, then byte seven should contain the extended key code and byte five should be zero. A field with two keystroke-select characters stores them in bytes five and seven.

To use a panel file from within a C program is not dissimilar to accessing the objects we have seen so far. First, a panel handle must be created via the *pan_new()* API call.

Once a panel handle has been created it must be associated with the panel file via the *pan_open()* API call. This call returns a status indicating success or failure. A failure at this point with a disk-resident panel file probably indicates that the file could not be found. An error from a RAM-resident panel file indicates that something is wrong with the format of the panel file.

After the panel file has been opened, an individual panel is invoked by *applying* it to an existing window. *Apply* is a verb we have not seen before. This stems from the fact that other objects are atomic (i.e., they have no substructure). Opening a timer object makes it ready for use. Opening the panel file object only makes the panels available. *Applying* an individual panel actually causes one of the panels to be found and displayed.

The arguments to *pan_apply()* are the panel handle associated with a panel file, a window handle, and the name of the panel. The name must match one of the panels in the panel file. This function also returns an error status. An error at this point almost surely indicates that the panel was not found within the panel file. (Dump the panel file using a hex-dump utility to see the names of the panels in the panel file directory.)

The function *pan_apply()* also returns the handle of the window that the panel occupies. If the panel opens a window of its own, then it is the handle of this new window that is returned. However, a panel may *adopt* an existing window, opening fields within that window. This is known as an *overlay panel*. In this case, *pan_apply()* merely returns the handle passed to it. Thus, the user program can use the returned handle, no matter what type of panel is being applied.

Let us use the concrete example of a word processor that uses DESQview windows to divide the display into its various areas. Far and away, the largest area is the display window that contains the text being edited. This panel, carrying the name *EDIT*, consumes all but the top and bottom few lines. Selecting the *Save* command drops a menu of save options over the display window. The program creates this new window by applying the panel *SAVE*. Since this panel creates a new window, it returns a new window handle to the editor program.

For printing, however, our word processor uses the display window to show the printing options since there are too many such options to fit within a small drop-down menu. The printing panel, *PRINT*, overlays the display window, temporarily overtaking it. When the user selects the *Print* command, the word processor applies the *PRINT* panel to the existing display window and no new window handle is created. Once the print is complete, the program must reapply the *EDIT* panel to the display window to return it to editing.

If there are any input or select fields in the panel, *pan_apply()* also opens a keyboard object and returns its handle as well.

Figure 8.6—Prototype Declarations for Major Panel API Calls

```
                              /*write to a field*/
void  fld_swrite             /*returns nothing*/
          (ulong winhan,     /*window handle*/
           int   field,      /*field number*/
           char *buffer);    /*string to write*/

                              /*open an individual panel*/
int   pan_apply              /*returns completion status*/
          (ulong  panhan,    /*handle of panel object*/
           ulong  winhan,    /*handle of window to use*/
           char  *name,      /*name of panel within panel file*/
           int    lname,     /*length of panel name*/
           ulong *retwin,    /*returned window containing panel*/
           ulong *retkey);   /*returned keyboard to get input*/

                              /*free panel object*/
void  pan_free               /*returns nothing*/
          (ulong  panhan);   /*handle of panel to free*/

                              /*create a new panel object*/
ulong pan_new                /*returns panel handle*/
          (void);            /*takes no arguments*/

                              /*open a new panel object*/
int   pan_open               /*returns completion status*/
          (ulong panhan,     /*panel object handle*/
           char *name,       /*name of panel file*/
           char  lname);     /*length of name*/^
                              /*get the type of a field*/
int   qry_type               /*returns field type = FLT_INACTIVE,
                                 FLT_OUTPUT, FLT_INPUT, FLT_SELECT
                                 or else FLT_DESELECT*/
          (ulong  winhan,    /*handle of panel window*/
           int    field);    /*field to read*/
```

A program can *read* a panel by simply reading the keyboard object returned from the *pan_apply()* call. (This keyboard object is in field mode, a mode that I avoided earlier in my discussion of *key_addto()* as it applies primarily to panels.) The panel object returns a message whenever the user completes input. The exact format of this message is dependent upon the two least significant bits of the second byte of the field-table header (byte one in Figure 8.4).

The panel object can simply send an empty message indicating that the user has completed input to a field (bits = 00). In this case, the program code must read the screen itself to determine what has changed. It may do this using the *qry_field()* API call. This function allows the program to read each field, in turn, by field number. The program must decide what (if anything) has changed.

Alternatively, the program can have the panel object dump the contents of all of the fields in the message (bits = 01), also without regard to what has changed. In this case, the fields are simply concatenated into a single message. Input fields are printed in their entirety and select fields print either a *Y* or *N,* or their contents. Once again, the program does not know what has changed, but at least all the information is in the one message. Since inactive and output fields are not included in the dump, interpreting this message can still get tricky.

To help in parsing this dump, the panel object can add the field numbers and their lengths to the beginning of each field within the message (bits = 10). Now the application need not keep track of which fields are active or have been temporarily turned off. The program can examine each message section by field number.

Finally, the panel object can restrict itself to only sending modified fields (with field number; bits = 11). In this case, selecting a select field or completing input to an input field generates a message containing the new contents of the single-modified field. For most applications this is the most desirable mode since the program no longer needs to decide on its own exactly what has changed.

In all four cases, input fields simply report their contents, padded to the full length of the field, if necessary, with spaces. If the select-format bit in the field-table header (byte one) is cleared, select fields report a *Y* if the field is selected and an *N* if deselected. When the select-format bit is set, select fields report their contents when selected and all spaces when deselected. This latter mode can be useful with programs that do not want to keep track of each select field individually, since the contents of the select field identifies its purpose.

Once the program has finished with the panel, it must *win_free()* the
associated window handle. The keyboard handle returned from the
pan_apply() should not be *key_free()*ed separately. When finished with
the entire panel file, the panel handle should be freed using the *pan_free()*
API call.

Panel Example

The program listing PANTST1.C shows an example panel program. This
program opens a single panel with six fields. Three are select fields containing the text *Option A*, *Option B,* and *Option C.* These fields may be
selected by pointing or by typing the single characters *A*, *B,* and *C*, respectively. Below these three fields is an output field containing the prompt
Enter Name:. To the right of this is an input field where users can enter
their names. A fourth select field appears below this initially containing
the prompt *Make Selection.* As soon as any input is made, the program
changes this output field to *Esc to Exit.* Selecting the select field at this location (either by pointing or via the Escape key), exits the program.

```
 1[ 0]: /****************************************************************
 2[ 0]:  Panel Test - create a panel in local memory by filling
 3[ 0]:                 in the proper structure definitions.  Since these
 4[ 0]:                 definitions are quite involved, the panels have
 5[ 0]:                 been reduced to the absolute minimum.  The actual
 6[ 0]:                 window must be opened and positions and all text
 7[ 0]:                 written to it from C API calls, although that is
 8[ 0]:                 normally handled from the panel itself.  Serviceable
 9[ 0]:                 panels can be built with this skeleton in the absence
10[ 0]:                 of the Panel Design Tool from Quarterdeck.
11[ 0]: ****************************************************************/
12[ 0]:
13[ 0]: #include <stdio.h>
14[ 0]: #include <string.h>
15[ 0]: #include "dvapi.h"
16[ 0]:
17[ 0]: /* prototype declarations of user functions*/
18[ 0]: void main (void);
19[ 0]: void program_body (void);
20[ 0]: ulong panel_window (void);
21[ 0]: void panel_text (ulong);
22[ 0]: void init_panel (void);
23[ 0]:
24[ 0]: /*minimum API version required is DESQview 2.00*/
25[ 0]: #define required 0x200
```

```
26[ 0]:
27[ 0]: /*main - standard pattern for DESQview programs*/
28[ 0]: void main (void)
29[ 0]: {
30[ 1]:   int  version;
31[ 1]:
32[ 1]:   version = api_init();
33[ 1]:   if (version < required)
34[ 1]:       printf ("This program requires DESQview %d.%02d or later.\n",
35[ 1]:               required >> 8, required & 0xff);
36[ 1]:   else {
37[ 2]:       /* tell DESQview what extensions to enable and start application
38[ 2]:       api_level (required);
39[ 2]:       program_body();
40[ 1]:   }
41[ 1]:   /*if DESQview present (even if wrong version), shut it down*/
42[ 1]:   if (version)
43[ 1]:       api_exit();
44[ 0]: }
45[ 0]:
46[ 0]: /*structure definitions for building panels within a program.
47[ 0]:   The panel file is defined by the structure PANEL.  The first field
48[ 0]:   is the panel directory (PANEL_DIR) which points to the inividual
49[ 0]:   panels or field tables (FTABLE).  A field table consists of
50[ 0]:   an initial fixed sequence followed by a header (FHEAD defined
51[ 0]:   in DVAPI.H include file) and an array of fields (FENTRY also
52[ 0]:   defined in DVAPI.H).  Notice that at least one of each type of
53[ 0]:   field has been included.  Otherwise, these panels have been reduced
54[ 0]:   to the absolute minimum.  Manipulating the actual text within the
55[ 0]:   panels must be handled from C.*/
56[ 0]: #define NO_PANELS   1      /*no. panels defined in this panel file*/
57[ 0]: typedef struct panel_directory {
58[ 1]:     unsigned preamble;           /*must be 0xC3C0*/
59[ 1]:     char     number;             /*number of panels (must
60[ 1]:                                    be equal to NO_PANELS)*/
61[ 1]:     struct {
62[ 2]:             char name [8];       /*name of each panel*/
63[ 2]:             ulong pan_address;   /*offset of panel in file*/
64[ 2]:             int  pan_length;     /*length of panel*/
65[ 1]:             } panels [NO_PANELS];
66[ 0]:     } PANEL_DIR;
67[ 0]:
68[ 0]: #define NO_FIELDS 6                  /*define space for 6 fields*/
69[ 0]: typedef struct field_table {
70[ 1]:                     char  escape;    /*window stream:*/
71[ 1]:                     char  zero;
72[ 1]:                     int   length;    /*length of stream*/
73[ 1]:                     char  E5;        /*define panel type:*/
74[ 1]:                     char  field_type;
75[ 1]:                     int   E5_18;     /*8 char fields*/
76[ 1]:                     char  FF;        /*starts field table*/
77[ 1]:                     FHEAD header;
78[ 1]:                     FENTRY entries [NO_FIELDS];
79[ 0]:                     } FTABLE;
80[ 0]:
81[ 0]: /*  Bit assignments for the field_type field of the FTABLE   */
```

```
 82[ 0]:
 83[ 0]: #define FT_NEWWIN 0xC0     /*create a new window*/
 84[ 0]: #define FT_NEWTBL 0x80     /*define a new table for existing window*/
 85[ 0]: #define FT_UPDATE 0x40     /*update existing table*/
 86[ 0]: #define FT_FTABLE 0x20     /*define a field table*/
 87[ 0]: #define FT_INPUT  0x10     /*define input fields*/
 88[ 0]: #define FT_SELECT 0x08     /*define select fields and does not
 89[ 0]:                                define any input fields*/
 90[ 0]:
 91[ 0]: struct PANEL_FILE {
 92[ 1]:                 PANEL_DIR directory;
 93[ 1]:                 FTABLE panels [NO_PANELS];
 94[ 0]:                 } panel_file;
 95[ 0]:
 96[ 0]: /*program_body - open a panel and a display window.  Display every
 97[ 0]:                 message which arrives from the panel until the
 98[ 0]:                 'Escape' entry selected*/
 99[ 0]: void program_body (void)
100[ 0]: {
101[ 1]:   ulong panhan, retwin, retkey, dispwin, fldwin;
102[ 1]:   int i, status, buflng;
103[ 1]:   unsigned char *buffer, *bufptr;
104[ 1]:
105[ 1]:   /*open a display window first*/
106[ 1]:   dispwin = win_new ("Message Display Window", 22, 15, 50);
107[ 1]:   win_move (dispwin, 5, 10);
108[ 1]:   win_logattr (dispwin, 1);
109[ 1]:   win_attr (dispwin, 1);
110[ 1]:   win_unhide (dispwin);
111[ 1]:   win_top (dispwin);
112[ 1]:
113[ 1]:   /*initialize the panel in memory*/
114[ 1]:   init_panel ();
115[ 1]:
116[ 1]:   /*now create and open a panel and apply it to the display window*/
117[ 1]:   fldwin = panel_window ();
118[ 1]:   panhan = pan_new ();
119[ 1]:   status = pan_open (panhan, &panel_file, sizeof panel_file);
120[ 1]:   if (!status) {
121[ 2]:       status = pan_apply (panhan, fldwin, "panel1", 6,
122[ 2]:                           &retwin, &retkey);
123[ 2]:       if (!status) {
124[ 3]:           /*put up the text for the fields*/
125[ 3]:           panel_text (retwin);
126[ 3]:
127[ 3]:           /*read messages from the panel until either the Escape
128[ 3]:            field is selected or 10 selections made.  Display the
129[ 3]:            messages received in the display window.  After at
130[ 3]:            least one selection is made, change the Output Field
131[ 3]:            from 'Make Selection' to 'Enter Escape to Exit'.*/
132[ 3]:           i = 10;
133[ 3]:           do {
134[ 4]:               key_read (retkey, &buffer, &buflng);
135[ 4]:               win_printf (dispwin, "Message %2d (length = %x) - ",
136[ 4]:                           i, buflng);
137[ 4]:               for (bufptr = buffer;buflng; bufptr++, buflng--)
```

```
138[ 4]:                          win_printf (dispwin, "%c(%x) ",
139[ 4]:                                          *bufptr, *bufptr);
140[ 4]:                    win_printf (dispwin, "\n");
141[ 4]:
142[ 4]:                    /*change the output field now that something input*/
143[ 4]:                    fld_swrite (retwin, 4, " Esc to Exit  ");
144[ 3]:               } while ((i--) && (*buffer != 4));
145[ 2]:          }
146[ 2]:          win_free (retwin);
147[ 1]:      }
148[ 1]:    win_free (dispwin);
149[ 1]:    pan_free (panhan);
150[ 0]:
151[ 0]: }
152[ 0]: /*Panel_window - put up the panel's window*/
153[ 0]: ulong panel_window (void)
154[ 0]: {
155[ 1]:    ulong fldwin;
156[ 1]:
157[ 1]:    /*now open a field window*/
158[ 1]:    fldwin = win_new ("Sample Menu", 11, 7, 22);
159[ 1]:    win_move (fldwin, 15, 45);
160[ 1]:    win_logattr (fldwin, 1);
161[ 1]:    win_attr (fldwin, 1);
162[ 1]:    win_unhide (fldwin);
163[ 1]:    win_top (fldwin);
164[ 1]:
165[ 1]:    /*now return the handle of this window*/
166[ 1]:    return fldwin;
167[ 0]: }
168[ 0]:
169[ 0]: /*Panel_text - put up the text for each of the fields*/
170[ 0]: char *texts[] = {"  Option   A  ",
171[ 1]:                  "  Option   B  ",
172[ 1]:                  "  Option   C  ",
173[ 1]:                  "Make Selection",
174[ 1]:                  "",
175[ 0]:                  "Enter Name:"};
176[ 0]: void panel_text (panwin)
177[ 0]:      ulong panwin;
178[ 0]: {
179[ 1]:    int i;
180[ 1]:
181[ 1]:    for (i = 0; i < NO_FIELDS; i++)
182[ 1]:          fld_swrite (panwin, i + 1, texts[i]);
183[ 0]: }
184[ 0]:
185[ 0]: /*Init_panel  -  build the panel in memory.  This could all
186[ 0]:                  be done with a VERY careful initialization
187[ 0]:                  statement back when the structure was declared*/
188[ 0]: void init_panel (void)
189[ 0]: {
190[ 1]:    unsigned i;
191[ 1]:
192[ 1]:    /*first build the directory*/
193[ 1]:    panel_file.directory.preamble = 0xC3C0;
```

```
194[ 1]:    panel_file.directory.number   = NO_PANELS;
195[ 1]:    strncpy (panel_file.directory.panels[0].name, "panel1  ", 8);
196[ 1]:    panel_file.directory.panels[0].pan_address =
197[ 1]:                               sizeof panel_file.directory;
198[ 1]:          .               /*this works for panels[0] only*/
199[ 1]:    panel_file.directory.panels[0].pan_length =
200[ 1]:                               sizeof panel_file.panels;
201[ 1]:
202[ 1]:    /*now init the panel itself*/
203[ 1]:    panel_file.panels[0].escape   = 0x1B;
204[ 1]:    panel_file.panels[0].zero     = 0x00;
205[ 1]:    panel_file.panels[0].length   = sizeof panel_file.panels[0] - 4;
206[ 1]:    panel_file.panels[0].E5       = 0xE5;
207[ 1]:    panel_file.panels[0].field_type = FT_NEWTBL +
208[ 1]:                               FT_FTABLE +
209[ 1]:                               FT_INPUT;
210[ 1]:    panel_file.panels[0].E5_18    = 0x18E5;
211[ 1]:    panel_file.panels[0].FF       = 0xFF;
212[ 1]:    panel_file.panels[0].header.fh_size   = NO_FIELDS;
213[ 1]:    panel_file.panels[0].header.fh_format = FTH_KEYSELECT +
214[ 1]:                               FTH_2BUTTON  +
215[ 1]:                               FTH_AUTORESET +
216[ 1]:                               FTH_MODIFIED;
217[ 1]:    panel_file.panels[0].header.fh_curin  = 0;
218[ 1]:    panel_file.panels[0].header.fh_cursel = 0;
219[ 1]:    panel_file.panels[0].header.fh_pntattr = 9;
220[ 1]:    panel_file.panels[0].header.fh_selattr = 2;
221[ 1]:
222[ 1]:    /*set up the select fields first*/
223[ 1]:    for (i = 0; i < 4; i++) {
224[ 2]:        panel_file.panels[0].entries[i].fe_srow   = 1 + i + (i / 3);
225[ 2]:        panel_file.panels[0].entries[i].fe_scol   = 1;
226[ 2]:        panel_file.panels[0].entries[i].fe_erow   = 1 + i + (i / 3);
227[ 2]:        panel_file.panels[0].entries[i].fe_ecol   = 14;
228[ 2]:        panel_file.panels[0].entries[i].fe_type   = FTE_SELECT;
229[ 2]:        panel_file.panels[0].entries[i].fe_key1   = 'A' + i;
230[ 2]:        panel_file.panels[0].entries[i].fe_norattr = 1;
231[ 2]:        panel_file.panels[0].entries[i].fe_key2   = 0;
232[ 1]:    }
233[ 1]:    panel_file.panels[0].entries[3].fe_key1 = 0x1B; /*give field 4 a
234[ 1]:                               select key of ESC*/
235[ 1]:
236[ 1]:    /*now set up the input field*/
237[ 1]:    panel_file.panels[0].entries[4].fe_srow   =  4;
238[ 1]:    panel_file.panels[0].entries[4].fe_scol   = 13;
239[ 1]:    panel_file.panels[0].entries[4].fe_erow   =  4;
240[ 1]:    panel_file.panels[0].entries[4].fe_ecol   = 21;
241[ 1]:    panel_file.panels[0].entries[4].fe_type   = FTE_INPUT;
242[ 1]:    panel_file.panels[0].entries[4].fe_inmode = FTE_ENTER +
243[ 1]:                               FTE_CLEARDFLT;
244[ 1]:
245[ 1]:    /*and finally the output field*/
246[ 1]:    panel_file.panels[0].entries[5].fe_srow   =  4;
247[ 1]:    panel_file.panels[0].entries[5].fe_scol   =  2;
248[ 1]:    panel_file.panels[0].entries[5].fe_erow   =  4;
249[ 1]:    panel_file.panels[0].entries[5].fe_ecol   = 12;
```

```
250[ 1]:    panel_file.panels[0].entries[5].fe_type    = FTE_OUTPUT;
251[ 0]: }
```

The principles in this program are important and bear careful study. The panel file used in this program is built in RAM using C statements only. Building panel files in separate assembly-language files that are assembled and then linked with the C-object files offers the programmer more control, but is also more difficult to get right. Besides, this technique assumes a familiarity with assembly language that is not a prerequisite for this book.

When building a large, complex data structure in memory, it is always tempting to simply declare a character array and start loading bytes into it. This tendency should be resisted. C allows detailed structure definitions that accurately reflect the data both in function and form.

The structure type *PANEL_TABLE* (variable *panel_table*) consists of two structures, *PANEL_DIR* (panel directory) and *FTABLE* (panel). The structure *PANEL_DIR* is defined to match the format of a panel directory as shown in Figure 8.2. The structure *FTABLE* describes the layout of a panel consisting of a single-window stream containing a field table. All window streams begin with the Escape character followed by zero and the length of the stream, the first three fields in *FTABLE*. The first stream in a panel must be the E5 window-stream command, which is the next entry in the structure. The *#defines* appearing below the *FTABLE* definition are used in the creation of the *FIELD_TYPE*, which is actually part of the *E5* command. Finally, a second window-stream command (*E5,18*) is used to indicate eight-byte field-table entries, which is what I have allocated.

Following this is the *FF* window-stream command that begins the field-table definition itself. The first entry beyond the *FF* is the field-table header, *FHEAD*. Its format is shown in Figure 8.4. *FHEAD* is defined in DVAPI.H. Following this are the individual field-table entries of type *FENTRY*, whose format is given in Figure 8.5. *FENTRY* is also defined in DVAPI.H.

The define *NO_PANELS* is set to one, to indicate that this panel file has a single panel. The define *NO_FIELDS* is used to specify the number of fields and is set to six to agree with the description (four select fields, an input field, and an output field). Unused fields can be declared and ignored, if desired, as C will initialize the space to zero, which specifies an inactive field to DESQview. (It has been said before but bears repeating, this structure must be byte packed if it is to generate something that DESQview will be able to understand. Be sure and select byte alignment in your compiler options.)

There are no variables in these structure definitions. Some fields have fixed values implied by their name (such as E5) and others have values that are user selectable but must be fixed at compile time (such as the position of a field). Therefore, it would be possible to assign the structure values with a single initialization statement. Such a statement might be horribly complicated, however. Therefore, the function *init_panel()* is used to initialize the structure to the proper values. Besides, it is easier for the reader to see the values assigned to the different fields when they are written out.

The elements of particular interest are the assignments to *field_type* and the *fe_* assignments. The *field_type* entry specifies the field table type and *must* specify an overlay panel (*FT_NEWTBL*). The *fe_* assignments position and type the individual field-table entries. The field entries one through four are the select field, entry five is the input field, and entry six is the output field. The sleight of hand in specifying the row (1 + i + (i / 3)) is only so that the first three select fields appear together on rows one through three with the fourth one row lower on row five.

With this minimum panel, the programmer must create the panel's window and position it using conventional API calls. This is performed by the function *panel_window()*. Once in place, the panel that *panel_init()* built is then overlayed on the existing window.

Even though the program must open and position the window itself, with care the majority of the window-format details can remain in the data. The user function *panel_text()* writes each of the text fields to the panel by field number using the *pan_swrite()* API call. In this context, it is helpful to declare an output field for every text string within the panel, as I have done for the *Enter Name:* prompt. Otherwise, carefully placed and sized *win_printf* calls are required to place the window text in just the proper places.

By leaving out the window-creation features, the structure presented is as simple and as general as possible so that the reader may have a clearer view of the panel's format. This same structure can be used by the reader to build any number and type of fields desired.

Our program initializes the panel by calling *init_panel()* and opens a display window where received messages will be displayed. The function *panel_window()* opens the panel window and places it appropriately, finally returning the window's handle. Next, the RAM-resident panel is opened with the *pan_new()* and *pan_open()* API calls. Finally, the panel is overlayed on the window using the *pan_apply()* API call. If all worked well (status equals zero), then the program outputs the text of the fields in the function *panel_text()*.

Next, the program enters a loop and awaits a message each time by reading the keyboard handle returned from *pan_apply()* using a conventional *key_read()*. Whatever message received is simply dumped to the display window both in hex and in ASCII using the *win_printf()* API call.

As soon as a message is received, the program writes the string *Esc to Exit* to the bottom select field (field number four), replacing the *Make Selection*. Presumably, the program wants the user to make at least one selection, hence the *Make Selection* prompt. Having made a selection, the user is reminded how to exit.

The while loop exits whenever field four (the Escape select field) is selected. This may be selected either by pointing at it or hitting the Escape key, which was set as its keystroke-select key in the panel initialization. Failing this, the program exits after ten inputs of any kind. (The latter is important because, when experimenting with the panel, it is easy to confuse the program into not properly recognizing the terminate message. In a real-world program, this check would not be necessary.)

Once the program exits the while loop, it frees the display window and then frees the panel window and panel objects. Notice that the panel keyboard object should not specifically be freed. Apparently this is freed when the window handle is freed.

When executing the program, select one of the first three select fields. Notice the format of the received message and compare it with the format listed in the *API Reference Manual.* By the way, do not worry about the holes that might open up in the display window for every *NULL* byte in the received message. Remember that character *\0* is the transparent character. You are actually just seeing through the display window into whatever might be behind it.

To get a feel for panels, I encourage you to play with this program. Notice the pointed at and selected colors of the select fields. Carefully examine the message generated as fields are selected and deselected. Set bit four in byte one of the field-table header to cause more than just a simple *Y* and *N* to be generated and rerun the program. Try generating the other message types and notice their format. Play with the status bits in the input field—input fields have an especially large number of controls. Try changing the select and pointed at attributes of the select fields.

As already noted, the structures have been set up to be as general purpose as possible in building overlay-style panels. Try adding additional fields to the panel or an additional panel to the panel file. Do not get discouraged if your new panel crashes the first time you try it. Go over the panel very carefully. If this still does not solve the problem, try commenting out the initialization of different fields in the *init_panel()* function one at a time. (Remember, a *NULL* panel is interpreted as an inactive panel and attempts to *fld_swrite()* to it are ignored.) If commenting out a field-table entry causes the problem to go away, then you know where the problem must lie.

As you gain familiarity with these structure definitions, you will find it progressively easier to build overlay panels using the template program provided.

Note: The structures described above build a panel file. With a single panel (or a small number of panels) this may not be necessary. It is possible to open and apply a single panel directly. This offers some simplification, since the programmer need only define the structure of type *FTABLE*. The structures of type *PANEL* and *PANEL_DIR* are no longer necessary.

To open a panel directly, the address of the panel (the *FTABLE* structure) is passed directly to the *pan_open()* call instead of the address of the panel file. In the *pan_apply()* call, the program must send a null-panel name with a length of zero. In PANTST1, the *pan_open()* and *pan_apply()* calls to open the example panel directly look like this:

```
status = pan_open (panhan, &panel_file.panels[0],
                   sizeof panel_file.panels[0]);
if (status) {
      pan_apply (panhan, fldwin, "", 0, &retwin, &retkey);
```

Other Field Operations

There are several other operations that may be performed on fields besides *fld_swrite()*. Just as with the other write operations, there is the more "Pascal-like" *fld_write()*, which accepts as its argument the length of the string, rather than using a *NULL* terminator. Notice that in both cases the text being written to the field should be the same length as the field itself. In fact, if the text is too short the field is padded out with spaces; however, it may be unwise to count on this fact. Programmers should pad their field texts with spaces to assure that the lengths match. Also remember that a program may write to select and input fields as well as output fields, despite what the names might imply.

A field may be more than one row in length. As such, a field may be scrolled either up, down, left, or right using the *fld_scroll()* API call. Scrolling a field is similar to scrolling a window.

In addition, a specific field may be cleared using the *fld_clear()* API call. In this case, the entire field is filled with blanks. If programmers would rather fill a field with some other character besides blanks, they may use the *fld_char()* API call instead. This function fills the indicated field with the specified character.

Finally, the attribute of a field may be changed using the *fld_attr()* API call. Notice that this call only changes the field on the screen. It has no affect on the normal, pointed at, or selected attributes in the field-table header and entries of select fields.

DESQview provides some cursor control within fields as well. The *fld_cursor()* API call places the logical cursor at the beginning of the specified field. This is very useful when first enabling an input field. For example, when the user selects *Back up enable*, a program might enable the *Filename* input field and then place the cursor at the beginning of this field using the *fld_cursor()* call. (Enabling an input field has no effect on the cursor, so it may in fact be somewhere out in left field unless specifically placed.)

The *fld_point()* API call also allows the program to position the mouse pointer within a field. This has roughly the same uses as the *fld_cursor()* call except that it affects the mouse pointer and it allows placement within the field as well.

DESQview also provides three API calls for controlling the fields themselves. The *fld_marker()* call allows the programmer to specify a marker character for select fields. Selecting a field is generally reflected to the user by a change in attribute (the selected attribute). This is acceptable on a color monitor, but on a black and white or monochrome monitor, there may not be enough different attributes to go around. For these cases, DESQview allows the programmer to declare a marker character. If the first character of a select field is a space, then it is replaced with the marker character whenever the field is selected. The space is put back when the field is deselected. Select fields that do not begin with a space are not affected. Restoring the marker character to a space disables this feature.

With autoreset enabled, the modified bits of fields are normally cleared after each message to the keyboard object. The program can allow the modified bits to stay set, if desired, until they are cleared by calling the *fld_reset()* API routine. This function clears the modified and selected bits for all fields in the panel.

In addition, the program may select or deselect a field from program control via the *fld_type()* API call. Setting the type of a select field to *FLT_DESELECT* or *FLT_SELECT* deselects or selects the field. The current type of a field may be read with the *qry_type()* API call. This function accepts a field number and simply returns its type.

These API functions can be particularly useful when select fields are being used to indicate a list of mutually exclusive choices, such as the baud rate of a serial port. Selecting one of these fields should clear the others, since only one of the fields can be true. Add the following statements to the bottom of the *DO WHILE* loop in PANTST1 and notice the effect.

```
/*clear other select fields and reselect our own*/
if (qry_type (retwin, *buffer) == FLT_SELECT) {
    fld_reset (retwin);
    fld_type (retwin, *buffer, FLT_SELECT);
}
```

Notice now that selecting Option *A, B,* or *C* automatically deselects the other two. Now when a field is selected, the *fld_reset()* is executed which automatically deselects all select fields. The *fld_type()* call then puts the single field that the user just selected back to its select state.

The *if* statement allows the user to deselect the selected field leaving none of the possible choices selected. Removing the *if* statement forces at least one field to always be selected. (Deselecting the selected field merely causes it to blink as DESQview first deselects it and the *fld_type()* call selects it again.)

A field may also be deactivated and later reactivated to one of the normal field types. This function may not change the type of a field from select to input type or back, however, because bytes five through seven of the field-table entry have different meanings for these two different field types. (It can change either type to an output field and back, however, as the output field does not use bytes five through seven for anything.)

To change a field in other ways, such as making it smaller or larger, the program may first query the field-table entry using the *qry_entry()* API call. This function call reads a particular field-table entry into the program's local memory. The program can then modify the field-table entry before writing it back with the *fld_entry()* API call. The *fld_entry()* call replaces the field-table entry with the structure provided.

Only field-table entries that already exist may be changed. New fields may not be created in an existing panel. However, several spare inactive fields may be defined and left null in the panel declaration. The program can later write new field declarations into these inactive slots using the *fld_entry()* call to *create* new fields in the window.

Finally, the field-table header may be changed as well using the *fld_header()* API call. Here again, the field-table header structure passed to this function is the same as was used in declaring our *PANEL* above. A program may read the field-table header using the *qry_header()* API call and modify it before writing it back. Programs do not routinely edit the field-table header. If the field table is that different, it is probably wiser to define two different panels and apply them independently.

Figure 8.7—Prototype Definitions for
Field-Related API Calls

```
                                /*fill a field with an attribute*/
void    fld_attr                /*returns nothing*/
                (ulong winhan,  /*handle of panel window*/
                 int   field,   /*number of field to fill*/
                 int   attribute);/*attribute to fill with*/


                                /*fill a field with a character*/
void    fld_char                /*returns nothing*/
                (ulong winhan,  /*handle of panel window*/
                 int   field,   /*number of field to fill*/
                 int   character);/*character to fill with*/


                                /*clear a field*/
void    fld_clear               /*returns nothing*/
                (ulong winhan,  /*handle of panel window*/
                 int   field);  /*number of field to clear*/


                                /*move cursor to a field*/
void    fld_cursor              /*returns nothing*/
                (ulong winhan,  /*handle of panel window*/
                 int   field);  /*number of field*/


                                /*change a field table entry*/
void    fld_entry               /*returns nothing*/
                (ulong winhan,  /*handle of panel window*/
                 int   field,   /*number of field to change*/
                 FENTRY *fentry); /*replacement field table entry*/


                                /*change a field table header*/
void    fld_header              /*returns nothing*/
                (ulong winhan,  /*handle of panel window*/
                 FHEAD *fheader); /*replacement field table header*/


                                /*declare a field marker*/
void    fld_marker              /*returns nothing*/
                (ulong winhan,  /*handle of panel window*/
                 char  marker); /*new field marker character*/


                                /*move pointer to position in field*/
void    fld_point               /*returns nothing*/
                (ulong winhan,  /*handle of panel window*/
                 int   field,   /*number of field*/
                 int   row,     /*row within field (0 relative)*/
                 int   col);    /*col within field (0 relative)*/


                                /*reset selected and modified bits*/
void    fld_reset               /*returns nothing*/
```

```
                  (ulong winhan);    /*handle of panel window*/

                                     /*scroll contents of a field*/
void   fld_scroll                    /*returns nothing*/
                  (ulong winhan,     /*handle of panel window*/
                   int   field,      /*number of field to scroll*/
                   int   direction,  /*equals SCR_UP, SCR_DOWN,
                                        SCR_LEFT or SCR_RIGHT*/
                   int   text);      /*1 -> scroll text, 0 -> attributes*/

                                     /*write a string into a field*/
void   fld_swrite                    /*returns nothing*/
                  (ulong winhan,     /*handle of panel window*/
                   int   field,      /*number of field to write*/
                   char *buffer);    /*ASCIIZ string to write*/

                                     /*change the type of a field*/
void   fld_type                      /*returns nothing*/
                  (ulong winhan,     /*handle of panel window*/
                   int   field,      /*number of field*/
                   int   type);      /*new type; one of:
                                            FLT_INACTIVE, FLT_OUTPUT,
                                            FLT_INPUT,    FLT_DESELECT,
                                         or  FLT_SELECT*/

                                     /*write to a field*/
void    fld_write                    /*returns nothing*/
                  (ulong winhan,     /*handle of panel window*/
                   int   field,      /*number of field to write*/
                   char *buffer,     /*ASCII string to write*/
                   int   length);    /*length of string*/^P^J
                                     /*retrieve a field table entry*/

int    qry_entry                     /*returns size of entry*/
                  (ulong  winhan,    /*handle of panel window*/
                   int    field,     /*number of field to query*/
                   FETRY *buffer);    /*address of buffer to hold entry*/

                                     /*read the contents of a field*/
void   qry_field                     /*returns nothing*/
                  (ulong  winhan,    /*handle of panel window*/
                   int    field,     /*number of field to query*/
                   char **buffer,    /*returns pointer to string*/
                   int   *length);    /*and length of string*/

                                     /*retrieve the field table header*/
void   qry_header                    /*returns nothing*/
                  (ulong  winhan,    /*handle of panel window*/
                   FHEAD *buffer);    /*address of buffer to hold header*/
```

```
                                  /*get the type of a field*/
int    qry_type                   /*returns field type = FLT_INACTIVE,
                                      FLT_OUTPUT, FLT_INPUT, FLT_SELECT
                                      or else FLT_DESELECT*/
                  (ulong  winhan,  /*handle of panel window*/
                   int    field);  /*field to read*/
```

Panel Design Tool

As mentioned earlier, writing a *complete* panel requires a thorough knowledge of the streams interface to DESQview, a skill that the DESQview C API programmer would not normally possess. In my example program, I pointed out how the labor could be reduced by opening the window and assigning text to the fields using API C calls. Defining the actual fields, which is about all that is left, is then reduced more or less to a formula that the C programmer simply fills out. However, writing a more thorough panel, especially one on disk, can be a bit tricky. This difficulty has done much to retard the acceptance of panels in the programmer community.

To address this problem, Quarterdeck began selling the Panel Design Tool in late 1988. As its name implies, the Panel Design Tool, also known as the PDT, is a utility designed to help build panels and panel files. With the PDT, programmers size and position a window using the mouse or keyboard. They then fill in the text and define any fields along with their type and assorted properties. Drop-down menus help in the development process along the way.

Once complete, the user simply presses a button and out pops a panel file. The PDT also includes a test mode by which the programmer can execute the panel and examine the messages generated by different user operations. This is a good way to make sure that the program is expecting the correct message. In fact, the test feature is a great way to play with panels to determine the effect of the various switches on their operation and the messages they generate. Changing one of the properties of a particular field and retesting the panel takes only a few seconds. (The message-display window of PANTST1 is loosely patterned after the test feature of the

PDT.)

It should be stressed that the PDT is a separate product and not a part of the API C Library. (The PDT is also not a prerequisite for this book.) However, if programmers decide to implement a project using panels, they will most certainly want to purchase the PDT. The savings in time will offset the cost. This is especially true for C programmers, since, unlike building panels by hand, with the PDT there is *no assembly required*.

The previous example program has been rewritten to use a PDT RAM-resident panel. It appears below as PANTST2.C. You will notice that this program is very similar to its predecessor except that it is considerably simpler. Gone are the involved structure definitions requiring initialization in the *init_panel()* function. Also gone is the *panel_text()* function to open the window using C calls and the *fld_swrite()* calls to fill the fields with text. All of this information is contained within the panel itself. Although considerably simpler, in operation this program executes identically to the previous example. (Note that PANTST2 must have a special-project file to include the *.OBJ* file created by the PDT containing the panel during the link step.)

```
 1[ 0]: /****************************************************************
 2[ 0]:   Object Panels - load a panel contained within a .OBJ file created
 3[ 0]:                   by the Panel Design Tool.  The Panel Design Tool
 4[ 0]:                   is much more powerful than what can be done by
 5[ 0]:                   hand.  There is no need, therefore, to create the
 6[ 0]:                   windows from within C - let the panel do it.
 7[ 0]:                   (Notice that the file MYPANELS.OBJ must be included
 8[ 0]:                   during the link step, probably by including it in
 9[ 0]:                   the project file.)
10[ 0]: ****************************************************************/
11[ 0]:
12[ 0]: #include <stdio.h>
13[ 0]: #include <string.h>
14[ 0]: #include "dvapi.h"
15[ 0]:
16[ 0]: /* prototype declarations of user functions*/
17[ 0]: void main (void);
18[ 0]: void program_body (void);
19[ 0]:
20[ 0]: /*minimum API version required is DESQview 2.00*/
21[ 0]: #define required 0x200
22[ 0]:
```

```
23[ 0]: /*main - standard pattern for DESQview programs*/
24[ 0]: void main (void)
25[ 0]: {
26[ 1]:   int  version;
27[ 1]:
28[ 1]:   version = api_init();
29[ 1]:   if (version < required)
30[ 1]:       printf ("This program requires DESQview %d.%02d or later.\n",
31[ 1]:               required >> 8, required & 0xff);
32[ 1]:   else {
33[ 2]:       /*tell DESQview what extensions to enable
34[ 2]:         and start application*/
35[ 2]:       api_level (required);
36[ 2]:       program_body();
37[ 1]:   }
38[ 1]:   /*if DESQview present (even if wrong version), shut it down*/
39[ 1]:   if (version)
40[ 1]:       api_exit();
41[ 0]: }
42[ 0]:
43[ 0]: /*The object file I created was given the name MYPANELS.OBJ with
44[ 0]:   the entry point MYPANELS and the length given as LMYPANELS.
45[ 0]:   Since these are defined in a different module they must be
46[ 0]:   defined here as EXTERNs.  The link step will provide the
47[ 0]:   address of MYPANELS to this module. */
48[ 0]:
49[ 0]: extern char  mypanels [];
50[ 0]: extern ulong lmypanels;
51[ 0]:
52[ 0]: /*program_body - open a panel and a display window.  Display every
53[ 0]:                  message which arrives from the panel until the
54[ 0]:                  'Escape' entry is selected*/
55[ 0]: void program_body (void)
56[ 0]: {
57[ 1]:   ulong panhan, retwin, retkey, dispwin;
58[ 1]:   int i, status, buflng;
59[ 1]:   unsigned char *buffer, *bufptr;
60[ 1]:
61[ 1]:   /*open a display window first*/
62[ 1]:   dispwin = win_new ("Message Display Window", 22, 15, 50);
63[ 1]:   win_move (dispwin, 5, 10);
64[ 1]:   win_logattr (dispwin, 1);
65[ 1]:   win_attr (dispwin, 1);
66[ 1]:   win_unhide (dispwin);
67[ 1]:   win_top (dispwin);
68[ 1]:
69[ 1]:   /*now create and open a panel and apply it to the display window*/
70[ 1]:   panhan = pan_new ();
71[ 1]:   status = pan_open (panhan, mypanels, (int)lmypanels);
72[ 1]:   if (!status) {
73[ 2]:       status = pan_apply (panhan, dispwin, "panel1", 6,
74[ 2]:                           &retwin, &retkey);
75[ 2]:
76[ 2]:       /*read messages from the panel until either the Escape
77[ 2]:         field is selected or 10 selections made.  Write
78[ 2]:         received messages to the display window.*/
```

```
79[ 2]:        if (!status) {
80[ 3]:            fld_swrite (retwin, 4, "Make Selection");
81[ 3]:            i = 10;
82[ 3]:            do {
83[ 4]:                key_read (retkey, &buffer, &buflng);
84[ 4]:                win_printf (dispwin,
85[ 4]:                            "Message %2d (length = %x) - ",
86[ 4]:                            i, buflng);
87[ 4]:                for (bufptr = buffer;buflng; bufptr++, buflng--)
88[ 4]:                    win_printf (dispwin, "%c(%x) ",
89[ 4]:                            *bufptr, *bufptr);
90[ 4]:                win_printf (dispwin, "\n");
91[ 4]:
92[ 4]:                /*once a selection is made, change output field*/
93[ 4]:                fld_swrite (retwin, 4, " Esc to Exit  ");
94[ 3]:            } while ((i--) && (*buffer != 4));
95[ 3]:            win_free (retwin);
96[ 2]:        }
97[ 1]:    }
98[ 1]:    win_free (dispwin);
99[ 1]:    pan_free (panhan);
100[ 0]: }
```

The PDT can also generate disk-resident panel files. The same program now written to access the same panel file as a disk-resident file appears as PANTST3.C. This program is identical to the RAM-resident version except for the single call to *pan_apply()*, which is now given the name of the panel file and not its address. (The disk-resident panel file along with the object file necessary to link PANTST2 are included on the distribution disk for this book.)

```
1[ 0]: /****************************************************************
2[ 0]: Disk Panels - load a panel contained within a panel library file
3[ 0]:               created with the Panel Design Tool. The Panel
4[ 0]:               Design Tool is much more powerful than what can be
5[ 0]:               done by hand. There is no need, therefore, to
6[ 0]:               create the windows from within C - let the panel
7[ 0]:               do it.
8[ 0]:               (Notice that the file MYPANELS.PLB must be in the
9[ 0]:               same directory as the .EXE file when the program is
10[ 0]:              executed.)
11[ 0]: ****************************************************************/
12[ 0]:
13[ 0]: #include <stdio.h>
14[ 0]: #include <string.h>
15[ 0]: #include "dvapi.h"
16[ 0]:
17[ 0]: /* prototype declarations of user functions*/
18[ 0]: void main (void);
19[ 0]: void program_body (void);
20[ 0]:
```

```
21[ 0]: /*minimum API version required is DESQview 2.00*/
22[ 0]: #define required 0x200
23[ 0]:
24[ 0]: /*main - standard pattern for DESQview programs*/
25[ 0]: void main (void)
26[ 0]: {
27[ 1]:   int  version;
28[ 1]:
29[ 1]:   version = api_init();
30[ 1]:   if (version < required)
31[ 1]:       printf ("This program requires DESQview %d.%02d or later.\n",
32[ 1]:                  required >> 8, required & 0xff);
33[ 1]:   else {
34[ 2]:       /*tell DESQview what extensions to enable
35[ 2]:         and start application*/
36[ 2]:       api_level (required);
37[ 2]:       program_body();
38[ 1]:   }
39[ 1]:   /*if DESQview present (even if wrong version), shut it down*/
40[ 1]:   if (version)
41[ 1]:       api_exit();
42[ 0]: }
43[ 0]:
44[ 0]: /*I previously used the Panel Design Tool to create the
45[ 0]:   panel library file MYPANELS.PLB.  This file must be in
46[ 0]:   the same directory as the executable file or else a full
47[ 0]:   path name must be provided if the program is to execute
48[ 0]:   properly - in this case, I have provided a full path.
49[ 0]:   (This is the same panel that created the .OBJ file
50[ 0]:   MYPANELS.OBJ.)*/
51[ 0]:
52[ 0]: char mypanels [] = "d:\\mypanels.plb";
53[ 0]:
54[ 0]: /*program_body - open a panel and a display window.  Display every
55[ 0]:                     message that arrives from the panel until the
56[ 0]:                     'Escape' entry selected*/
57[ 0]: void program_body (void)
58[ 0]: {
59[ 1]:   ulong panhan, retwin, retkey, dispwin;
60[ 1]:   int i, status, buflng;
61[ 1]:   unsigned char *buffer, *bufptr;
62[ 1]:
63[ 1]:   /*open a display window first*/
64[ 1]:   dispwin = win_new ("Message Display Window", 22, 15, 50);
65[ 1]:   win_move (dispwin, 5, 10);
66[ 1]:   win_logattr (dispwin, 1);
67[ 1]:   win_attr (dispwin, 1);
68[ 1]:   win_unhide (dispwin);
69[ 1]:   win_top (dispwin);
70[ 1]:
71[ 1]:   /*now create and open a panel and apply it to the display window*/
72[ 1]:   panhan = pan_new ();
73[ 1]:   status = pan_open (panhan, mypanels, sizeof mypanels);
74[ 1]:   if (!status) {
75[ 2]:       status = pan_apply (panhan, dispwin, "panel1", 6,
76[ 2]:                               &retwin, &retkey);
```

```
77[ 2]:        if (!status) {
78[ 3]:
79[ 3]:            /*read messages from the panel until either the
80[ 3]:             Escape field is selected or 10 selections made.
81[ 3]:             Display any messages received in  the display
82[ 3]:             window.*/
83[ 3]:            fld_swrite (retwin, 4, "Make Selection");
84[ 3]:            i = 10;
85[ 3]:            do {
86[ 4]:                key_read (retkey, &buffer, &buflng);
87[ 4]:                win_printf (dispwin,
88[ 4]:                            "Message %2d (length = %x) - ",
89[ 4]:                            i, buflng);
90[ 4]:                for (bufptr = buffer;buflng; bufptr++, buflng--)
91[ 4]:                    win_printf (dispwin, "%c(%x) ",
92[ 4]:                            *bufptr, *bufptr);
93[ 4]:                win_printf (dispwin, "\n");
94[ 4]:
95[ 4]:                /*once a selection is made, change the
96[ 4]:                 output field*/
97[ 4]:                fld_swrite (retwin, 4, " Esc to Exit  ");
98[ 3]:            } while ((i--) && (*buffer != 4));
99[ 3]:            win_free (retwin);
100[ 2]:        }
101[ 1]:    }
102[ 1]:
103[ 1]:    /*now free any assets allocated*/
104[ 1]:    win_free (dispwin);
105[ 1]:    pan_free (panhan);
106[ 0]: }
```

Is it Worth it?

With all of the discussion about the pitfalls of panel files, the question must arise, "Is it really worth all this?" After consideration, the answer must be an unequivocal, "Yes!" For one thing, imagine how much more complicated this discussion would be if we were considering how to read the mouse pointer, move the cursor, and manipulate the window to perform the same operations that input, select, and output fields do for us. But beyond that there is another consideration.

No new idea is ever easy the first time. The programmer must first cast off previously held prejudices and venture down the unfamiliar logical corridors of the new paradigm. For example, the first time the programmer is presented with the concept of multitasking, perhaps in this book, it takes time to fully grasp its advantages. At first it may not seem like the benefits justify the difficulties. Panels are a new concept to DOS programmers. Once grasped, however, panels are not difficult. Even when developing panels by hand using the C technique outlined in this chapter, the programmer quickly gets the hang of it. With the Panel Design Tool, building panels is easier than programming!

The trend in programming through the decades has been towards ever-increasing modularity and encapsulation. Divorcing the code from the data, the function from the form, represent another step in this evolution. Programmers or their representatives can adapt displays to fit the needs of individual customers at their sites, if necessary. If a particular user should not have access to a particular command, the programmer can remove the field that invokes the command from the panel given that user, and the user will no longer be able to access it. Even were the need not foreseen, equipped with the PDT it could not possibly take longer than a few minutes to accomplish.

Need a superuser as well as a normal version of your program? Why not write one version of the program and two versions of the panel file, one equipped with extra fields to invoke the superuser capabilities? Do you have a requirement to support several languages or, as often happens in the defense world, do your programmers speak a different language than your users? If properly written, your program can change language merely by rewriting the panel files.

We as programmers are failing. Today programmers are using essentially the same programming techniques as they used to develop DOS programs six years earlier when the PC was first introduced. This might be understandable were it not for the fact that the problem is increasing in difficulty all the time. Users are expecting more than ever from their applications.

The panel-programming paradigm, along with the multitasking paradigm discussed so many times before, represent new and powerful ways of looking at the programming problem, of getting more production per programming hour, and of developing a better, more adaptable product. This, more than any *compile-in-the-background* circus tricks, is the real promise of multitasking, second-generation operating systems like DESQview.

Appendix

DESQview Switches

Most aspects of the DESQview user interface are documented within the Quarterdeck manuals. One undocumented feature of DESQview 2.0 and later is the collection of command-line switches that can be used to slightly modify DESQview's execution. These switches are included on the same command line that loads DESQview. For example:

```
XDV /CV
```

The /CV is by far the most important of these switches since it is critical to executing under a debugger programs that spawn subtasks.

Except for the /L switch, all switches are equivalent when used with *DV* or with *XDV*.

Switch	**Explanation**
/OK	sets original IBM keyboard. Default is to check the ROM for original or extended keyboard. Use this switch if *SETUP* works but *DV* only beeps when keys entered, especially on some Phoenix's BIOS, such as those found on the Olivetti 6300.
/CV	(CodeView switch) changes the rules for determining keyboard ownership. Normally the forground task receives all keystrokes. When executing a newly

335

spawned task under a debugger, the problem arises that the debugger can no longer see keystrokes from the programmer. Debugger stops at a breakpoint and appears to die. With */CV,* the task that owns the window to which the mouse points tends to be the keyboard owner. By pointing at the window containing the debugger with the mouse, the programmer can allow the debugger to get regain control of the keyboard.

/EE   only access EEMS through driver calls. Default is for DESQview to access some EEMS I/O ports directly for greater performance.

/L   (*XDV* only) makes *XDV* display the high memory ranges being used and pause for a key press. This can be useful when debugging *XDV* failure.

/LD   lock out multitasking during disk accesses. This switch can be helpful with hard drive controllers that are less than 100 percent compatible

filename.DVP   load the API program specified in the *.DVP* file. User program becomes the controller of the system. Default is to allow user to control system.

Bibliography

Davis, S. R., *Turbo C: The Art of Advanced Program Design, Optimization, and Debugging*. Redwood City, CA: M&T Publishing, Inc., 1987.

Kuppin, Michael, *DESQview, Version 2*. Santa Monica, CA: Quarterdeck Office Systems, 1985.

DESQview API Reference. Santa Monica, CA: Quarterdeck Office Systems, 1987.

Tannenbaum, Andrew S., *Operating Systems—Design and Implementation*. Englewood Cliffs, NJ: Prentice-Hall, Inc., 1987.

Vigoritta, Howard, "Memory Management and EMS." *Micro/Systems Journal* (May 1988): 34—41.

About the Author

Stephen Randy Davis graduated cum laude from Rice University in Houston. Since 1979 he has worked in the defense industry as a systems programmer, and has established North Texas Digital Consulting, Inc., his own consulting firm. Davis is the author of *Turbo C: The Art of Advanced Program Design, Optimization, and Debugging* (M&T Books 1987) and several popular public-domain programs. He is also a regular contributor to *PC Magazine*.

Index

More Programming Tools from M&T Books

The Programmer's Essential OS/2 Handbook

by David E. Cortesi

The Programmer's Essential OS/2 Handbook provides the OS/2 technical information necessary to write efficient, reliable applications in C, Pascal, or assembler. Two indexes and a web of cross-referencing provide easy access to all OS/2 topic areas.

Inside you'll find an overview of OS/2 architecture and vocabulary; a look at the 80286 and a description of how the CPU processes data in real and protected mode; an overview of linking, multiprogramming, file access, and device drivers; and an in-depth discussion of important OS/2 topics, including dynamic linking, message facility, the screen group, inputs, outputs, the queue, the semaphore, and more.

No programmer developing in the OS/2 environment can afford to be without this valuable reference.

Book & Disk (5-1/4" & 3-1/2" OS/2)   Item #89-5 $39.95
Book only   Item # 82-8 $24.95

Building Local Area Networks

by Patrick H. Corrigan and Aisling Guy

From the basic components to complete network installation, here is the practical guide that PC system integrators will need to build and implement PC LANs in this rapidly growing market. The specifics of building and maintaining PC LANs, including hardware configurations, software development, cabling, selection criteria, installation, and on-going management are described in a clear "how-to" manner with numerous illustrations and sample LAN management forms.

Building Local Area Networks gives particular emphasis to Novell's Netware, Version 2.1. Additional topics covered include the OS/2 LAN Manager, Tops, Banyan VINES, internetworking, host computer gateways, and multisystem networks that link PCs, Apples, and mainframes.

Book & Disk (MS-DOS)   Item #025-7 $39.95
Book only   Item #010-9 $24.95   *Available JUNE 1989*

More Programming Tools ...

Graphics Programming in C

by Roger T. Stevens

Graphics Programming in C details the fundamentals of graphics programming for the IBM PC family and its clones. All the information you need to program graphics in C, including source code, is presented. You can either use the included graphics libraries of functions as is or modify them to suit your own requirements.

Inside, you'll find complete discussions of ROM BIOS, VGA, EGA, and CGA inherent capabilities; methods of displaying points on a screen; improved, faster algorithms for drawing and filling lines, rectangles, rounded rectangles, polygons, ovals, circles, and arcs; graphics cursors; and much more!

Graphics Programming in C carries a complete description of how to put together a graphics library and how to print hard copies of graphics display screens. Both Turbo C and Microsoft C are supported.

Book & Disk (MS-DOS)   *Item #019-2*   *$39.95*
Book only   *Item #018-4*   *$24.95*

Public-Domain Software and Shareware, Second Edition

by Rusel DeMaria and George R. Fontaine

Why pay $150 or $300 for software when you can buy a comparable package for only $15 or $30? This book critically reviews the public-domain and Shareware gems that are available, and provides all the information you'll need on how and where to find them. The new 498-page second edition contains twice as many program reviews with expanded software categories. You'll find accounting, database, graphics, and entertainment software, as well as editors, utilities, DOS shells, desk managers, menu programs, and much more. Sample public-domain programs are available on disk.

Book & Disk (MS-DOS)   *Item #014-1*   *$34.95*
Book only   *Item #011-7*   *$19.95*

More Programming Tools ...

Taming MS-DOS,
Second Edition

by Thom Hogan

If you need to go beyond the basics, *Taming MS-DOS, 2nd Edition*, is for you. Here is an advanced user's guide to enhancing the MS-DOS environment. By following Thom Hogan's instructions and advice, you will quickly become an MS-DOS expert.

This new and improved second edition has been updated to cover MS-DOS 3.3. You will learn how to maximize your batch file routines using redirection, filters, and pipes; prevent the accidental formatting of your hard disk; redefine function keys; and locate files within subdirectories. Other batch files will implement an MS-DOS help system. There is also a demonstration of how to create configurable AUTOEXEC.BAT files and how to customize CONFIG.SYS and use ANSI.SYS to suit your needs.

Included are nearly 50 ready-to-use BASIC programs that enhance MS-DOS. You can easily rename directories and disk volumes, change file attributes, check available RAM and disk memory, display a memory-resident clock, and assign MS-DOS commands to ALT keys.

The programs, including batch files and MS-DOS enhancements, are available on disk with full source code.

Book & Disk (MS-DOS)   *Item #92-5*   *$34.95*
Book only   *Item #87-9*   *$19.95*

To Order: Return this form with your payment to **M&T Books**, 501 Galveston Drive, Redwood City, CA 94063 or **CALL TOLL-FREE 1-800-533-4372** Mon-Fri 8AM-5PM Pacific Standard Time (in California, call 1-800-356-2002).

☐ **YES!** Please send me the following: ☐ Check enclosed, payable to **M&T Books**.

Item#	Description	Disk	Price

Charge my ☐ Visa ☐ MC ☐ AmEx

Card No. _____ Exp. Date _____

Signature _____

Name _____

Address _____

City _____

State _____ Zip _____

Subtotal _____

CA residents add sales tax __ % _____

Add $2.99 per item for shipping _____

TOTAL _____

7023

M&T BOOKS